CHILD RIGHTS

THE MOVEMENT, INTERNATIONAL LAW, AND OPPOSITION

Child Rights

The Movement, International Law,

and Opposition

⤝ EDITED BY CLARK BUTLER ⤞

Published in cooperation with
The Human Rights Institute of the Center for Applied Ethics,
Indiana University-Purdue University Fort Wayne

PURDUE UNIVERSITY PRESS
WEST LAFAYETTE, INDIANA

Printed in the United States of America.

Library of Congress Cataloging-in-Publication Data
Child Rights: The Movement, International Law, and Opposition / edited by
Clark Butler.
    p. cm. -- (Purdue University Human Rights Studies)
  Includes bibliographical references and index.
  ISBN 978-1-55753-549-8 (pbk. : alk. paper) -- ISBN 978-1-61249-205-6
(epdf) -- ISBN 978-1-61249-204-9 (epub) 1. Children's rights. 2. Convention
on the Rights of the Child (1989) 3. Children (International law) I. Butler,
Clark, 1944-
  HQ789.C42745 2012
  342.08'772--dc23
                            2011047726

Contents

PART 3: CHILDREN'S RIGHTS IN THE DEVELOPING WORLD

UNITED NATIONS CONVENTION ON THE RIGHTS OF THE CHILD
http://www2.ohchr.org/english/law/crc.htm

This book is dedicated to the children of the world, to those who can speak for themselves, and to others who sincerely endeavor to advocate for their rights and interests.

Acknowledgments

We express appreciation to Indiana University for the New Perspectives Grant received in support of the 2006 conference on Moral Education, the United Nations, and Human Rights. That conference, organized by the Human Rights Institute on the Indiana University-Purdue University Fort Wayne (IPFW) campus, resulted in the research team behind the present book. We also express our appreciation for grants received from the campus Office of Research and External Support, from the College of Arts and Sciences, and from the Philosophy Department, which houses the Human Rights Institute, now expanded as the Center for Applied Ethics. Mark Savio, in his work as an Institute research assistant, is to be thanked for the painstaking work he did to put the annotation in proper form. To Mary Arnold Schwartz the editor is grateful for having reviewed his own essay from an external perspective, which was more difficult for him to gain than in the case of the other essays.

Introduction

Multidisciplinary Responses to the International Rights of the Child

⌒ CLARK BUTLER ⌒

The essays in this volume largely express ways in which the United Nations Convention on the Rights of the Child (CRC) has been interpreted and used by those who are active in disciplines other than international human rights law. A large body of literature shows that there is considerable precedent for nonlegal, pedagogical, political, psychological, anthropological, and ethical reflection on the use of human rights law. Much of the moral conscience of humanity has been stored away in such law, and remains in that law ready to be retrieved by being interpreted as a statement of moral law. Historically, the concept of human rights arose as an ethical concept which preceded and inspired international human rights law. The ethical concept then led to a social, political, and pedagogical human rights movement, which only then led to the body of international human rights law as we know it. But the ethics and the movement never entirely dissolved into the law. Ethical human rights norms remain as the norms by which human rights law is justified, created, extended, qualified, or repealed. The movement and the opposition remain the larger context of the law. It uses the law as a tool, and critically evaluates, positively as well as negatively, the law from various nonlegal perspectives. Thus the essays in this volume largely fall into what has come to be known as critical philosophy of law.

Michael Freeman is an example of a scholar working in human rights studies not limited to the discipline of law. He reflects that "the lawyers who

1

dominate human rights studies" sometimes limit themselves to the view that "human rights are what human rights law says they are."[1] He notes that "the concept of human rights is, to a considerable extent, though not wholly, *legal*," and that "the UN introduced the concept of human rights into international law and politics."[2] But the United Nations introduced human rights into international law because they already had an important place in moral philosophy. Richard Pierre Claude, founding editor of *Human Rights Quarterly*, writes that "human rights are no longer the solitary domain of lawyers, but increasingly the central agenda for action and inquiry for thinking people worldwide."[3] Yet it is equally true that, because of international human rights law, human rights are no longer the solitary domain of ethicists.

The Convention on the Rights of the Child makes reference to itself as legally "binding" (article 50). That is how the discipline of international law interprets the convention, which should never be discounted. It is a strict constructionist textual interpretation of the wording of the law. But this formal interpretation of the legal text is only one way of interpreting it. If we take it as the only way of interpreting it, we discount the importance of complementing such an interpretation by contextual interpretation, specifically in the international social context in which the convention is only weakly enforced. Thomas Hobbes and legal positivists generally have argued that the text of the law is correctly interpreted contextually and sociologically, not merely textually. Wherever it is disobeyed with impunity, it is at most paper, not genuine law.

From this perspective, what is a true legal text depends on going beyond the text to see whether penalties actually exist for disobeying it. The convention is admittedly legally binding in the heaven of international human rights law, but that heaven—though it has begun to descend to earth in certain world regions, especially the European Union—is still far from fully doing so around the world in any way that would justify the actual existence of children's rights, as distinct from sometimes contested ethical norms. As a matter of sociological fact, the convention clearly fails to bind the behavior of many nations that have nonetheless ratified it. But the less the convention is able to justify itself as enforceable law, the greater the importance of shifting attention to its function as a pedagogical instrument and standard for further moral education.

We need to be clear, however, about what it means to say the CRC is "legally binding." It does not mean that all ratifying nations are legally bound to legislate the children's rights in the convention as domestic law. It means, rather, that ratifying nations are legally bound to participate in the monitoring procedure spelled out in the convention. They are legally bound to show that they are seriously trying to legally implement children's rights, to file reports on their success in implementing those rights, to be examined by the UN Child Rights Committee, and to receive recommendations from the committee. They are not legally bound to follow the recommendations or to actually pass domestic legislation, however great the displeasure which the committee may show toward such countries in future reports. States sometimes feel conflicting pressures from different governmental or nongovernmental agents of the world human rights movement, and sometimes have to make hard decisions and set their own budgetary priorities.

Yet even in this weaker sense of a "legally binding" human rights convention, the CRC fails to consistently bind in fact the action of ratifying nations that fail to submit reports in the required time frames, that submit frivolous or unresponsive reports, or that do not seriously attempt to follow the committee's recommendations. No punitive actions beyond shaming and blaming exist to enforce compliance with what nations have legally bound themselves to do. The committee issues recommendations, but the CRC regime provides for no court empowered to issue legally binding verdicts. It may be difficult for the committee to judge whether a nation has made serious efforts. In part this is because the Child Rights Committee can more easily verify concrete external governmental actions than the inner commitment of government office holders. And it may be difficult for the committee to judge whether a government is justified in claiming it must limit funding for the promotion of children's rights in favor of a higher level of funding for what it says is the more urgent promotion of other human rights. Human rights are said to be indivisible, not standing in a hierarchical order of priority. Yet actions on behalf of one right may be placed in a higher or lower level of priority than another right, depending on what is most urgent given the current situation of the nation.

Part 1 of the volume explores ways in which the global children's rights movement has positively interpreted and used the Convention on the Rights of the Child. The first chapter extends views expressed in Clark Butler's *Human Rights Ethics: A Rational Approach* into the area of child rights. The chapter defends the neo-humanist concept of children's rights dating from the early nineteenth century, as advocated by William von Humboldt and G. W. F. Hegel. Neo-humanist education protested a prior child rights movement initiated by Jean-Jacques Rousseau, who upheld child-centered pedagogy. Rousseau pleaded the innocent virtue of children and advocated education by play and problem solving responding to the immediate challenges of the natural environment. Chapter 1 gives an account of the neo-humanist concept of adult-centered education for children who, sensing their disadvantage in interchanges with adults, accept the discipline of school education in order to be gradually inducted into adult culture. The chapter notes, as a second feature of neo-humanist education, the attempt to emancipate children from their immediate cultural environment by foreign language study, providing them with an ability to communicate with a diversity of adult perspectives on a level playing field. It is argued that if children fail to claim a right to education in dialogical skills, it may be viewed either as a putative right or a past-tense adult human right to have been educated at an early age in skills serving them as equal dialogue partners in adulthood. The chapter equates such a right with the CRC participation rights of children.

Since this right, as well as supportive provision (subsistence) and protection (security) rights, is violated with impunity in many nations, universal children rights are alleged not yet to exist. What exists, it is maintained, is rather a child rights movement making use of a UN convention monitoring to which ratifying nations are legally bound to respond. It is held that the United States should ratify the CRC if it would help the United States better respect children's rights. Sovereignty and the US Constitution are not seen as obstacles to ratification, since treaty-making powers are part of the Constitution, and since the CRC is a treaty that can prod but not force the United States to follow its recommendations. The chapter concludes that the CRC allows homeschooling with a parental right to give children an initial cultural identity, as long as such schooling also teaches human rights supporting dialogical skills by which children may inquire beyond their initial cultural identity.

According to Katherine Covell, Professor of Psychology at Breton Cape University (Canada) and Executive Director of its Children's Rights Center, the CRC, ratified by most states in the 1990s, reflects a near-global consensus on what childhood should be and an almost global commitment to make laws, policies, and practices consistent with its provisions. But she sees a large gap between promise and reality.[4] In chapter 2, she gives an overview of the significance of the CRC in elevating the status of children into persons with fundamental rights, and describes the benefits of understanding children as bearers of morally inalienable rights, rather than as merely beneficiaries of concern and charity. Criticisms and myths about children's rights are addressed with a focus on how they hamper progress toward full implementation of the CRC. Were the convention taken seriously, it is argued, the conditions in which children grow would be more optimal for their healthy physical and psychological development. Covell suggests that one route toward closing the gap between the promise and reality of the convention, toward its fuller implementation, is through the provision of children's rights education in schools.

In chapter 3 Katherine Covell and R. Brian Howe (author of chapter 7) examine the value of teaching children's rights in schools, keeping developmental considerations in mind. The value of children's rights education, they explain, is not only that children gain knowledge of their own rights, but also that they gain a sense of responsibility in support of others' rights. Developmental considerations they consider include age, the relevance of the rights taught to a given age group, and pedagogical methods. They believe the optimal age to formally teach rights is during adolescence, when children have the cognitive capacity to understand and internalize the value of rights. By holding that the rights taught need to be relevant, they intend a focus on children's own rights, not on those of people in a distant country or those of grown-ups which they cannot yet exercise. The pedagogy they support needs to be consistent with the exercise of and respect for rights, which means the use of a democratic teaching style where children can exercise their rights of participation.

Marie-France Daniel, author of chapter 4 and Professor of Kinesiology at the Université de Montréal, addresses the problem of violence to which young children are exposed. She extends the Philosophy for Children (P4C) approach, as conceived by Gareth Matthews and Matthew Lipman, to preschool children, developing the approach as an important tool for such children as well as one for protecting them from violence. She finds the essence of P4C to lie in philosophical (critical) dialogue among children in a community of peers. Daniel presents the results of an experiment with preschool children, showing that, even at five years old, children are capable of developing the discursive skills and attitudes required by philosophical dialogue. The evolution of discursive skills among children is shown to begin with anecdotal exchanges, to pass through monological exchanges, and finally to arrive at dialogical and quasi-critical exchanges. She examines the relationship between P4C and specific articles contained in the CRC, highlighting self-protection by participation rights, which lend support to the P4C approach.

Part 2 of the book is devoted to criticism of the CRC and its implementation. Critics come both from countries that have ratified the convention and from those that have not, and both from scholars who support it and those who do not. Some think it goes too far, while others think it has not gone far enough. Michael Farris, the founding president of Patrick Henry College, who has successfully defended homeschooling before the US Supreme Court, objects to the CRC due to limitations he claims it would impose on the sovereignty of the United States. He notes that colonial Americans, with a long-standing belief in local self-government, rebelled against the usurpation of this power by London. They created a written Constitution with checks and balances to protect self-government. A Bill of Rights was added, blocking government interference with freedom of belief through an established church. He argues that all countries that have ratified the CRC have done so with reservations, depriving it of the force of binding law. Because article 6 of the US Constitution makes treaties part of the supreme law of the land, superseding all incompatible federal law, he maintains that ratification of the convention in the US case would transfer important elements of American self-government to the UN Committee on the Rights of the Child, an international advocacy group. Through the federal power of the purse, the convention could become legally binding on states that never ratified it.

He agrees that some articles in the convention are praiseworthy, but implementation by an international authority bodes ill in further matters for the future of US self-government. He notes that internationalists argue that widely ratified treaties become part of the customary international law, and thus apply to the United States even when it has not ratified them. However, the Founding Fathers held to restricting the application of customary international law to law with a basis in natural law as interpreted by Christian nations, serving to govern the international relations implications of domestic law. Yet recent US court decisions have assigned persuasive authority to customary international law, and in particular to the Child Rights Convention, without the above restrictions intended by the Founding Fathers.

Michael Farris also believes that the CRC would improperly interfere with parental authority. US courts cannot legally intervene between parents and children except in cases of abuse, neglect, divorce, or separation. But article 12 of the convention would authorize the UN Child Rights Committee to intervene with recommendations in any case of a difference of opinion between parents and children. He interprets article 12 to mean that full weight must be given to the child's views as to what is in his or her best interest as decided not by the parents, but by a UN committee, with members sometimes drawn from countries with unsavory child rights records. He expresses concern that US ratification would oblige homeschooling, and not just private and public schooling, to respect the freedom of belief and religion of children, thus violating a right which some parents exercise in not sending their children to public schools.

Perry Glanzer, of the Baylor University School of Education, is in essential agreement with Michael Farris. In chapter 6 he criticizes the CRC for excessive limitations on the rights of parents. He holds that, when it comes to the education of children, a tension always exists between the roles of the important parties involved. The tension concerns the proper balance between the rights and interests of the child, the parents, and the state. If one looks to human rights documents for answers to this balancing act, one will not necessarily find a clear answer. The Universal Declaration of Human Rights appears to give priority to parents when it states: "Parents have a prior right to choose the kind of education that shall be given to their children." Understandably, proponents of parental choice in education, particularly defenders of private schooling and homeschooling, tend to defend this right. Some of these defenders, however, remain concerned about legal efforts that might attempt to elevate the rights of children or the interests of the state above parental rights. For example, the Home School Legal Defense Association has identified particular stipulations in the CRC as a legal standard that could cause states to significantly curtail the freedom of homeschooling parents.

He intends to show that these concerns should not be dismissed as right-wing paranoia. Beyond a government report in England arguing for increased regulation of homeschooling based on the CRC, a substantial number of prominent scholars make arguments that would reduce the importance of parental interests and rights in ways that would have a practical influence on how educational policy and law are structured in the United States and around the world. The first part of Glanzer's chapter describes the views of three prominent scholars who justify extensive state intervention and control over children's education at the expense of parental rights and interests. After describing the arguments, Glanzer concludes by pointing out problematic aspects of these arguments for the well-being of parents, children, and society.

Unlike Perry Glanzer and Michael Farris, R. Brian Howe—Professor of Political Science and Cape Breton University in Canada—supports the convention in chapter 7. Both he and Claire Cassidy in the following chapter—who also supports the convention—document a lack of political will, if not organized opposition, to fully implement the convention, even in nations that have ratified it. Howe argues that though ratification of the CRC was a significant step forward for Canada, it has not assured children major progress in their rights. He holds that, compared with the United States, which has not adopted the CRC, Canada has been helped by the convention to promote action on behalf of children. But Canada still has a mixed record. Child poverty remains high, child care remains inadequate, the youth justice system allows for the adult sentencing of juvenile offenders, and aboriginal children continue to face third-world conditions. Together with a complicated system of federalism, a chief reason for the lack of implementation of children's rights is a lack of public pressure due in part to lack of public knowledge and education about the rights of the child.

Claire Cassidy—from the University of Strathclyde in Scotland Department of Education and Professional Studies—focuses in chapter 8 on resistances to implementation of the CRC in relation to the United Kingdom. The United Nations' last committee report on the United Kingdom's progression of the CRC was published in 2008. She presents the recommendations for reform contained in that report together with examples of how the four UK member states with mixed success are currently responding. Obstacles in the United Kingdom to full implementation of the CRC are discussed with emphasis on the need for real participation on the part of children. Participation, she argues, is fundamentally allied to what a child actually is, and this ultimately impacts children's status in society. She stresses that childhood is a period in life when children should enjoy rights of play and participation specific to them, without viewing children's rights as merely a means to the exercise of adult human rights. She advocates child-centered child education, which is closer to Rousseau than the adult-centered child education promoted by the neo-humanist school. Yet without true participation rights and an implied reallocation of resources to address persistent child poverty in a highly developed country, she maintains that the prospects for enhancing the status of children will remain poor, that children will remain relatively powerless, and that enactment of the CRC will remain somewhat limited.

The last chapters in part 3 address children's rights in the developing world. Stephen L. Esquith, an applied ethicist at Michigan State University, examines in chapter 9 how children are often caught in the middle of civil wars, severe poverty, and other forms of violence, especially but not exclusively in poorer developing countries. They can be forcibly conscripted to fight as child soldiers, sold as slaves and prostitutes, or employed as indentured servants. They can be sent away or even sold by their families to protect them from poverty. Their parents can be murdered or disappear and their identities can be changed through adoption procedures with or without their knowledge. All of these constitute violations of children's rights and they raise important philosophical questions that have practical significance. One question is, who is responsible for the protection of children against these acts of violence? Equally important, how can those who are responsible be motivated to desist, repair, or otherwise morally respond to these harms? While many of the responsible parties are states, and often are the very states in which these harms take place, this is not always the case.

Esquith distinguishes two types of responsibility for the violation of children's rights. Cause responsibility refers to the direct and indirect moral and legal responsibility that perpetrators and collaborators have for such harms. Benefit responsibility refers to the political responsibility that other parties (for example, expatriate employers, international adoptive parents, and foreign donors to orphanages) have for benefiting from rather than causing such violations under the convention. After analyzing the difference between these two concepts of responsibility, he turns to the ways in which benefit-responsible parties can be motivated to help change the political conditions that make their benefit from often systematic child rights violations possible. Here he distinguishes between a method of simulation and a method of reenactment. The method of simulation, he argues, can result in little more than a knee-jerk act of rationally unregulated compassion. The second method, however, is more promising in engaging those who are benefit responsible in greater reflection and dialogue about reforms that may be needed to empower children to exercise more fully their participatory and other rights.

Krisjon Olson, an anthropologist, focuses in chapter 10 on the implementation of human rights norms (like the CRC) by humanitarian organizations and the absorption of those principles in a Guatemalan youth movement for peace. Her narration of her own field experience illustrates the ambiguities which can arise when attempts are made to apply the CRC in a developing nation. Part of her work has been to trace the establishment of one nongovernmental association, called *Apoyo*, for the protection, education, and social welfare of children during the Guatemalan armed conflict (1960-1996) and to examine its impact on the Ixil area of Nebaj. This influential association is part of a major philanthropic venture in The Hague to improve the well-being of young people in adverse circumstances with a strategy to redress the impact of genocide. Her two years of on-site ethnographic research (August 2003-August 2005) focused on the complex relationships between children and humanitarian organizations.

Olson explores how such organizations contribute to the elaboration of rights and invest in efforts to prevent death and promote human life within a new legal orthodoxy. She documents the conditions of humanitarian assistance after genocide and the emergence of a new ethics, praxis, and public policy. In postwar Guatemala, where children are both the survivors and perpetrators of violence, with a view to the future young people have become a focal point of local, national, and international humanitarian policies. Donors and peace workers often discuss the difficulties of building "moral community" in the aftermath of genocide, while developing a model of the "right child" in contemporary Guatemala. Although human rights center around diversity and the right of maximally diverse people to express themselves diverse ways, efforts to implement them are sometimes reduced to the promotion of changing models of "the right human being" and by extension of "the right child." Her essay explores the tension between the development of this notion of the "right child," the logic of protection presupposing the value we attach to human life, and assumptions about the vulnerability of life that continue after war.

Jennifer Caseldine-Bracht, in chapter 11, examines the capabilities approach to development ethics and to the implementation of human rights in the developing world, with particular attention to children's rights in the light of Dewey's distinction between aims and ends. She inquires into the flexible policies that developing in contrast to developed countries might adopt to ensure positive outcomes for children. The chapter gives concrete examples of the diversity of programs directed at reducing poverty that can be successfully implemented in diverse countries using the capabilities approach coupled with a pragmatic methodology. Caseldine-Bracht makes the case that children's rights ethics may develop over time and in different real world situations. The result is to view the UN Convention on the Rights of the Child as a living instrument of development ethics, rather than as merely a legal text with a fixed meaning interpreted though the lens of a strict constructionist approach in the discipline of international law.

Clark Butler
Center for Applied Ethics
Indiana University-Purdue University Fort Wayne Campus

Notes

1.   M. Freeman, *Human Rights: An Interdisciplinary Approach* (Cambridge, UK: Polity 2002), 9-10.

2.   Ibid., 4.

3.   R. P. Claude, "Michael Freeman, Human Rights: An Interdisciplinary Approach," *Human Rights Quarterly* 25, no. 2 (2003): 563-66.

4.   The descriptions of the different chapters of this book in this and the following paragraphs are based on abstracts provided by the authors.

PART 1

THE MOVEMENT AND THE UN CONVENTION

One

Children's Rights: An Historical and Conceptual Analysis

⟐ CLARK BUTLER ⟐

THE CHILD RIGHTS CONVENTION IN THE LIGHT OF TWO MOVEMENTS FOR THE RIGHTS OF THE CHILD

There was a time, exemplified by early Roman law, when children were considered property of the family father, who had a life-and-death power over them. This was no longer the case by the time of the French Enlightenment. Yet the enthusiastic reception given to what Jean-Jacques Rousseau (1712-1778) considered his most important work, *Emile,*[1] was nothing less than the discovery of preschool childhood by the reading public of Europe in the eighteenth century. This was an important and lasting discovery. Before Rousseau, children were often viewed within the upper classes as little adults, and were dressed accordingly, but not allowed the freedom to express themselves as adults. The child rights movement, which Rousseau founded, soon spread to the German speaking world, and eventually to the English speaking world, through writers such as Johann Heinrich Pestalozzi (1776-1827),[2] Friedrich Froebel (1782-1852),[3] and Elizabeth Peabody (1804-1894)[4]—child rights activists to whom we owe kindergarten. The peculiarity of Rousseau's child rights movement was that it proclaimed the essential goodness and innocence of preschool children. Quite legitimately, it promoted the right of such children to be children, to play and explore and not merely to be seen and not heard. Yet it also aspired to perpetuate childhood as a model of virtue for children into the school years and even

13

into adulthood. Children were virtuous, and adults were corrupt and degener-
ate, unless they preserved something of the innocence of the child. Rousseau
initiated a kind of children's liberation movement. However, it was not a movement to liberate children from childhood and to enable them to exercise, even
as children, adult human rights, like the right to work, as advocated in recent
decades by some child liberationists.[5] Rousseau's aim was precisely to liberate
children from the exercise of such adult human rights. His aim is reflected in
article 31 of the United Nations Convention on the Rights of the Child, which
declares the child's right to leisure and to learning by play.

This Rousseauean child rights movement, however, is not the only one that
has come to fruition in the UN Convention on the Rights of the Child. What
is most striking about the convention, what goes beyond the 1959 UN Declaration of Children's rights is, I suggest, the result of a very different children's
rights movement—one upheld, for example, by Georg Wilhelm Friedrich Hegel
(1770-1831) in express opposition to Rousseau. This essay will defend the neo-
humanist concept of children's rights more commonly associated with Wilhelm
von Humboldt (1767-1835), but to which Hegel also subscribed. Hegel did not
write extensively on children's rights.[6] Yet what he does say, developed in close
association with his particular philosophy of education, points to respect for a
basic right of the child to education in dialogical skills for adulthood, and not
merely as an end in itself to be enjoyed by children in deliberating and deciding their own life conditions as children. This is a right that does not depend
merely on our universal compassion for the millions of children who continue
to suffer in this world due to insecurity and a lack of life's necessities. Children
consciously suffer from starvation. But they may not consciously suffer from
violation of their basic right to nonvocational education, which their rights to
security and subsistence of course serve to support. Children already appreciate
that basic right to the extent that they want to be the equals of adults, but they
will fully appreciate it only when they are no longer children.

That there is a "basic" human right may seem to contradict United Nations
documents that consistently deny a hierarchy in such rights and hold all such
rights to be not only interrelated but indivisible. But we avoid affirming a basic
adult human right in the sense of a right which appears at the top of a hierarchy
of rights. It can be argued that there is only one adult human right (freedom of
expression in dialogue) which "other" rights serve to support. In other words,
they are the same universal right under different particular descriptions. Thus,
the right to freedom of expression is under one description that very right under
the more particular description of a right to food, since the exercise of freedom
of expression is severely restricted by starvation. But the same basic right also

assumes the form of a right to vote, since governments which we freely elect are less likely to persecute us. The basic universal moral right along with all its particular forms can be justified all at once. They all promote dialogue open to all on an even playing field. Such dialogue results in true belief, and thus in successful action in the world, more than the appeal to self-evidence or dialogue before a restricted audience.

Is There a Basic Right of the Child?

If we are correct about the basic adult human right, there would seem to be an implied basic child's right. Hegel rejected the notion, championed by Rousseau and Pestalozzi, that school should be a mere playground in which school-age children learn not merely by the games they play with one another but also, and more fundamentally, by solving problems directly posed by the natural environment.[7] He rather held that school-age children learn chiefly by increasing association with adults, by participating increasingly in adult activities. Thus, the most intelligent thing children can do with their toys is to break them.[8] He held that Rousseau's belief in the essential virtue of children was misguided. Virtue for him was a learned habit. Children perceive themselves as failing to live up to what they ought to become as adults. Educators should focus on helping children realize their potential for adulthood. Children, once they realize the gap between themselves and adults, take the standpoint of their educators and likewise view adulthood as their essential unrealized potential. Achievement of this goal is the central purpose of school education. And if this is the central purpose of K-12 education, it is all the more so the purpose of university education. University educators err if they view entering freshmen and women, during the last stage of childhood, as "their kids" and allow the act of taking their standpoint to gain the upper hand over the expectation that the students should take the standpoint of their educator. The fact that this happens less often in American universities today education reflects a failure of education from the first grade on.

According to Hegel's hard saying, the natural impulsiveness of school children must first be broken and discipline imposed.[9] Obedience must be imposed not merely because it is a potential threat to others and to themselves as children, but even more importantly because it is a threat to their own future as adults. It is a mistake for educators to merely encourage play beyond the earliest childhood. However much video games give training in adroit motor skills, they do not induct children into the adult discussion of issues affecting them.

Commentators on the UN Convention commonly divide children's rights into the so-called three Ps: protection, provision, and participation. Infants and young children, due to their vulnerability, need to be protected and provided for. Their claim to protection and provision, since it is socially validated by a well-nigh universal consensus, establishes specific children's rights from birth onward in customary international law. Participation rights, increasing participation by children in adult deliberations, gradually come to be exercised by children only in the course of growing up. Participation rights progressively allow children to engage in dialogue about decisions affecting them. They enable children to offer their opinions, if not always to decide. They give them a right to be informed of alternatives between which to choose and of known indirect consequences of their choices insofar as they are able to understand them. The child flees child-hood by discontent with his or her childlike state.[10]

Participatory rights are declared in articles 12-17 of the convention as rights to freedom of thought, expression, communication, and access to informa-tion on all questions affecting the child. Such rights distinguish the convention from the 1959 United Nations Declaration of the Rights of the Child, which is restricted to protection and provision rights. If the convention is interpreted as setting a moral standard, the child's rights to protection and provision reappear as supports to the basic right of children to participation. The child exercises the dialogical right to participation only by way of exercising rights to freedom from fear and freedom from want.

Children are not yet adults. The list of children's rights in the convention omits certain adult human rights listed in the Universal Declaration of Human Rights. Children do not have the same right to marry, to vote, to work, or to move freely within and outside the borders of their country—all adult human rights according to the Universal Declaration. But the child rights movement does not define children's rights merely negatively as *not* being adult rights. Participatory child rights are conceived positively as rights in support of the adults children will become. Assuming freedom of expression as the basic adult human right,[11] the basic children's right is a right to a kind of nonvocational education already includ-ing some scope for freedom of expression, an education that will enable him or her to one day fully exercise the right to freedom of expression. There could be no closer relation between the basic adult human right and the basic right of the child.

A place for play, we noted, needs to be preserved alongside the academy even if school is more than a playground. But children should not be left to be-lieve that everything must be fun and games. Child education should be adult centered and child centered. In part, we grant participatory rights to children because we can learn from them. But children have a right to participation, in part, because the perpetuation of adult cosmopolitan inquiry requires ever new generations of adult dialogue partners.

A child cannot be educated merely through exposure to a diversity of sensory experiences, study tours, or field trips exploring different regions of the natural or increasingly cultural environment. Education should include memorization of words the child does not yet fully understand, encouraging the respect for what only adults understand.[12] Children have a publicly protected right to skills empowering participation in dialogue even against the will of their parents, and even against the will of the child. Children have a duty to develop skills making participation in dialogue a real option, although they have no duty to take that option on any given issue. No duty exists to dialogue under duress; the credibility of dialogue depends on its voluntary character.

Given this concept of the basic right of the child, which ethically the children's rights movement should support, I want to address six questions about the movement's use of the convention: Can child rights declared to exist in the convention really exist? If they do exist, how are they "inalienable," as the convention claims in its preamble? Assuming that the right to education in dialogical skills is the principal right of the child, what form should that education take? Is homeschooling compatible with the convention, and, if so, what kind? Could the United States ratify the convention consistently with the US Constitution? How can the convention be used by the child rights movement in the developing or non-Western world?

Do Children's Rights Actually Exist?

Since the entire UN human rights regime is committed only to the "promotion" of human rights, the convention does not oblige us to assume that the human rights of the child which it cites actually exist.[13] The convention itself invokes the norm of acting in the "best interests of the child."[14] But acting in the best interests of the child may mean paternalistically deciding in the place of the child for his or her own welfare without any assumption that the child has any rights. "Interests" may be translated as "benefits" or "advantages." An individual who acts to preserve his or her health acts in the best interest of his or her cells, that is, to their advantage. Healthy cells benefit by not being attacked by cancerous cells, but since cells are not persons they have no rights.

Whether or not universal children's rights exist, it is clear that children have some rights. Rights are, minimally, socially validated claims within some group, and children stake out tacit claims. A baby does in screaming for the attention of his or her parents when in need. Babies acquire genuine social rights to the extent that their parents recognize the validity of such claims and respect them to the extent of their ability. Parents normally respect the infant's right to successfully pursue satisfaction of natural propensities like the food drive. The baby has an inalienable natural propensity to pursue nutrition, though without a natural right to succeed in this pursuit enforced by any natural law.[15] At least within the family he or she lays down a claim to food and normally has a socially validated right to succeed in this pursuit. The baby itself lays claim to this right as soon as it enters into two-way communication with a parent, so it is not a right exercised by others merely on the child's behalf.

A universal right of all children to education in dialogical skills might seem to be a so-called "putative right" of infant children, a right imputed to them by adults, since it is a right to which they do not yet lay claim. Yet such a right is not a putative right in the usual legal sense. Your right to the security of your house is putative in the usual sense because your neighbor, in protecting your house from burglary during your absence, acts as you would act if you knew the clear and present danger which he or she knows. Yet no matter how much we warn young children of the threat to their future due to deficient education, some may not appreciate the warning or act on the threat upon being informed. Instead of saying such children have a putative right, we might say they have a prospective past-tense adult human right to have received an education in dialogical skills as a child. Grown human beings have a *past-tense adult human right* to have received as education in dialogical skills as a child. As an adult, one can discover that his or her parents or schools have violated this right. The right to have received an education in dialogical skills is, like the right to food, an important form of the basic adult human right to an equal opportunity for freedom of expression. Parents and schools need to act on behalf of the adults whom children will become. Yet this is not to deny that children also have a present-tense human right to freedom of expression on matters that they perceive to be of concern. We only say that they have a prospective past-tense right to have received an education in dialogical skills even if, as children, they do not actually perceive such education to be a matter of concern to them.

I suggest that the actual existence of children's rights must meet four conditions. Universal children rights will exist only when they are claimed by virtually all children either directly, by others on their behalf, or by the adults whom children become; when the claim is recognized by a general human consensus to be valid; when the claim insofar as possible is customarily respected; and when a violation of children's rights in exception to that general consensus threatens negative consequences for the violator. Universal children's rights will exist only when violations set in motion procedures aiming, insofar as possible, at effective punishment and enforcement. Whether or not children's rights exist is thus an empirical question. If, in any nation or region of the world, children's rights declared in the convention are violated while the violators face no consequences, universal children's rights do not really exist. They are then moral ideals or at most obligations insofar as steps exist to realize them. Yet, even without the real existence of children's rights, there remains a children's rights movement supported in part by the monitoring provided by the convention. Because the convention is not well enforced, it has not crowned the child rights movement with success; nevertheless, the convention represents the continuation of the movement under another form, guided by internationally ratified and monitored ethical norms.

Child rights, like adult human rights, insofar as they are also economic rights, may exist by virtue of seriously attempted enforcement, even if it is not fully effective. But a mere half-hearted effort at enforcement does not prove the existence of those civil or due process rights of the child which, not needing any financing, solely depend on an act of good will by individuals, or by the states to which we individuals delegate some responsibility for enforcement. For example, the child's right not to be subjected to humiliating or degrading punishment (article 37) can be enforced merely by a voluntary decision to refrain from such punishment. But the child's right to an education in participatory dialogical skills is, in part, an economic right which the nations of the world are obliged to respect not only progressively but also conscientiously, according to their resources and according to their careful judgment as to which child rights claims are most pressing.

By Thomas Hobbes's (1588-1679) legal positivist criterion for verifying law, if one breaks "the law" without a well-grounded fear of consequences, it is not really the law. Merely intended enforcement leaves us with merely intended law. Hobbes's legal positivist legal theory is valid only for law in a strong domestic sense. International human rights law, including child rights law, is law only in a weaker sense—however legally binding it is from a purely international law perspective sometimes out of touch with conditions around the world on the ground. Thus, the child's weaker but universal right to an education can exist simply by the worldwide enforcement of one doable step after another toward full observance of the right—qualified only by the obligation to finance the most pressing child rights claim at the time, which might be the right to food and hence to life itself rather than the right to education.

Many children learn that they have participation rights (such as the right to nonvocational education) as well as protection and provision rights locally if not universally. The usual way learn this is not by being taught the Convention on the Rights of the Child, but by working through life situations with the consistent help of others. Children who in their home life achieve security, sustenance, and inclusion in dialogues of concern to them may be stricken with fear, deprivation, and exclusion when they venture out alone among strangers.

They begin to learn that they have universal children's rights by gradually finding that strangers consistently protect them, like other children, from deprivation, danger, and exclusion from discussion of matters of concern to them. As
long as these rights are violated anywhere with impunity, universal children's
rights do not yet fully exist.

Children's rights, like all human rights, are said to be inalienable by the
convention (preamble). But, if they were truly inalienable, they would not need
to be protected. A rational interpretation of the text can only mean that they
are inalienable from children in a morally ideal situation. What we today call
children's rights have been alienated from countless children throughout history, and this alienation continues despite the convention. Yet the convention
reflects a revolution of rising moral expectations. When the convention is held
in mind, there is greater awareness that violations have occurred.

ADULT-CENTERED CHILD EDUCATION

Children begin to view themselves as aspiring adults as soon as they try to enter serious discussions with parents, teachers, or other adults. They aspire to
acquire adult dialogical skills after they have made such an attempt, only to
discover that they have participated in discussion at a disadvantage, due to the
superior skills and background information of their adult discussion partners.
In the worst cases, when they fail to express themselves effectively, their questions are dismissed as lacking in seriousness. Adults may help empower the
budding adult in the child by carefully listening to questions without implying
that the answer is "obvious," that is, not worth asking. Children feel disrespect
when adults respond in a condescending manner.[16]

If the right to freedom of thought and expression for children takes the
form of a right to education in dialogical skills for adulthood, to what kind of
education does a child have a right? Two simple models exist for education. Either children may receive instruction dispensed from the standpoint of school-
masters and parents as authoritative external dispensers of truth. Or the teacher
ceases to posture as the high priest of truth, as the sighted one leading the blind,
in favor of dialogical facilitator.[17] The facilitator takes the child's standpoint non-
condescendingly and, through dialogue, accompanies him or her down a path
to reflection on issues of perceived concern to the child.

Critical educators, like Paulo Freire (1921-1997), fear that the schoolmaster's approach of inculcating obedience to commanding authority may create in
children a desire to simply dish out, upon attaining adulthood, what they have
received as children. The strict discipline to which school children are subjected
even today in a country like France tends to brand a good part of the population

for life. Teachers receive obedience in the classroom, but adult citizens outside the teaching profession play with less success the role of the schoolmaster, with regular cutting criticisms of one another as well as those under their supervision. If we wish to create a population of citizens with a large store of knowledge, but who can also work together cooperatively rather than with a largely competitive mindset of mutual fault-finding, we should begin education from elementary school based neither on mere lecturing nor on leaderless discussion, but on lecturing placed in a clear dialogical context.

Inducting children into the mere appearance of dialogue is not enough. Even the devil can draw children into a semblance of dialogue that really amounts to manipulation. We must refrain from engaging them in phony dialogue.[18] Children are smart enough to know when dialogue is not sincere. Dialogue in which one does not put oneself at risk as an educator, but in which one knows beforehand the conclusion of the dialogue, is not authentic. It is authentic only when educators perceive themselves as capable of learning from children and students as well as of teaching them. When teachers cannot suspend the presumption of superior knowledge, they should not pretend to dialogue.

Dialogue about the multiplication tables may not be appropriate. The child should simply memorize them on authority. Yet if rote memorization is not to be irksome and off-putting, the child needs to perceive it as directly connected with his or her own aims in life. A negative aim can be to escape inferiority, while a positive aim can be the desire to grow up. The young Mozart cannot create music without first learning the scales. Yet the child's right to liberating education is a right to accept only a necessary minimum of obedience training. Hegel held that educators must break the impulsive will of young children who do not yet see where their higher interest lies by forcing obedience to rote memorization in reading, writing, and arithmetic.[19] Freire adds that the child will harness him- or herself to the discipline of a definite task, such as literacy, more willingly when the task is seen as a means to liberation from oppression,[20] that is, to equality with adults.

Dialogue with young children allows the educator to be educated by the child about his or her perceptions, fears, and anxieties. Freire was influenced by Hegel's dialectic of lordship and bondage in his ideal dialogical education as emancipatory.[21] Yet Hegel retained a role for the "banking model" of education which Freire criticizes.[22] Banking remains primarily important in that children and students become frustrated with aimless classroom discussion that leaves them with nothing to take to the bank.

The oppression to which Freire objects is not oppression by parents or educators as such. It is social oppression. The authority of parents may channel

sexism, racism, ethnocentrism, or Western chauvinism. Hegel himself com-
municated oppressive social structures to his illegitimate son Ludwig in suggesting that he was not destined for the liberal professions.[23] He also conveyed
the oppression of women in his attitude towards his wife, and towards girls for
whom he did not think that academic secondary or university education was
appropriate.[24] He opposed despotism in general, but, illogically, not always despotism in particular.

In dialogue educators and children alternately pose questions and reply.
Questioning eliminates the schoolmaster's authoritative position as a source of
enlightenment beyond appeal. If the adult respondent fails to be convincing,
the child questioner begins to assume dialogical leadership with a responsibility to respond to further questions. Overall equality in dialogue does not mean
equality between dialogue partners at any given time, but implies an alterna-
tion between temporary self-subordination to the other's dialogical leadership
and one's own temporary responsibility for such leadership. Temporary self-
subjection to apparent passive listening to lectures becomes active participatory
listening when placed in the larger dialogical context. The lecturer is open to
questioning, and to being the recipient of another's lectures. One pursues truth
by alternately speaking in awaiting a time to listen and listening while awaiting a time to speak.

Leaderless dialogue is the initial form assumed by dialogue. It paves the
road to dialogical leadership when the group identifies someone as a messenger. Whereas leadership not acclaimed by the group is authoritarian, democratic
leadership justifies itself by the lure of special knowledge that the children begin
to feel will come from someone. This lure may be based on the intrinsic interest
of some special knowledge, or the interest may be extrinsic and the lure diminished, based on the child's realization that reading, writing, and arithmetic are
obligatory if he or she is someday to assume dialogical leadership on some issue.

The onset of the lure for special knowledge begins the transformation of
pupils into students. Pupils do not at first recognize the division of knowledge
into areas of specialized knowledge. The messenger holds a finally dispensable
authority over the group. Once students assimilate the message, the messenger is
dispatched as the child acquires the ability to verify its truth. For a child, no lure
of special knowledge for children should become an exclusive passion. (Doctoral
students are different.) The forms of specialized knowledge, reflecting the various
environments in which teachers know an adult human being will need to operate, are different but related. The world of knowledge is like a chest of drawers,
and the student must know how to pull out one drawer, study its contents, and
put it back. Beginning in middle school, and then in high school, the zone of

free student inquiry gradually expands to new forms of specialized knowledge, and by the time students reach a university-level education the protective authority of the teacher, preventing pupils from pursuing specialized knowledge for which they are unprepared, is virtually eliminated.

HUMAN RIGHTS EDUCATION

Unlike primary school children, middle school and especially high school students become ready to study the adult Universal Declaration with its emphasis placed on freedom of expression, the "freedom of belief" which already has a place of privilege in the preamble, as in Franklin Delano Roosevelt's 1941 Four Freedoms Speech. If high school students do not yet exercise all the adult human rights declared in support of that basic right, they foresee that they may soon be able to do so. The discouraging "Not yet!" with which parental or school human rights educators, as Katherine Covell and Brian Howe see,[25] would have to confront young children becomes a more encouraging "Not quite yet."

We may distinguish pre-adolescent, adolescent, and adult human rights education. Basic human rights education, as contrasted to applied human rights education for adults, is remedial if only introduced in adulthood. We must assure early education for the child in his or her child rights as a precursor to the optimal exercise of adult human rights. More than any other special human rights convention, the Convention on the Rights of the Child is an essential complement to the UN universal covenants on human rights.[26] We were all children, and the child is the parent of the adult.

The induction of a child into dialogue requires dialogical role models. Initiating dialogue with children on matters of concern to them fosters in them a new self-identity as dialogue partners consciously empowered with the basic participatory right of freedom of expression. Such induction is possible for children who have never studied human rights law. The Universal Declaration of Human Rights should not be taught to children who cannot exercise several of them, and who do not yet understand their importance to their future adult lives. The failure to recognize this is a problem with the United Nations' own attempt to teach human rights to children by providing a plain language version of the Universal Declaration for use in primary and secondary schools.[27] Nor should children's rights be taught to children by didactically teaching the Convention on the Rights of the Child. Teachers inspired by the convention usually teach best by example.

Children's rights are limited by the fact that children are not able to assess the fuller implications of their choices. Since a young child does not always realize the implications of a choice not to attend school, being dialogical about such a matter may not be appropriate. Compulsory school attendance obliges the child to respect the right of the adult, whom he or she will become, to have had an education as a child; however, the year in which one reaches adulthood is indefinite. Adults are allowed a human right to make apparently foolish choices, and so why are not children who are close to being adults allowed to make choices which are questionable to others, such as the choice to end their schooling? It is paternalistic to disallow an adult a right to make choices which others find to be foolish. Such choices may objectively be foolish in some cases, in which cases adults still have a right to those choices and to learn from their foolishness. But, in other cases, the choices might not be foolish at all.

Homeschooling as Education in a Faith Tradition

One adult human right supporting the exercise of child rights is the parents' right to educate their children in their own cultural tradition (article 26, Universal Declaration of Human Rights). There is even a moral duty to exercise this parental right, assuming that every child has a right to be educated in a tradition, providing her or him with a nonanonymous personal initial identity and point of departure in dialogue. No child is obliged to maintain that identity in adult life, since dialogue may lead one to revise one's original standpoint. The parental right and duty helps perpetuate among children as many ways of life as possible as a resource for future dialogues, educating new generations of individuals representing those ways of life.

Education in a tradition or faith community is thus not antithetical to child and human rights education. The first is supportive of the second. On the surface, public schooling seems better able to guarantee child and human rights education, while homeschooling appears better able to assure education within a tradition. Parents who send their children to public school also commonly engage in homeschooling in a tradition, but parents who for whatever reason engage in exclusive homeschooling prima facie bear a burden of proof to show that they also provide child and human rights education. Public schools also bear a similar burden of proof to show that they do not undermine homeschooling in a tradition.

Secular human rights education in public schools is not identical with Christian human rights education at home. Two differences exist between secular human rights ethics taught as a universal moral minimum and Christian ethics. First, those who restrict themselves to secular human rights ethics believe that we can justify human rights, centered on freedom of expression and choice, without appeal to theology, as the precondition of the fullest possible dialogical pursuit of truth before a universal audience. By contrast, Christian ethics, like ethics in other theistic ethical traditions, holds that human rights are grounded in a particular theology assigning some divine excellence to each human being.

A second difference is that secular human rights ethicists believe that the fate of human rights depends only on the efforts of finite human beings, while theistic human rights moralists believe that the cause of human rights is assured of ultimate success by divine providence. These differences mean that Christian homeschooling goes beyond secular human rights education in public schools without being incompatible with it, since there is a secular human right to freedom of worship.

Some objectors to the Convention on the Rights of the Child in the United States, such as Michael Farris, question the compatibility of homeschooling in a faith tradition with the convention. Two types of homeschooling need to be distinguished. In most of the world and through most of history homeschooling, due to the lack of public schools or inadequate public schools, has been the only kind of schooling available. Homeschooling was traditionally homeschooling by private tutors if not by parents. Rousseau's Emile received such homeschooling. Hegel dispensed such homeschooling in the 1790s in Berne and Frankfurt in wealthy households. This old form of homeschooling has continued to exist in regions where universal elementary education is not been available, where it is not free, where the quality and funding of such education is inadequate, or where it violates minority rights or even practices ethnic cleansing.

Hegel participated in the fateful transition from private education for those who could afford it to mandatory public education under the impetus of Frederick the Great in Prussia. From 1808 to 1816 Hegel served as rector of the Nuremburg Gymnasium, strongly supporting compulsory and free elementary education and state-supported secondary education free from church control. By the middle of the nineteenth century this impulse from Germany reached the United States. It is true that public education was assigned a conservative ideological function by government officials during and after the Restoration. Examples include Karl Auguste von Hardenberg, under whom Hegel would serve as a Berlin philosophy professor,[28] and Victor Cousin (1792-1867), who as Minister of Education in Paris would introduce mandatory philosophy instruction in French lycées in the 1830's with the mission of thwarting revolutionary ardor among the young.[29] But William von Humboldt and Hegel assigned an emancipatory function to secondary education in the spirit of neo-humanism.[30] Classical education in ancient language and literature was emphasized in nineteenth century neo-humanism to free citizens from their immediate cultural environment and from purely vocational education in the service of the demands of the labor market.

The ancient Greeks were original, coining from direct experience the words to express that experience.[31] We in the modern world are dominated by book learning, the textbook, passing from words to an expanded range of borrowed, imaginary experience. Romantics in the tradition of Rousseau regretted the loss of originality implicit in book learning. Classical neo-humanists reconciled themselves to the irretrievability of what was lost, making book learning the basis of school education. Nonvocational education becomes cultural education or *Bildung*, reconstructing the complex world-historical cultural tradition in the mind of the child, originally through the study of ancient languages but more commonly today in the study of modern foreign languages.

The contemporary homeschooling movement in America sometimes differs from traditional homeschooling by the availability of quality public schooling. It is sometimes motivated negatively by suspicion of a possible authoritarian mind control of children exercised by the state, or positively by the desire to see children educated in a particular religious or cultural tradition. From the standpoint of many educators in the public schools, if not always from the standpoint of the state, public education seeks to promote dialogical freedom of thought and speech in both private and public life. There is no duty to dialogue on all matters, especially because dialogue under duress is not credible in any quest for truth. A contemporary human rights-based regime centering on the right to freedom of expression is compatible with the free choice of children who, while being given by their parents the opportunity to investigate other faiths, still prefer to exercise their right to uphold without questioning the faith of their parents.

Homeschooled children, like other children and even adults who value the religious identity of their parents, thus have a right to be nondialogical theologically. They are free to reject the view that those who disagree theologically with them have something to teach them. They are free to believe that they are self-evidently right on those issues, and that others are simply wrong, even damned.[32] Yet in the modern post-seventeenth-century human rights tradition they tolerate the equal rights of those who believe differently as the price to pay for noninterference in their own freedom of worship by others. They may have little concern for what others think or do as long as they are left alone. The Convention on the Rights of the Child does not deny the right to homeschool by withdrawing children from public schools. But it does assign to homeschoolers an obligation to educate children in human rights-promoted dialogical skills, even if it does not insist that those skills be exercised on matters theological. A growing child, having applied such skills on other issues, will then be equipped to apply these skills someday to theology, if he or she so chooses.

The responsibility to teach dialogical human rights is delegated to each sovereign state by the United Nations. A democratic citizenry educated in respect for human rights delegates to the state the same responsibility as a backup to its own direct responsibility for such teaching. In public education this responsibility is carried out directly by the government. In homeschooling the responsibility is delegated by the state back to parents, and the burden of proof lies on parents to demonstrate that they are discharging this obligation, which did not originate in the family as an institution. Parents have no right to dispense just any kind of homeschooling. The Universal Declaration states: "Education shall be directed to the full development of the human personality and to the strengthening of respect for human rights and fundamental freedoms. It shall promote understanding, tolerance and friendship among all nations, racial or religious groups" (article 26).

No belief is held rationally unless it is held dialogically with openness to criticism. UN human rights culture is secular, but secularism is not atheism.[33] Freedom of worship as a secular right includes the freedom to believe creationism even by a dogmatic leap of faith. Secular rights are compatible with nonsecular faith. Homeschooling in a faith tradition allows a right to dogmatic faith.

Subject to the qualification that "States Parties agree that the education of the child shall be directed to: . . . (b) The development of respect for human rights and fundamental freedoms . . . (article 29)," the convention explicitly declares a right to homeschool: "no part of the present article [article 29] or article 28 shall be construed so as to interfere with the liberty of individuals and bodies to establish and direct educational institutions." Yet the qualification authorizes some state monitoring of homeschooling, which must also meet other state standards even if education is not dispensed by the state.

A difference exists between the obligation to give education in dialogical skills and the obligation to feed children. The family, however structured, is the most ancient human institution. Given an infant's inability to survive by instinct, the family has a natural function in respecting protection and provision rights of the child. The marketplace and the state are more recent, based on convention rather than natural law. But when about six thousand years ago the sovereignty of the state emerged to replace that of the family, the family agreed to add to its natural functions certain conventional state functions delegated to it. The family acquired the duty of paying taxes and submitting some disputes between family members to state arbitration. In the present time it has acquired the duty to respect insofar as possible universal human rights.

But the state cannot delegate to the family, without further supervision, responsibilities so specialized that the family has no effective natural competence to fulfill the obligation on its own. Children should learn to respect human and child rights at an age when moral character formation can best take place. It follows that parents have an obligation to allow for education in children's rights and human rights, whether they dispense this education or not. This is relevant to the question as to where the burden of proof in homeschooling lies. The burden of proof that parents provide food and shelter does not lie with the parents. Rather, the state has the burden of proof to show that the parents are not doing this, since the natural presumption is that the parents are. But it is difficult to say that they have no such burden in the matter of obligations delegated to them by the state. Yet just as there is a right to revolution if the state should violate basic human rights, a parental right to homeschool is clear if the state should indoctrinate public school pupils in an ideology, religion, or value system other than respect for child and human rights.

THE UNITED STATES AND THE CONVENTION ON THE RIGHTS OF THE CHILD

The fact that the United States has not ratified the Convention on the Rights of the Child does not mean that it has been or is insensitive to various particular rights of children. It has ratified international conventions for the protection of selected children's rights, especially the first two protocols to the Convention on the Rights of the Child, one protocol protecting children from being recruited as soldiers in armed conflict and the other protecting them from servitude and exploitation in child pornography.[34] Further, it has passed numerous federal laws promoting the interests of children, such as the 1946 National Lunch Act and other legislation promoting education.

The United States has declined to ratify the convention because, for one thing, it has not ratified the United Nations Convention on Economic, Social, and Cultural Rights (UNCESC), which the Convention on the Rights of the Child presupposes.[35] Yet quality freedom of speech is an empty rhetorical abstraction unless it includes the child's right to any necessary funding of the right. The philosopher Immanuel Kant (1727-1804) said that no one really wills the end if he or she fails to will the means.[36] If particular child rights like the right to nutrition are necessary to support optimal exercise of freedom of inquiry of the child, the failure to will such economic rights is a failure to seriously will freedom of inquiry.

In 2001, the Bush Administration was quite willing to commend the Child Rights Convention with its economic rights to other nations,[37] but with mounting federal deficits, today's Congress is ever more wary of entitlement rights. Although the Obama Administration has a full plate, it has placed ratification of the convention on its agenda, but there is little expectation that it will be presented to the Senate for ratification in the near future.[38]

A relative decline in American economic power in the twenty-first century means that the nation is less capable of asserting its military preeminence as the chief agent of world security, costing 40% or more of federal tax receipts. Multilateralism with a fairer distribution of the cost of world security would place the United States more on a plane of equality with other traditional and emerging world powers, and establish it as more nearly an equal dialogue partner within the international community. The effect may be to reduce American exceptionalism and the nation's aversion to ratifying conventions like the Convention on the Rights of the Child.

Many child rights activists continue to believe that the United States could benefit from monitoring by the Childrens' Rights Committee as along as, for example, children are still imprisoned with adults, tried in courts of law with adults, and until 2005, executed.[39] For Americans to believe that they cannot use the help from a UN Convention which they believe may be good for other nations, and which contains rights absent in the US Constitution, smacks to such activists as arrogance.

Some claim that United States ratification of the convention would violate sovereignty and the Constitution.[40] Yet article 6 of the Constitution grants treaty-making authority to the government of the United States, and characterizes treaties as belonging to the supreme law of the land. American courts have found that human rights and humanitarian treaties are not self-executing in domestic courts without further federal legislation,[41] but there is no basis for such a judgment in article 6. Conservatives in fact need to be concerned that a future Congress and Supreme Court might reverse the current view, which is really more a matter of policy than of law.[42] Placing the United States under the authority of international human rights law remains a prerogative of the Senate. That Congress would have to change conflicting federal law if the Convention on the Rights of the Child were implemented would be no objection to the convention if the United States would thereby gain help in providing greater respect for legitimate children's rights.

RIGHTS OF THE CHILD IN THE NON-WESTERN WORLD

If the right to education for dialogical skills is the basic children's right, we can criticize a failure in many developing nations to observe it. If a nation does not respect the adult human right to freedom of expression, it is not apt to respect the children's right to education for such freedom. All the attention to food, medical care, and even literacy for children falls short when totalitarian, authoritarian, or fundamentalist regimes provide food, social services, health care, and even literacy, but indoctrinate children instead of educating them to exercise and respect freedom of expression and choice. Western civilization also educated for religious indoctrination until the Enlightenment. The West in the seventeenth and eighteenth centuries, after the European religious wars and the Treaty of Westphalia, converted to the modern human rights of reciprocal religious tolerance, the principle of live-and-let-live or peaceful coexistence. The second, higher stage of human rights, dialogical human rights, in which we embrace fallibilism and engage in a cooperative search for the truth, began to emerge only after World War II.

Distinguishing between these two concepts of human rights, an ethically motivated stress on participation rights in the Convention on the Rights of the Child can only be justified by privileging contemporary dialogical human rights. Note the incongruence which arises if we try to found them on modern human rights. The motive by which adults would have to respect child rights would be a concern to restrict interference by children as well as adults in one another's freedom of action and belief! Child rights would presuppose that children are a threat to adults, which can be countered only by contracting peaceful coexistence with them, allowing them freedom of action and belief based on reciprocity. Although some parents, due to an exaggerated permissiveness, may actually have entered into such a contract with their own children, fearfulness of one's children or the toleration of brats is not the basis of child rights according to the convention.

The casual multiculturalism or diversity training of public schools is not as dialogically productive as parentally guided insertion of the child in an initial tradition as a starting point for the development of future dialogical capabilities. A child can learn dialogical skills without starting out with a perspective within a particular tradition, but can learn more easily by starting out with such a perspective, putting him or her on a global map of alternative traditions.

When we speak of child rights in developing nations, the developmental deficit is educational because it is more fundamentally economic. Dialogical rationality is a universal human value, although a great world-historical movement for such rationality happened to have begun in ancient Greece. However, there is nothing inherently antidialogical about non-Western cultures. Buddhist culture in economically underdeveloped Southeast Asian countries is dialogical without being Western.[43] Sufi culture in Islam is also dialogical.[44] Societies in which Buddhist or Sufi culture is prominent are often relatively poor economically. Respect for those who disagree and dialogical openness to what others say do not require huge investments of money. They require a moral choice. Such a choice is not compatible with starvation, which reduces thought to the thought of survival, but it is compatible with low income.

From this perspective, the challenge in the developing world is to discover the conditions under which the horrendous civil wars of the Balkans, Africa, and Latin America, along with sectarian religious conflicts in the Islamic and Eastern Orthodox world, might yield to something similar to the Enlightenment, which arose in Western Europe, but which also independently arose in Buddhist and Sufi enlightenment. No clash of civilizations makes this transition impossible for the non-Western world. A clash internal to the West between medieval mindsets and the seventeenth- and eighteenth-century Enlightenment was not insurmountable for medievals. If peaceful coexistence and eventually dialogical rationality are essential human interests, we may hope for a gradual decline of terrorist jihadism. Only dialogical enlightenment raised to the level of customary international law creates an understanding of the basic right of children. Yet, however good the case is for enlightenment, it may not come if global macro-economic conditions are not favorable. As we shall see, it is incompatible with dire poverty.

The dire poverty of much of the developing world effectively eliminates the American debate over homeschooling. The question is no longer whether exclusive homeschooling is a right whose exercise may sometimes be necessary if education in a parental tradition is undermined by public schools. The problem in the developing world is that of creating the universal availability of public education in the first place. Poverty may mean that parents lack the resources to provide for education at home, that is, that a parental cultural tradition maintained merely by homeschooling is likely to be marginalized in global civil society. Certain sectarian groups may of course opt for marginalization rather than assimilation to the secular world culture. But many more parents in the developing world want little more for their children than to become competitive in the global labor market. In many developing countries, public school education is needed to assure access to a borrowed international language opening children to global lines of communication and employment. In these countries, the cause of the education of children, and hence of children's rights generally, depends on the achievement of millennial development goals raising living standards and combating poverty.[45]

Due to dire poverty, it is common in the developing world for individuals to receive child rights and human rights education dispensed largely to the victims of abuse. Yet the least developed nations also often give more official publicity to child and human rights. A consequence of their poverty is the need for foreign aid. Child and human rights education is often more explicit in the governmental policies of a nation like Burkina Fasso, which has a Ministry for the Promotion of Human Rights, than in the West. The United States and the West in general are the historical sources of the dominant world human rights movement. Governments in the movement's historical homes, such as France or the United States, may rest on their laurels domestically while imposing higher human rights standards on developing nations depending on them for aid. Hence the attraction of Chinese foreign aid without human rights strings attached.

A second consequence of dire poverty is the abuse of child labor and its negative effect on the exercise of citizenship rights by the adults children one day will become, as Jorge Bula has amply shown.[46] Traditional political citizenship, suffering from the inability of many developing countries to afford universal public education, may be replaced by a new, socially validated citizenship through personal consumption. Children are lured into the labor market by a mirage of purchasing power, even though any such empowerment it gives vanishes upon closer inspection. Enfranchisement by conspicuous consumption among peers is a failed substitute for political citizenship. Industrialization in the United States a century ago on the Henry Ford model, with secure jobs, radically differs from the current process of capital accumulation in developing nations. Child labor even more than adult labor is precarious, intermittent, and even uncompensated.

The fact that some developing countries, such as those in the Balkans, never fell within the colonial domain of a historical Western European human rights homeland also reduces the capacity of its political leadership and for nongovernmental organizations in civil society to dispense such education. The United Nations and the Council of Europe have been attempting to fill this void in Kosovo since the end of the air war in 1999. But a native Kosovar human rights culture, which for the international community was posed as a precondition of Kosovo's acceptability as a sovereign entity, takes root with difficulty. It is not easy to create any culture in committee or merely by governmental edict. Yet, despite such hurdles, the children's right movement continues. As with the adult human rights movement, child rights workers in developing nations, as Krisjon Olson has shown,[47] continue to struggle to resist the temptation of stoic resignation. Good evidence of this is provided by Krisjon Olson's story in this volume.

NOTES

1.   J.-J. Rousseau, *Emile: Or Treatise on Education*, trans. William Payne (Amherst, NY: Prometheus Books, 2003).

2.   K. Silber, *Pestalozzi: The Man and His Work*. (London: Routledge and Kegan Paul, 1960).

3.   F. Froebel, *Froebel's Chief Writings on Education*, trans. S. S. F. Fletcher and J. Welton (London: Edward Arnold, 1912).

4.   M. T. P. Mann and E. Palmer Peabody, *Moral Culture of Infancy, and Kindergarten Guide* (New York: J. W. Schemerhorn, 1870). http://www.archive.org/details/moralcultureinf00peabgoog.

5.   H. Cohen, *Equal Rights for Children* (Totowa, NJ: Littlefield, Adams, 1980); R. E. Farson, *Birthrights* (New York: MacMillan, 1974). Claire Cassidy defends a more moderate form of liberationism in chapter 8 of this volume. In the present essay I view existing children's rights as past-tense adult rights to a particular upbringing. However, I am persuaded by Cassidy that children should have a present-tense dialogical right with possible impact on their life conditions when it is not incompatible with the adult past-tense right to have received as a child an education making them effective interlocutors as adults. They should be able to enter dialogues, together with other children as a minority in assembly, and not merely with their parents but with adults generally. But such a child right does not yet exist, since is not recognized as valid by a general consensus of humanity, but is only the aim of a legitimate special rights movement.

6.   See G. W. F. Hegel, *Philosophy of Mind*, trans. W. Wallace and A. V. Miller (Oxford: Oxford, 1971), §396, §405; G. W. F. Hegel, *Philosophy of Right*, trans. T. M. Knox (London: Oxford, 1951), §173-§179, §187; C. Butler, "Hegel's Nuremberg Rectorship," in *Hegel: The Letters*, trans. C. Butler and C. Seiler with commentary by C. Butler (Bloomington: Indiana University Press, 1984), ch. 8; A. Wood, "Hegel on Education," in *Philosophy as Education*, ed. A. Rorty (London: Routledge, 1998), 300-17. Available online at www.stanford.edu/~allenw/webpapers/HegelEd.doc.

7.   K. Olson in this volume discusses use of the UN Convention in the context of the developing world. Hegel's concept of child remains valid here. Yet the immediate priority in this context needs to be given to the economics of poverty reduction, but while not acting against the end of dialogical skills on an even playing field. Only on this condition does the end justify the means.

8.   G. W. F. Hegel, *Philosophy of Right*, §396, Addition.

9.   Ibid., §174, Addition.

10.   Ibid., §396, Addition.

11.   C. Butler, *Human Rights Ethics: A Rational Approach* (West Lafayette: Purdue University Press, 2008), 165. The present essay seeks to extend my treatment of adult human rights in *Human Rights Ethics* into a compatible treatment of children's rights. The basic human right to freedom of expression in a dialogi-

cal quest for the truth—supported by the right to life, to democratic elections, and to all the other rights of which one commonly hears—is justifiable to all human beings as goal seekers. It is justifiable as a precondition to the rational and successful pursuit of any goals. Such success depends on true knowledge of the world to be transformed if the goal is to be realized. Ruling out self-evidence as a source of knowledge, since it has time and time again proven untrustworthy, the only remaining alternative path to true belief is dialogue—and ideally dialogue including dialogue partners from any quarter of the world.

12.   G. W. F. Hegel, *Philosophy of Mind*, §60-61.

13.   The question which David William Archard raises as to the existence of children's rights is motivated by a desire not to multiply rights beyond necessity. See *The Stanford Encyclopedia of Philosophy online, s.v.* "Children's Rights," accessed February 27, 2009, http://plato.stanford.edu/archives/win2008/entries/rights-children.

14.   United Nations Convention on the Rights of the Child, articles 3, 9, 18, 20, 21, 27, 37, 40.

15.   C. Butler, "Natural Rights, Human Rights," *Human Rights Ethics*, 25-36.

16.   "What the child is to learn must . . . be given to him on and with authority; he has the feeling that what is thus given to him is superior to him. . . . [W]e must describe as completely preposterous the pedagogy which . . . demands that the educator should lower himself to the childish level of intelligence . . . instead of lifting them up to an appreciation of the seriousness of the matter at hand." G. W. F. Hegel, *Philosophy of Right*, §396, Addition.

17.   A. Darder, M. Baltodano, and R. D. Torres, eds. *The Critical Pedagogy Reader* (New York: Routledge, 2003).

18.   G. W. F. Hegel, *Philosophy of Mind*, 60; G. W. F. Hegel, *Philosophy of Right*, 118.

19.   G. W. F. Hegel, *Philosophy of Right*, §174, Addition.

20.   P. Freire and D. P. Macedo, *Pedagogy of the Oppressed* (London: Continuum International, 2000).

21.   G. W. F. Hegel, *Phenomenology of Spirit*, trans. A. V. Miller (Oxford: Oxford University Press, 1974), ch. 4.

22.   P. Freire, *Education: Authority and Authoritarianism Dialogue Versus "Banking" Education* (Victoria, Australia: Move Records for the A.C.C. Commission on Christian Education, 1974).

23.   C. Butler, "Hegel's Natural Son Ludwig," in Hegel, *The Letters*, 423-39.

24.   C. Butler, "Hegel's Idea of Marriage, Science or Ideology," in Hegel, *The Letters*, ch. 9, 234-52.

25. K. Covell and R. B. Howe, "Human Rights Education: *Developmental Considerations in Teaching Children's Rights*," in this volume.

26. United Nations Covenant on Civil and Political Rights (UNCCPR); United Nations Covenant on Economic, Social, and Cultural Rights (UNCESCR).

27. *ABC, Teaching Human Rights: Practical Activities for Primary and Secondary Schools*, Office of the United Nations High Commissioner for Human Rights, accessed June 3, 2009, www.unhchr.ch/html/menu6/2/abc.htm.

28. Hegel, *Hegel: The Letters*, 575.

29. L. Sève, "Philosophie et Politique," in *La Philosophie française contemporaine* (Editions Sociales, 1962), ch. 1.

30. D. Sorkin, "Wilhelm Von Humboldt: The Theory and Practice of Self-Formation (*Bildung*), 1791-1810," *Journal of the History of Ideas* 44, no. 1 (1983): 55-73.

31. G. W. F. Hegel, "On Some Characteristic Distinctions of the Ancient Poets," trans. C. Butler, in *Miscellaneous Writings of G. W. F. Hegel*, ed. J. Stewart (Evanston, IL: Northwestern University Press, 2002), 14-18.

32. C. Butler, *Human Rights Ethics*, 3-8.

33. Ibid.

34. The United States ratified the optional protocol on the sale of children, child prostitution, and child pornography in 2002. It ratified a second protocol protecting the rights of children in armed conflict in 2003.

35. Preamble, Convention on the Rights of the Child (CRC).

36. "Whoever wills the end, wills also (so far as reason decides his conduct) the means in his power which are indispensably necessary thereto." I. Kant, *Fundamental Principles of the Metaphysic of Morals*, trans. T. M. Abbott., ch. 2, 33, accessed December 21, 2011, www2.hn.psu.edu/faculty/jmanis/kant/Metaphysic-Morals.pdf.

37. "The Convention on the Rights of the Child may be a positive tool for promoting child welfare for those countries that have adopted it. But we believe the text goes too far when it asserts entitlements based on economic, social and cultural rights. . . . The human rights-based approach . . . poses significant problems as used in this [convention] text." Quoted from the official United States statement in response to the preliminary UNICEF draft in second preparatory meeting for a Special Session on Children by M. J. Anderson, "Bush Team Signals New UN Direction: Decries 'Erosion of Parental Authority,' in Internationalization of Family Policy," *World Net Daily*, February 2, 2001, accessed July 16, 2011, www.wnd.com/?pageId=8046.

38. J. Heilprin, "Obama Administration Seeks To Join UN Rights Of The Child Convention," *Huffington Post*, June 23, 2009, accessed August 27,

2010, http://www.huffingtonpost.com/2009/06/23/obama-administration-seek_n_219511.html.

39.   See, for example, "Reform the Nation's Juvenile Justice System," A. E. Casey Foundation, January 2009, accessed February 27, 2009, www.aecf.org.

40.   M. Farris, "Nannies with Berets: The CRC and the Invasion of National and Family Sovereignty," in this volume.

41.   T. Buergenthal, D. Shelton, and D. Stewart, *International Human Rights* (St. Paul, MN: West, 2002), 371.

42.   Ibid., 359-77.

43.   "It is in the essence of Buddhism to be a developing process in dialogue. The initial steps of the dialogue are in the presumed earliest records of Buddhism." A. Watts, *Buddhism the Religion of No-Religion: The Edited Transcripts* (North Clarendon, VT: Tuttle, 1999), 14.

44.   H. Kim, "Gulen's Dialogic Sufism: A Constructional and Constructive Factor of Dialogue," in *Islam in the Age of Global Challenges: Alternative Perspectives of the Gulen Movement,* Conference Proceedings, Rumi Forum, Georgetown University, 2008, 374-406, accessed February 27, 2009, http://www.rumiforum. org/server/images/stories/events/conference/georgetown2008_gulenconference/ Materials/ConferenceProgram.pdf.

45.   Regarding the Millennial Development Goals, see "We Can End Poverty 2115: Millennial Goals," accessed July 16, 2011, www.un.org/millennium-goals. See also C. Butler, "The Coming World Welfare State Hegel Did Not See" in *Hegel and Global Justice* (New York: Springer, 2012).

46.   J. Bula and L. F. Camacho, *Ciudadanía y trabajo infantil. La lógica económica y la dimensión ética del problema del niño trabajador* (Bogotá: Universidad Externado de Colombia, 2006).

47.   K. Olson, *"The Right Child:" Challenges and Opportunities of Child Rights Legislation in Theory and Practice,* in this volume.

Two

The Case for the Convention on the Rights of the Child from the Perspective of Child Psychology

⌒ Katherine Covell ⌒

During the latter part of the twentieth century there was a growth of human rights consciousness, and of knowledge about and legislation to protect healthy child development.[1] These trends converged to produce a changing view of children from one of parental property to one of independent persons with dignity and basic rights of their own.[2] During this time, recognition of the status of children as persons with rights increasingly was reflected in the incorporation of a children's rights perspective into new legislation, legal principles, and court decisions.[3] That status received official recognition with the adoption by the General Assembly of the United Nations of the Convention on the Rights of the Child (CRC) in 1989, and with ratification of the convention by virtually all countries of the world during the 1990s. The convention is a landmark document in the history of childhood and of international law and public policy dealing with children. My purpose is to describe the significance of the convention and how the rights approach to providing for children differs from the needs approach. I also examine the myths and misperceptions about the convention that hamper its full implementation. I end by outlining how childhood development would be healthier were children's Convention rights fully realized, and suggest that one route to this is through the systematic provision of children's rights education.

What is the Convention on the Rights of the Child?

The major significance of the convention is that it officially elevates the status of children worldwide to persons in their own right, and puts to rest lingering assumptions about parental and state paternalism with regard to children.[4] By ratifying the convention, states are agree that children are not simply "noble causes" but "worthy citizens."[5] Ratifying states put on record their agreement that children are claim holders who have fundamental rights as individual persons, and that parents, adults, and state authorities are duty bearers who have obligations for providing for those rights.[6]

As the most quickly and widely ratified international convention in world history, the Convention on the Rights of the Child reflects a near global consensus on what childhood should be, and a near global commitment to make laws, policies, and practices consistent with the provisions of the convention, if not immediately, then over time in the case of economic, social, and cultural rights. It is only a near global consensus and commitment because there remain two countries which have signed, but not yet ratified, the convention.

Somalia has been unable to ratify the convention due to its ongoing state of civil war. The United States, which signed the convention in 1995, has made no move toward its ratification. It has been argued that a major reason for the US failure to ratify the convention, other than political complexities, is based in public concerns that the rights of children would override the rights of parents, and that the convention would override American sovereignty.[7] Nonetheless, the convention remains an important guide for much child advocacy in the United States and for professional practice.[8] States such as Vermont have passed resolutions in support of the convention and of its ratification, and the convention has been used as a basis for developing child policies and practices at local, state, and federal levels.[9] And importantly, since the United States did sign the convention, it is at least obligated not to adopt policies internationally contrary to its purposes.[10]

The convention is also significant in that it is the first document of international law in which the psychological needs of children are given equal primacy with their physical and material needs. It seems likely that this attention to the psychological needs of the child is an outgrowth of the increasing knowledge about child development. Consistent with previous declarations and charters, the convention articulates children's rights to provision of their basic needs (for example, education, health care) and to protection from all forms of harm (for example, sexual and physical abuse). In a radical departure from earlier documents, the convention also articulates children's rights to participation. In fact, a fundamental guiding principle of the convention, described in article 12, is that children have the right to participate in all matters that affect them with their views being given weight according to their age and maturity. Yet under article 5 the child does so subject to measured parental guidance in accordance with his or her evolving capacity. Participation has a potential for meeting the child's psychological needs through enabling the development of a positive sense of self, effective decision making, a sense of efficacy, self-confidence, and a sense of belonging to family and community.[11] It is noteworthy also that the right to participation promotes the recognition of children as contemporaneous rather than merely future citizens, as citizens who must be given a voice.

The convention has two other guiding principles. The principle of non-discrimination, described in article 2, requires that all appropriate measures be taken to ensure that every child is protected from negative discrimination of any kind, including but not limited to criteria such as race, language, religion, or sex. The principle of the best interests of the child, stated in article 3, requires that these interests are to be a primary consideration in all actions concerning children, whether undertaken by public or private social welfare institutions, courts of law, administrative authorities, or legislative bodies.

The convention thus provides a standard for legislation, policy making, and programs. It is a standard that is different in nature and in its implications from one based on paternalistic notions of children's needs. When it comes to economic, social, and cultural rights in the convention, states parties are required to progressively realize such rights through the adoption of rights-based laws, policies, and programs according to their evolving resources.

NEEDS VERSUS RIGHTS

The key differences between adopting legal rights-based practices and needs-based practices have been well identified.[12] In essence, a needs-based approach is a paternalistic or welfare approach in which children, as objects of pity, are the passive recipients of others' benevolence. Children's ostensible needs are identified, a hierarchy of their importance is determined, and practices are implemented to supply children with their most pressing needs. Although needs are recognized as creating obligations, meeting these obligations is motivated only by moral or charitable considerations. The needs approach focuses on dealing with the overt manifestations or proximal causes of problems; it does not concern itself with the participation or empowerment of its target group. A needs approach does not recognize its target group as bearers of rights. In contrast to this approach are the four essential principles of a children's rights-based approach to program, policy, and practice.

First is the recognition that each and every child is a bearer of rights, a claim holder of rights that are morally inalienable. A child can neither give up nor lose his or her rights regardless of behavior, family context, or parental wishes. Children should be empowered through skills building and provision of knowledge to lay claim to their rights and to exercise them. This may require some alteration to existing practices and institutions in order to allow meaningful participation for children, participation that is directed to and likely to affect real outcomes.

Second is the recognition of the obligations of those who can be held accountable and against whom a claim can be made. Thus there are legal, rather than merely moral, obligations to work for the betterment of children, to respect, protect, and fulfill all child rights to which ratifying states are committed.[13] Such recognition is most apparent in those few state parties, such as Belgium, where the convention is self-executing, that is, where its effect without further implementing legislation is immediate upon ratification and it can be invoked as the basis of a claim in a court of law.[14] In other states parties, pressure from advocacy groups, capacity building, and empowerment through training are commonly prerequisites to the realization of the obligations of states parties. At the very least, all states parties are accountable to the UN Committee on the Rights of the Child to whom they must report their progress and by whom their efforts to implement the convention are monitored.

Third is the recognition that the rights of the convention are indivisible. Rights cannot be prioritized and considered in hierarchical order. This does not require that in efforts to improve children's lives it is necessary to target all rights at the same time. However, it does require that in the targeting of any one area, for example, the right to health care, there be due consideration of how the focus on that right may undermine or contribute to the realization of others, whether in general or for subgroups of children. Thus, changes in health care policy and practice should be undertaken in ways such that they can be shown not to undercut the exercise of children's rights to education and to protection from harmful substances.

Fourth is the recognition of the need to be proactive by addressing the distal as well as proximal causes of rights infringements. Rights approaches not only focus on the overt and immediate manifestations of problems, but also examine and address their underlying causes.[15] Considering the rapidity of child development and the possible consequences of rights violations, it is not enough to react to an infringement of a child's rights. It is important to affect programming and policy that prevents infringements. Preventive interventions should always be evidence based. The Committee on the Rights of the Child has recommended the use of child-impact statements in the evaluation of policies and programs and in the assessment of changes to them. These together with existing research in the social sciences can provide an excellent foundation for proactive programming.

It is important to note also that the criterion for success differs between the two approaches. Using the same example of changes in health care, a needs-based approach would measure success in terms of what proportion of children had better access to health care after changes to policies and programs. An outcome showing that the changes resulted in sixty-five percent more children having access to health care would be considered a highly successful outcome. The criterion of success with a rights-based approach, however, is more stringent. Beyond the requirement that improvements in health care be shown not to undermine improvements in other areas of rights, there are two further requirements for success. First, in accordance with the principle of participation is the requirement that changes be made with children or with the chosen representatives of children. Secondly, in accordance with the principle of nondiscrimination, changes must provide a benefit for every child. The sixty-five percent would not be considered adequate. It would be necessary to identify obstacles to inclusion, for example, by age, gender, ethnicity, religion, or geographic area. It would be necessary to show how discriminatory practices, if any, are being sustained, and to ascertain what is being done to address them.

CRITICS OF RIGHTS-BASED APPROACHES

Some critics of children's rights continue to argue that children are better served by the needs or welfare approach. Onora O'Neill, for example, believes that identifying adult moral obligations to children will provide the optimum means of bettering children's lives.[16] There are two fundamental flaws with her argument. First, as Michael Freeman notes, such an approach places the obligated parent rather than the child at center stage, and importantly denies the child the agency and participation that are inherent in the exercise of human rights by the child.[17] Participation is not only a fundamental human right; it is essential to the child's healthy growth.[18] Second, O'Neill appears to assume that parents will exercise their child-rearing obligations in the best interests of the developing child. As evidenced in high rates of abuse and neglect, especially in North America, this too often is not the case.[19] Moreover, it would seem that O'Neill is discounting the empirically demonstrated link between early rearing experiences and subsequent developmental outcomes. When children's rights are not recognized and respected, children are at risk of a range of poor developmental outcomes, including the intergenerational transmission of violence.[20] The costs to the individual child and to society are enormous.

Other critics of children's rights argue against rights in general. They believe that rights can result in excessive demands made by certain individuals at a cost to the group. This perspective is exemplified in the writings of ethicist Norman Daniels in the context of health care.[21] The essential concern is one of resource allocation. Is it fiscally responsible, or even possible, to provide the best possible health care, or education, or housing, and so forth to each and every child? Will the rights of a particular child, perhaps one whose medical condition requires extensive and expensive interventions, result in injustice, a lack of resources, to others? The issue of resource allocation, particularly with regard to health care, is a complex one, a detailed analysis of which is well beyond the scope of this essay. However there are two general points that can be made from the perspective of children's rights.

First, age rationing has been suggested as a possible response to resource scarcity. Although a contentious issue, existing agreements indicate that in any resource allocation, priority is to be given to children.[22] In 1990, the World Summit for Children was held as a follow-up to adoption of the Convention on the Rights of the Child by the UN General Assembly. At the summit, leaders of seventy-one states developed a global plan of action in which the principle of "first call for children" was agreed upon. The principle states that children should be given highest priority in the allocation of resources regardless of economic conditions.[23] This principle calls to mind the convention's article 4 obligation of states to allocate resources "to the maximum extent of their available resources" in realizing the economic, social, and cultural rights of children. Resources vary among states. In consequence, the convention obligates each state party to respect such rights by the highest standard uniformly affordable for all children.

Thus there is no requirement that any particular child should receive more expensive medical care than other children in the same situation, or have the privilege of free access to an ideal high school, or live in a large affluent suburban home. Rather each child has a right to the highest attainable uniform standard of health care (article 24), the highest attainable uniform free primary level education (article 28), and an adequate uniform standard of living (article 27). In addition, all children with disabilities have the right to the same standard of special care which available resources allow (article 23). So children's rights do not legitimize excessive demands made by any individual. Rather, resource allocation must provide maximal uniform affordable standards for healthy development to all children. However, assuming that each state should realize uniform affordable economic, social, and cultural rights for all children while giving preference to children in general as the 1990 World Summit called for, the difficult problem remains as to how to allocate available resources between different kinds of such rights, and even more particularly between the right to health care of children affected by HIV versus the rights of children affected by tuberculosis.

MYTHS ABOUT RIGHTS-BASED APPROACHES

In addition to the types of criticisms summarized above, rights-based approaches also have been misinterpreted in ways that threaten the integrity of the rights approach and undermine the acceptance of the convention. Some seem to believe that the convention means giving only children a voice. Others, perhaps due to a misunderstanding of participation and due to an overreaction to the need to move beyond the concept of children as in need of charity, seem to believe that a consistent approach to children's rights means focusing only on the strengths of children.

A primary problem stems from a misunderstanding of article 12's participation rights. Many groups have used Roger Hart's ladder of participation as their standard for initiating rights-based programs.[24] In Hart's ladder, the early rungs describe nonparticipation. There is movement from manipulation of children by adults—for example having young children wear placards for an adult cause they probably do not understand—to tokenism, where children's voices are solicited but not listened to. This is seen often when children are included as conference panelists solely to demonstrate the involvement of children. The highest rungs are said to reflect true participation, and here projects are child initiated. Here adults do not have a decision-making role, but are involved only in a supportive role.

On the basis of Hart's ladder, what often has become not only the measure of participation, but also the defining criterion of a rights-based approach is having child-initiated and child-led projects. And in their desire to ensure that projects and programs are rights based, those working with children adopt a supportive role and in essence promote the self-determination of the child rather than participation.

Self-determination, while consistent with the developmental adult result of participation, is not consistent with the convention's goals for children, but due to misunderstanding it provides fuel for opponents of the convention. With a conviction that child-initiated and -led programming is the ideal, adults abdicate their article 5 obligation to provide guidance and to take into account the evolving capacity of the child and context in which the child is developing. Instead, adults take the role of resource persons. I have observed a growing tendency for organizations to alter their policies, procedures, and interventions—many of which have a history of success—in favor of new ones simply because these new ones are child initiated or can be child led. There is a real danger here of throwing out the baby with the bathwater. Whatever children say must be given primacy over anything adults say. Whether we are talking program development, implementation, or evaluation—children always know best. It is as wrong to always assume children know best as it is to never take into account their perspectives. And it is a real obstacle to public acceptance of the convention to perpetuate the myth that self-determination is a convention right.

Listening to children helps us understand their lives and their concerns and provides us guidance on what supports and programs they would find useful. Listening to children provides decision makers with an understanding of how different polices, programs, and practices may affect children. And listening to children helps promote their healthy psychosocial development. But children's perspectives must be taken into account in accordance with the age and maturity of the child, neither rejected without consideration, nor followed without consideration. It must be remembered that according to article 12 children are not even obligated to participate directly; participation in a judicial or administrative procedure can be indirect through a representative. There are contexts and circumstances, for example, a highly contested custody dispute, in which indirect participation may be the better option for the child.

There are also many problems associated with a focus on children's resilience, their strengths, their coping strategies, and their capacity for being agents of social transformation. While such a focus can be used to justify excessive or inappropriate participation, it is a focus that is not consistent with the spirit of the convention. The convention regards childhood as a legally protected part of the lifecycle, protected by adults. The very existence of many children is threatened by war, by hunger, and by HIV/AIDs; many children are also threatened by lack of education, by sexual exploitation, by economic exploitation, or by the need to prematurely adopt adult roles in caring for themselves and siblings. To focus on the resilience and strengths of such children is helpful to understanding them as active subjects with rights, but to do so exclusively is to deny their rights to protection and provision. The convention obligates states parties to work toward respecting all the rights of every child so that each and every child can develop in a physically, socially, and mentally healthy manner. For that, children have a right to childhood.

Myths Hamper Progress

The full realization of children's rights in Canada, as in many other states parties, remains a hope for the future. Although there is evidence of progress in areas such as juvenile justice and child protection, there appears to be an ongoing reluctance to afford Canadian children their full status as independent bearers of rights. As noted, there has been a changing view of children from parental property to persons with rights.[25] It is, however a view that, while changing, is not yet changed. It seems most likely that the obstacles to the full realization of children's rights in Canada stem in large part from myths and misperceptions about the nature of the convention. These misperceptions have fueled fears about the loss of parental rights and family autonomy, of anarchy among children, and of unwelcome United Nations intrusions into sovereignty. Critics have described the convention as UNICEF propaganda and as an antifamily document that serves only to indoctrinate children into unquestioning acceptance of United Nations policy.[26] As stated by one British Columbia school trustee, "It [the convention] undermines the integrity of the family and involves children in a political undertaking. There is a gradual erosion of parental authority and this is one more step in that direction."[27]

This comment was made in an effort to prevent children from learning they have rights. In celebration of the tenth anniversary of the adoption of the convention, UNICEF Canada and Elections Canada jointly organized an election for school children. A key purpose of the election was to stimulate thinking about children's rights and to educate young people about the rights of the child as described in the convention. School students across Canada were to be given the opportunity to discuss and to vote on the relative importance of children's rights in the general areas of education, family, food, shelter, health, safety, name, nationality, and the expression of opinions. The participation of many students was prevented by vociferous opponents, who argued that allowing children to know and to discuss their rights would undermine family and adult authority, involve children in undesirable political activity, and invite an undue degree of state intrusion into the family.[28] Nonetheless, three-quarters of a million students in over 1900 schools across Canada were informed about their convention rights and then voted on the rights that they thought were most important. But contrary to expectations that students would give priority to personal freedoms, the results of the election showed that the right held to be most important to children and youth was the right to a family upbringing. This was followed by the right to food and shelter, and the right to health care. The importance of such rights to Canadian children was consistent with patterns obtained in other countries where the election also had been held.

In the years that have passed since the unanimous adoption of the convention by the General Assembly of the United Nations in 1989, there have been relatively few reports that awareness of rights has led children into defying the legitimate authority of parents or religious leaders or teachers.[29] In fact there is no reason to suppose that children will become more rights demanding or defiant if they learn about their rights.[30] At the same time, one may wonder what child rights are worth if there is no opportunity for children to exercise them against the illegitimate exercise of authority. Marie-France Daniel in this volume argues persuasively that children who know their rights are better able to protect themselves from abuses.

WERE CHILDREN'S RIGHTS FULLY RESPECTED

The rights articulated in the convention are consistent with the developmental needs of the child. Were they fully respected, the conditions in which children grow would be optimum for healthy physical and psychological development. A comprehensive analysis of the fit between developmental needs and convention rights is beyond the scope of this presentation. A brief summary, however, may be helpful.

Urie Bronfenbrenner described an ecological model of development that allows for an understanding of how the full realization of children's rights would benefit not only the development of the individual child but also of society.[31] Of essential importance are the two underlying premises of his model. One is that child development always occurs in an environment that impacts the course of that development. The second is that child and the environment have a transactional influence; there is continual bidirectional influence. The model comprises four environments with the child at the center. The extent to which each environment impacts either positively or negatively on the rights of the child will have a determining influence on the development of the child, who in turn affects that environment. Let us briefly examine a few examples.

First, although the convention does not provide for fetal rights, it does recognize the importance of a healthy prenatal environment. Children born with compromised brain development or low birth weight due to maternal alcohol use, illicit drug use, or tobacco use are more likely than healthy infants to cause difficulties in their environments with corresponding negative effects on themselves and others. For example, maternal smoking has been associated with the development of childhood conduct disorders and adult criminality.[32] Likewise, children born with Fetal Alcohol Spectrum Disorder find themselves on a developmental path that reflects increasingly serious problems in coping daily for themselves, with their caregivers and with their communities.[33]

The first postnatal environment for development is the one that is closest to the child, the social microsystem. The *microsystem* includes the child's direct relationships with those in his or her family, day care, school, church, and play areas. While each of these is important, arguably the most important predictor of child outcomes is family socialization style. The convention, under article 19, requires that children be protected from all forms of abuse and neglect, specifi-cally including the use of physical punishment and exposure to domestic vio-lence. When the article 19 rights are violated, problems permeate all environ-ments. Socialization through physical punishment is associated with increased rates of childhood behavior problems,[34] aggression, and antisocial behaviors,[35] dating or intimate partner violence,[36] criminal violence,[37] depression, and low self-worth.[38] The impact of neglect includes poor health, malnutrition, poor school performance, emotional disorders, and developmental delays.[39] Children who are exposed to domestic violence are at risk for a number of emotional and behavioral difficulties, and are at increased risk of becoming victims of domes-tic violence themselves.[40] A cycle of rights violations and societal costs ensues.

The next environmental system in Bronfenbrenner's model is the *meso-system*, which describes mutually supportive relationships between those in the child's microsystem. The background of supportiveness and safety provided gen-erally by the child's neighborhood, his or her school, play spaces, and childcare are important here. Supportive relationships among the child's teachers, family members, neighbors, and peers are clearly in the best interests of the child (ar-ticle 3), are likely to contribute to the optimum development of the child (article 6), and prepare children for an active life as an adult (article 29).

The *exosystem* refers to the social settings that affect the child but with which the child does not interact. It includes the media, parents' workplaces, school boards, and municipal governments. Are children provided a daily diet of violent media? To what extent are workplaces family friendly? Are school board policies consistent with the goals of education described in article 29, which require that education be directed toward the development of the whole child, that it include respect for the child's parents, for human rights, for the natural environment? Are there special services for especially vulnerable children, for children who have been abused (articles 20 and 39), and for children with dis-abilities (article 23)? Are there environmental protections to combat the growing rates of childhood asthma and cancers, and to protect children's right to health (article 24)? How such questions are answered will indicate the existing balance between risk and protective factors, and in turn the probability that children grow to be productive and healthy members of their communities.

Finally there is the *macrosystem*, the attitudes and ideologies of the culture in which the child is growing. The convention requires that the best interests of the child shall be a primary consideration in all policies and practices that affect children (article 3). Does this happen? What portion of social spending is targeted to promote the healthy development of children? Are programs for children given less priority because of other budgetary demands, perhaps of military spending? Is there, at the societal level, enough attention to support for families and the building of protective factors necessary to promote healthy child development?

The reality is that we do not live in Pleasantville or any other utopia of choice.

The convention's assertion of legally binding obligations by states parties is not enough. It is a powerful tool and standard against which we can assess our progress in meeting these obligations in respecting children and providing conditions for their optimum development. Moreover, there is a way that we can work toward closing the gap between the promise and reality of children's rights, a way in which our changing views of children from being property to being persons can really evolve, namely, children's rights education.

CHILDREN'S RIGHTS EDUCATION

Children's rights education is education whose goals, content, and pedagogy are consistent with the convention. It is education that fully recognizes the citizenship and rights-bearing status of the child, in the classroom and out of it. From the perspective of child psychology, the convention should be taught in a democratic classroom environment characterized by mutual respect among students and between teacher and students. The rights of the convention should provide an overarching framework into which topics, policies, and practices are introduced. For example, children should not simply learn that they have a right to have their voice heard (article 12), they should actually be listened to and participate meaningfully in school decision making, classroom charters, school councils, and school newspapers. Children should not simply be told to "say no to drugs," but should be provided opportunities for peer deliberation about how experimentation with drugs may interfere with their right to maintain a high standard of health (article 24) along with their right to be protected from the production, use and trafficking of illicit substances (article 33). Children are not simply taught about governments, geography, and history, but can examine such issues as sustainable development, war, labor conditions, world religions, art, music, and literature from a rights-based perspective. The goal of children's rights education, consistent with the convention, is to provide the knowledge, attitudes, values, and skills that promote a society characterized by an appreciation of cultural diversity and the values of tolerance, social justice, peace, and democratic governance. In essence, children's rights education subsumes the goals of character education, environmental education, citizenship education, human rights education, peace education, and moral education.

As detailed elsewhere there is growing evidence of the benefits of children's rights education.[41] Overwhelmingly, the evidence shows that children who learn about and experience their rights are children who demonstrate the fundamentals of good citizenship. They gain knowledge not only of their basic rights but also of their corresponding social responsibilities, they develop attitudes and values that are necessary to the promotion and protection of the rights of others, and they acquire the behavioral skills necessary for effective participation in democratic society. The success of children's rights education today can be attributed in large part to four factors.

First, children's rights education provides a coherent set of values based upon a legally binding document. As noted by British educator and philosopher John Clarke, the convention provides an overarching framework for secular schools; such schools have been disadvantaged by their lack of universal values and principles.[42] The convention gives coherence to school regulations, codes of conduct, mission statements, classroom charters, and student council activities. And the legitimized values of the convention lessen or eliminate the difficulties facing value-free teaching.[43]

Second, the convention provides students with a coherent set of principles that they can apply to understanding the world around them and to decision making. Education researchers consistently have shown that children do not generalize from morals or principles that are taught in specific contexts, such as environmental protection or antiracism. Nor do children extrapolate underlying principles from teaching in moral or character education.[44] Rights-based teachings explicitly provide children with a common principle, a principle that they can and do use. Examples may be helpful. In Hampshire, England, where rights education is well integrated into the school ethos as well as across curricula, children have been observed using rights discourse to assert their rights not to be bullied on the playground and to settle disputes. In the classroom, the assertion of rights has resulted in the acceptance of more personal responsibility for behavior and for learning. As one boy commented on his improved concentration and performance, "knowing that I have the right to learn . . . it's up to me not to be distracted."[45]

Third, the pedagogy required by the convention has been shown to improve self-esteem and a sense of belonging to the school and classroom. Cooperative learning, role-play, and discussion of social issues are the core of rights consistent pedagogy. These have been demonstrated to increase students' opportunities to experience success, a sense of being valued, and emotional well-being and to promote mutually supportive relationships among students.[46]

Finally, children's rights education engages students because it teaches rights which they now have as children, rather than adult rights and responsibilities they will one day have. What they are learning is linked with their current reality and is of self-interest.[47] When children know that it is legitimate for them to be concerned about themselves, they are more likely to be concerned about others.[48] When children learn that they have a right, they understand that for their right to be realized they must respect the rights of others. Negatively oriented proscriptions for behavior—"Don't discriminate, don't litter, don't kill the whales"—do not always meaningfully connect with children's everyday experiences.[49] Nor do they promote the same engagement or motivation for prosocial behaviors.[50]

In summary, children's rights education has the potential to close the gap between the promise and reality of children's rights. As more children grow with the knowledge of their convention rights, there will be more rights-based approaches to law, policy, and programming, and increasingly there will be rights-respecting societies. There will be a progressive realization of rights and concomitant decrease in domestic and global rights violations. This may well be the greatest significance of the Convention on the Rights of the Child.

NOTES

1.   M. Grude Flekkøy and N. Hevener Kaufman, *The Participation Rights of the Child: Rights and Responsibilities in Family and Society* (London: Jessica Kingsley, 1997).

2.   S. N. Hart, "From Property to Person Status: Historical Perspective on Children's Rights," *American Psychologist* 46, no. 1 (1991): 53-59.

3.   K. Covell and R. B. Howe, *The Challenge of Children's Rights for Canada* (Waterloo, ON: Wilfrid Laurier University Press, 2001); M. Freeman, *The Rights and Wrongs of Children* (London: Frances Pinter, 1983); M. Schmidt, and N. D. Reppucci, "Children's Rights and Capacities," in *Children, Social Science, and the Law*, ed. B. Bottoms, M. Kovera, and B. McAuliff, 76-105 (Cambridge: Cambridge University Press 2002).

4.   K. Covell and R. B. Howe, *Empowering Children: Children's Rights Education as a Pathway to Citizenship* (Toronto: University of Toronto Press, 2005).

5.   K. E. Knutsson, *Children: Noble Causes or Worthy Citizens?* (Florence, Italy: UNICEF, 1997).

6.   M. Freeman, "Introduction: Children as Persons," in *Children's Rights: A Comparative Perspective*, ed. M. Freeman, 2-3 (Aldershot: Dartmouth Publishing, 1996); R. B. Howe, "Do Parents Have Fundamental Rights?" *Journal of Canadian Studies* 36, no. 3 (2001): 61-78; E. Verhellen, *Convention on the Rights of the Child* (Kessel-Lo, Belgium: Garant Publishers, 1994).

7.   C. Price, "Monitoring the United Nations Convention on the Rights of the Child in a Non-Party State," in *Monitoring Children's Rights*, ed. E. Verhellen (The Hague: Martinus Nijhoff, 1996), 486-88.

8.   M. Small, and S. Limber, "Advocacy for Children's Rights," in *Children, Social Science and the Law*, ed. B. Bottoms, M. Kovera, and B. McAulifff, 64-72 (Cambridge: Cambridge University Press 2002).

9.   Howe and Covell, *Empowering Children*.

10.   G. Melton, "Starting a New Generation of Research," in *Children, Social Science and the Law*, ed. B. Bottoms, M. Kovera, and B. McAulifff, 449-53 (Cambridge: Cambridge University Press, 2002).

11.   Covell and Howe, *The Challenge of Children's Rights for Canada*.

12.   For example, T. Collins, L. Pearson, and C. Delany, "Rights-Based Approach," Discussion Paper, Senate of Canada (2002); C. M. Ljungman, "Applying a Rights-Based Approach to Development: Concepts and Principles" (2004), accessed December 1, 2008, www.sed.manchester.ac.uk/research.

13.   Ibid.

14.   E. Verhellen, ed. *Monitoring Children's Rights* (The Hague: Martinus Nijhoff, 1996).

15.   Collins et al., "Rights-Based Approach."

16.   O. O'Neill, "Children's Rights and Children's Lives" *Ethics* 98 (1998): 445-63.

17 M. Freeman, "Why it Remains Important to Take Children's Rights Seriously," *International Journal of Children's Rights* 15 (2007): 5-23.

18.   C. C. Helwig, "The Development of Personal Autonomy throughout Cultures," *Cognitive Development* 21, no. 4 (2006): 458-73.

19.   K. Covell, "Violence Against Children in North America: United Nations Secretary General's Study on Violence Against Children" (Toronto: UNICEF Canada, 2005); P. S. Pinheiro, "Summary Report of the Independent Expert for the United Nations Study on Violence Against Children," Report to the General Assembly 61st Session, (October 2006), A/61/299.

20.   K. Covell and R. B. Howe, *Children, Families and Violence: Challenges for Children's Rights* (London: Jessica Kingsley Publishers, 2009).

21.   For example, N. Daniels, and J. E. Sabin, *Setting Limits Fairly: Learning to Share Resources for Health*, 2nd ed. (Oxford, Oxford University Press, 2008).

22.   See S. Brauer, "Age Rationing and Prudential Lifespan Account in Norman Daniels' *Just Health*," *Journal of Medical Ethics* 35 (2009): 27-31, for a detailed critique of age rationing.

23.   Covell and Howe, *The Challenge of Children's Rights for Canada*.

24.   R. Hart, "Children's Participation: From Tokenism to Citizenship," in *Innocenti Essays* (Florence: UNICEF International Development Centre, 1992).

25. S. N. Hart, "From Property to Person Status: Historical Perspective on Children's Rights."

26. K. Steel, "One Child, One Vote: UNICEF and Elections Canada Team up to Enthuse Kids on Their 'Rights,'" *BC Report,* August 9, 1999, 28-31.

27. Howe and Covell, *Empowering Children,* 3.

28. Ibid.

29. P. David, "Implementing the Rights of the Child. Six Reasons Why the Human Rights of Children Remain a Constant Challenge," *International Review of Education* 48, nos. 3-4 (2002): 259-63.

30. Knutsson, *Children: Noble Causes or Worthy Citizens?*

31. U. Bronfenbrenner, *The Ecology of Human Development* (Cambridge, MA: Harvard University Press, 1979).

32. P. A. Brennan, E. R. Grekin, E. L. Mortensen, and S. A. Mednick, "Relationship of Maternal Smoking During Pregnancy With Criminal Arrest and Hospitalization for Substance Abuse in Male and Female Adult Offspring," *American Journal of Psychiatry* 159, no. 1 (2002): 48-54; R. Loeber, S. M. Green, B. B. Lahey, P. J. Frick, and K. McBurnett, "Findings on Disruptive Behavior Disorders From the First Decade of the Developmental Trends Study," *Clinical Child and Family Psychology Review* 3 (2000): 37-59; L. Wakslag, B. Leventhal, D. S. Pine, K. Pickett, and A. S. Carter, "Elucidating Early Mechanisms of Developmental Psychopathology: The Case of Prenatal Smoking and Disruptive Behavior," *Child Development* 77, no. 4 (2006): 893-906.

33. Covell and Howe, *The Challenge of Children's Rights for Canada*; R. Galindo, P. A. Zamudio, and C.F. Valenzuela, "Alcohol is a Potent Stimulant of Immature Neuronal Networks: Implications for Fetal Alcohol Spectrum Disorder," *Journal of Neurochemistry* 94 (2005): 1500-11.

34. M. L. Keiley, T. R. Howe, K. Dodge, J. Bates, and G. Petit, "The Timing of Child Physical Maltreatment: A Cross-Domain Growth Analysis of Impact on Adolescent Externalizing and Internalizing Problems," *Development and Psychopathology* 13, no. 4 (2001): 891-912.

35. M. K. Eamon and C. Mulder, "Predicting Antisocial Behavior Among Latino Young Adolescents: An Ecological Systems Analysis," *American Journal of Orthopsychiatry* 75, no. 1 (2005): 117-27; S. R. Jaffee, A. Caspi, T. Moffitt, and A. Taylor, "Physical Maltreatment Victim to Antisocial Child: Evidence of an Environmentally Mediated Process," *Journal of Abnormal Psychology* 113 no. 1 (2004): 44-55.

36. D. Wolfe, C. Wekerle, K. Scott, A. Straatman, and C. Grasley, "Predicting Abuse in Adolescent Dating Relationships Over 1 Year: The Role of Child Maltreatment and Trauma," *Journal of Abnormal Psychology* 113, no. 3 (2004): 21-43.

37.   G. T. Harris, M. Rice, and M. Lalumiere, "Criminal Violence: The Roles of Psychopathy, Neurodevelopmental Insults, and Antisocial Parenting," *Criminal Justice and Behavior* 28, no. 4 (2001): 402-25.

38.   A. Bowlus, K. McKenna, T. Day, and D. Wright, "The Economic Costs and Consequences of Child Abuse in Canada," Report to the Law Commission of Canada (2003).

39.   Ibid.

40.   Ibid.; G. A. Bogat, E. DeJonghe, A. A. Levendosky, W. S. Davidson, and A. von Eye, "Trauma Symptoms Among Infants Exposed to Intimate Partner Violence," *Child Abuse and Neglect* 30 (2006): 109-25; J. Brzozowski, ed. *Family Violence in Canada: A Statistical Profile, 2004* (Ottawa: Canadian Centre or Justice Statistics, 2004); S. A. Koblinsky, K. A. Kuvalanka, and S. M. Randolph, "Social Skills and Behavior Problems of Urban African American Preschoolers: Role of Parenting Practices, Family Conduct, and Maternal Depression," *American Journal of Orthopsychiatry* 76, no. 4 (2006): 554-63; K. J. Mitchell, and D. Finkelhor, "Risk of Crime Victimization Among Youth Exposed to Domestic Violence," *Journal of Interpersonal Violence* 16, no. 9 (2001): 944-64; Wolfe et al., "Predicting Abuse."

41.   Howe and Covell, *Empowering Children.*

42.   Ibid.

43.   L. Burwood and R. Wyeth, "Should Schools Promote Toleration?" *Journal of Moral Education,* 27, no. 4 (1998): 465-73.

44.   Covell and Howe, *Empowering Children.*

45.   Ibid.

46.   S. Berman, *Children's Social Consciousness and the Development of Social Responsibility* (New York: State University of New York Press, 1997); S. Harter, "The Construction and Conservation of the Self: James and Cooley revisited," in *Self, Ego and Identity: Integrated Approaches,* eds. D. K. Lapsley and F. C. Power, 44-70 (New York; Springer-Verlag, 1988); C. A. McNeely, J. M. Nonnemaker, and R. W. Blum, "Promoting School Connectedness: Evidence from the National Longitudinal Study of Adolescent Health," *Journal of School Health,* 72, no. 4 (2002): 138-46.

47.   J. Beane, *Affect in the Curriculum: Towards Democracy, Dignity, and Diversity* (New York: Teachers College Press, 1990); M. Griffiths, and L. Davies, *In Fairness to Children: Working for Social Justice in the Primary School* (London: David Fulton Publishers, 1995); C. Holden and N. Clough, *Children as Citizens: Education for Participation* (London: Jessica Kingsley, 1998).

48.   N. Haan, E. Aerts, and B. Cooper, *On Moral Grounds: The Search for Practical Morality* (New York: New York University Press, 1985); Howe and Covell, *Empowering Children.*

49. W. Damon, and A. Gregory, "The Youth Charter: Towards the Formation of Adolescent Moral Identity," *Journal of Moral Education,* 26, no. 2 (1997), 117-31.

50. S. T. Hauser and M. K. Bowlds, "Stress, Coping and Adaptation," *At the Threshold: The Developing Adolescent,* ed. S. S. Feldman and G. R. Elliott, 388-413 (Cambridge, MA: Harvard University Press, 1990).

Three

Developmental Considerations in Teaching Children's Rights

Katherine Covell and R. Brian Howe

The value of human rights education cannot be overestimated. Human rights are of fundamental importance to a just and democratic society and knowledge of human rights is fundamental to the achievement of human rights. Successful human rights education not only provides knowledge of rights and the responsibilities that go with them, but also on a practical level engages learners and engenders rights respecting attitudes and behaviors. For human rights education to be successful it should start early, be integrated into school curricula, and engage children by providing human rights knowledge of direct relevance to them. Most relevant to children is knowledge of their own human rights as described in the United Nations Convention on the Rights of the Child.

The present essay is not written from the perspective of international law. Though legally binding, the convention is widely unenforced. We write from a perspective within the international children's rights movement and seek to develop a concept of human rights education beginning in childhood that is consistent with the convention viewed as an ethically supportive standard-setting document beyond its successes and failures judged purely as law. As a morally compelling document, the case for its relevance to teachers can be made even in the remaining few nations which have not ratified it.

The impact of children's rights education in promoting positive human rights attitudes and behaviors is found in a number of recent studies.[1] When children are taught about their rights in an age-appropriate manner, they become more respectful of the rights of all others. They demonstrate the fundamentals of good citizenship through displaying awareness not only of their basic rights but also of their corresponding social responsibilities.

In this chapter, we examine the developmental considerations that account for variation in successful human rights education. We start by describing the nature of children's rights education and the common obstacles to the provision of human rights education for children. We then focus on developmental considerations essential to the effective teaching of children's rights. To be systematic, rights education should be provided in schools as part of the curriculum and should be integrated into the school ethos as a guide to policy and practice.

THE UN CONVENTION AND CHILDREN'S RIGHTS EDUCATION

The convention, approved by the General Assembly of the United Nations in 1989, provides guidelines for both the content and pedagogy of age-appropriate human rights education for children. It informs children of their basic rights, which has been described as the three Ps: provision rights (for example, to health care and education), protection rights (against abuse and exploitation) and participation rights (to be heard in matters that affect them).[2] But it does more than this. With its emphasis on participation rights, it calls for a child-centered pedagogy in which adults actually listen to the voices of children in the educational process. The convention is the best available guide for teaching human rights.

Of primary consideration as an instrument for teaching human rights is the nature of the convention itself. First, the convention is legally binding in most nations. What has been suggested for the context of rights education, and what has most often been used is the 1948 Declaration of Human Rights.[3] However, declarations do not have the same legal status as conventions. They do not therefore have as much legitimacy as a standard or basis for teaching. Where declarations of rights are documents that describe goals or ideals, conventions are basic standards of human rights and legally binding pieces of international law.[4] Second, the Convention on the Rights of the Child is the most widely and the most quickly ratified convention in world history. All member nations of the United Nations have ratified the convention except for the United States and Somalia. Even the United States, because it has signed the document, is often considered to have an obligation at least not to act contrary to its purpose.[5] The convention has elicited a near-global consensus on the human rights of children. Children will learn that there is such a consensus and that the rights described in the convention are declared to apply to all children in the world—including them, even though the convention has not been universally ratified. Third, the comprehensiveness of articles in the convention relevant to education (rights to education, rights in education, and rights claimed through education) allows it to be used, particularly in nations that have ratified it, as a guide for teaching human rights to children in all school settings.

The participation rights of the convention, as described in articles 12 through 15, identify the appropriate pedagogy. These articles obligate educators to provide opportunities for children to be heard in matters that affect them (article 12). They call for the age-appropriate exercise of rights to freedom of expression, access to information, freedom of thought and religion, and freedom to association and peaceful assembly (articles 13-15). The rights in the convention must be respected by the teacher and reflected in teaching and classroom management style, as well as explicitly taught.[6] We note also that limitations on these freedoms are articulated. Pedagogical considerations thus require taking into account articles 3 and 5. Article 3, the overarching principle of the convention, states that in all decisions concerning the child, the child's best interests shall be a primary consideration. Article 5 obligates teachers to provide direction and guidance in the exercise of the rights of the child in accord with the child's evolving capacities.

OBSTACLES TO CHILDREN'S RIGHTS EDUCATION IN THE SCHOOLS

A fundamental consideration for effective human rights education is that learners be provided information of relevance to them. The teaching of human rights is less effective when the subject matter is abstract and remote and more effective when it is of direct concern to the learner. Teaching children about human rights is more effective when it begins with teaching children about their own rights. However, there has been considerable reluctance among parents and teachers to educate children about their convention rights, a reluctance driven by fears of defiance and demands. For the most part, the underlying concern appears to be a fear that if children are aware of their rights, teachers, parents, and adult authorities will lose authority and their ability to control children. But there is no evidence to support such a concern.

In the years that have passed since the unanimous adoption of the convention by the General Assembly of the United Nations in 1989, there have been few reports that awareness of rights has led children into defying the authority of parents or religious leaders or teachers.[7] In fact, there is little reason to suppose that children will become more rights demanding or defiant if they learn about their rights.[8] First, for better or worse it is unlikely that children will come together and form a widespread rights-demanding movement comparable to that of the American civil rights movement of the 1960s or the women's movement of the 1970s. As Karl Knutsson points out, the variations in children's socialization and resources make it highly unlikely that there would be enough children together at one time and place who share the sense of purpose and efficacy, or who have the resources to effect the formation of a critical mass.[9] Second, where there is evidence of action taken by children after learning about their rights, that action has been prosocial, and for the most part other oriented. Children do not demand more rights for themselves, but attempt to take action in response to knowledge of the rights violations of other children.[10]

Nonetheless, there remains reluctance among many teachers to include rights education in their curricula. Like adults in the general population, many teachers believe that children are unable to competently exercise rights. Thus the resistance or ambivalence about teaching children's rights, or allowing the practice of participation and children's rights in the classroom, most often comes from fears of loss of authority.[11] Some teachers are concerned that if children are made aware that they have rights, there will be rebellion and chaos in the classroom. In Australia, when a rights information kit was distributed to students, it was met with derision, resistance, and comments such as "The kit could lead to United States style schools where weapons and drugs are common and the enforcing of school rules may turn into a lawyer's picnic."[12] Other teachers are less concerned with potential anarchy, but wish to maintain their dominance in the classroom. As Kathy Bickmore of the Ontario Institute for Studies in Education notes, educators, like other adults, are not often disposed to sharing their power with children.[13] Misunderstanding the nature of children's rights, or perhaps the nature of childhood, many teachers have expressed a strong belief that their students need to be taught about responsibilities, and that the teaching of rights is antithetical to what is needed.[14]

Teachers' concerns may well be a joint function of their own lack of knowledge about children's rights and the failure of teacher training to provide the necessary pedagogy. For children's rights to be taught effectively, they must be modeled in the classroom and in the school. This implies the need for democratic leadership, cooperative learning, and controversial social issues discussion. The overwhelming evidence throughout the education literature is that teachers are poorly prepared to teach in other than traditional ways.

Fundamental to democratic teaching is teachers' ability to listen to their students. Building on Dewey's concept of reflection, Carol Rodgers stresses the importance of teachers developing their capacity to think critically about what and how their students are learning.[15] Part of this requires that teachers respect the participation rights of their students. Teachers should solicit, take into account, and value student feedback as critical to their understanding of students' learning. As Rodgers says, teachers must create conditions that "reveal learning rather than just answers."[16] This is an evaluation practice quite different from the usual testing procedures. Rather, it involves engaging the students in dialogue and it requires using students' comments to guide future teaching and students' further learning. Rudduck and Flutter also stress the need for teachers to be trained to listen to their students, to help students express their learning needs, and to respect the participation rights of the child.[17] In the absence of the necessary training, and with the fears of student anarchy, what often happens is inappropriate human rights education in schools.

COMMON TYPES OF HUMAN RIGHTS EDUCATION

Priscilla Alderson identifies characteristic approaches to rights education in schools. The most common is the "not-yet" approach.[18] Children are educated for the roles and responsibilities they will assume as future citizens and adult members of their society. As Alderson notes, there may be some acknowledgement that children do have human rights, but most frequently in a trivial manner such as teaching children they have a right to a clean environment so they have a responsibility to pick up litter. This approach fails to recognize the citizenship and rights-bearing status of children. Rather, it assumes them to be future citizens in need of preparation. A second approach is that of "constrained rights education." This approach gives grudging recognition to the rights of children, but at the same time, it assumes that children generally are insufficiently rational to understand them. Children may be taught that they do have rights under an international convention, but many of their rights will not be respected at the school, and children will not be provided opportunity to exercise their rights. In a third approach, children's rights education is selective and tends to focus narrowly on such issues as how fortunate children are to have the convention's rights to protection. The fourth approach is essentially "rights violations education." Students are taught about developing countries as places that are rife with the abuses of children. They learn that there is a convention of rights for children that is supposed to protect children in the developing world, but that it fails to do so.[19]

"Full-blown rights education" is the least common of all approaches to rights education. It is, however, the only approach that takes children's convention rights seriously, and as Alderson states, "combines talk with action."[20] The convention is taught in a democratic classroom environment characterized by mutual respect among students and between teacher and students. Students are provided with both the knowledge and skills that provide the foundation for effective democratic citizenship. This is a classroom in which children's rights are not just taught, but are recognized, respected, and modeled.

Across ages, it is this latter classroom atmosphere that is needed for human rights education. Achieving this atmosphere requires particular attention to developmental considerations. Phillip Payne, Australian environmental activist and educator, has written extensively on the need to take into account the student's developing identity in education.[21] He notes that educators have focused excessively on the end state of education with concomitant insufficient, if any, attention given to the current state of their students. In her discussion of human rights education, Felissa Tibbitts also points to the importance of developmentally appropriate teaching.[22]

DEVELOPMENTAL CONSIDERATIONS

A major consideration for children's rights education is when it should occur. There is some disagreement in the literature on the appropriate age for introducing children's rights education. UNESCO recommends including rights education at the preschool level, a recommendation supported by the Fortieth Council of Europe Teachers' Seminar and by the Committee of Ministers of the Council of Europe.[23] Many would agree with John Humphrey that it is important to instill the value of human rights in children before they experience prejudice or have time to develop biases.[24] Judith Torney-Purta suggests that middle childhood is the optimal time to introduce rights education.[25] As she points out, the attitudes and values of children between the ages of seven and eleven years are not yet determined. Others, similarly, have identified this period as the optimum age for developing attitudes toward human rights and global issues.[26] The cognitive capacities of middle childhood are considerably more advanced than are those of preschool children, so at least some understanding of rights should be possible.

We believe that the ideal situation may be to introduce the concept of rights at a very basic level in the early grades, but to delay the more comprehensive teaching until early adolescence. There is evidence that even young children have some general understanding of the concepts of rights, fairness, and justice.[27] However, it is only in adolescence that children's cognitive capacity, identity development, and interests in social issues converge to allow both the motivation to learn about and the ability to fully understand the implications of rights education. Prior to early adolescence, no matter how effectively they are taught, there will be some limitations on children's capacity to understand rights. This was well demonstrated in Rahima Wade's research.[28]

Wade notes that students in social studies often misunderstand important concepts such as the nature of rights. As she states, when assessing children's understanding of rights, researchers previously found that children under eleven may understand "'free' to mean without payment or the word 'equal' to mean numerically balanced."[29] The concepts were interpreted by the children's existing knowledge and within the children's existing experiences. Interested in examining how children might understand rights when they were specifically taught about rights in a concrete manner, Wade developed and introduced a month-long curriculum unit on children's rights to a class comprising seventeen children between the ages of nine and eleven. She based the content of the curriculum on the 1959 UN Declaration of the Rights of the Child. Her curriculum incorporated the elements known to be the most effective in rights education, including discussion, a democratic pedagogy, cooperative learning, and role-play. To reinforce classroom learning, the students undertook social action projects, and held weekly class meetings to address rights and responsibilities in the classroom. Her evaluation data, collected after the completion of the curriculum, indicated that despite this best possible teaching situation, the children had difficulty comprehending rights in ways that were different from their initial conception of rights as freedoms. They had particular difficulty appreciating that there was a link between the rights they were learning about and their own lives. Although by the end of the curriculum, most of the children were able to recognize applications of rights in their daily lives, most could not independently think of an example of a children's rights issue. Torney-Purta previously had stressed the importance of integrating the study of human rights with concrete experiences in the children's daily lives.[30] Wade did so in her study, but understanding was not changed. Overall, her data demonstrate that prior to age eleven, children's understanding of rights is likely to be nominal and limited by cognitive capacity.

Such findings do not mean, however, that there can be no human rights education in the early years at school. Even very young children have an understanding of fairness and justice and are quite capable of distinguishing which behaviors reflect fairness. Children between ages five and eleven can learn much about human rights through child-friendly posters and books with age-appropriate language, and through artwork, games and role-play. The most important means of teaching human rights at the younger age groups is through modeling of rights. Preschool and young elementary-aged children can learn the value of human rights through classroom and teacher respect for their rights. In our work with human rights education in Hampshire County Education Authority, England, we have been impressed with the capacity of four-year-olds to participate in school decision making through membership in school councils, where they discuss school policies and procedures, and through rudimentary decision making about classroom activities. The cognitive limitations imposed by immature neurological development do not preclude the use of rights discourse, although they likely limit the generalization of rights understanding beyond the specifics learned.

Rights Education in Adolescence

Around the age of eleven, children have developed the cognitive skills necessary to understand the nature of rights and the impact of rights violations. Jean Piaget's work suggests that the ability to reason in a hypothetical-deductive way, what Piaget called "formal-operational thought," develops between the ages of eleven and fifteen.[31] Formal-operational thought allows children to consider possibilities as well as reality, to understand abstract concepts such as rights, and to understand relativism. In essence, the child's world expands with the growing ability to consider how the world could be, and how the world should be. Although others subsequently have found variations in the ages at which children achieve such thought, there is significant evidence that pre- to mid-adolescence is a period of growth in a number of cognitive skills such as empathic understanding, perspective taking, and rights understanding.[32] The improved cognitive skills of late childhood have a significant impact on social understanding because they evoke improved perspective taking and empathic understanding.

Starting around age ten to eleven, children become able to consider their own and another's opinion and realize that the other person can do the same. In addition, children are able to assume the perspective of a third party and to anticipate how each person may react to the other's perspective.[33] This improved role-taking ability, together with an understanding of relativism, allows an appreciation that rights can be in conflict, that rights for one person subsume responsibilities toward others, and that it is important to protect the rights of all. As role-taking skills develop, so does sensitivity to the needs and feelings of others. Unlike in earlier childhood, direct experience with another's distress is no longer necessary to arouse empathy. Empathy can now be elicited through information about another's distress.[34] The empathy elicited by information about the impact of rights violations is expected to impact the child's emerging social and political ideologies and act as a stimulus for the development of a rights-respecting self. It is interesting to note also that it is during this same developmental period that children come to understand that conflict in the political or social system is "as inevitable as it is undesirable."[35] Changes in understanding provoke not only questioning about the social and political domain, but also questions about the self.

Changes in identity occur throughout life, but they are of particular salience in early adolescence because it is the first time the child has the cognitive ability to examine and construct a set of personal goals and values. How these values are delineated depends on the child's experiences and the values to which she or he has been exposed.[36] Experience with rights (learning you have rights, being treated with respect for your rights, learning how to protect your own and others' rights) can be the catalyst for the development of a rights-based identity. Roy Baumeister and Mark Muraven note that there tends to be a broad range of values choices for young people in contemporary society and no clear basis for choice among them.[37] Rights education can fill this void and take advantage of a critical period in development. In turn, the value of rights respect as an integral part of self can provide a framework for interpreting experience and deciding appropriate behaviors.

In essence, the development of identity in adolescence is impelled by maturation in physiological and neurological systems as well as by related increases in the capacity for abstract thinking and the broadening of the social world. Defining the self in the context of the UN Covenant on Civil and Political Rights (article 25), as an upholder of democratic ideals, requires that adolescents have opportunities to critically reflect on democratic values, to participate in democratic decision making, to understand social issues, and to feel empowered to exercise their citizenship responsibilities.

The implications of this for human rights education are as follows. Adolescent students increasingly should be provided opportunities for cooperative learning in peer groups, for critical thinking, for debate and discussion about social issues and values of relevance to them, and for meaningful participation. Another important developmental consideration stems from the heightened introspection and self-focus that accompanies the definition of a personal identity. Adolescents need very much to believe in and feel good about the self that is developing.[38] It is particularly important, and consistent with the convention, that education promote a sense of efficacy or empowerment rather than helplessness. Given these considerations, it is important that there be allowance in the educational process for self-focus and self-interest. It is important that subject matter be personally relevant.

In a number of surveys, Cathie Holden and her colleagues found adolescents to be very concerned with such social and human rights issues as environmental degradation, social inequalities, and violence.[39] They were, however, dissatisfied with what they were learning. Students complained that their schools were not teaching them the information they needed to understand their role in shaping the future. Quotes are illustrative. One fourteen-year-old said, "We

learnt the facts about what's happening but we don't learn what you can do."[40]
Similar sentiments were expressed by students in Payne's study. For example,
"Some of my inaction can be attributed to a sense of helplessness . . . and the way
in which I am made to feel part of the problem but not part of the solution."[41]
Students want to translate their learning into action, but feel disempowered.
They become increasingly cynical and disengaged.[42] Sheldon Berman notes that,
despite allowing his students to select which current social topics they wished
to study, they always appeared to be bored and ready to move on to a new issue after a few weeks.[43] He discovered that their wish to examine a different issue was not a result of boredom, but was in fact elicited by a sense that there
was nothing that they could do to deal with the problem under discussion. For
education to increase respect and support for human rights, students must feel
empowered and efficacious.

Engagement and empowerment are more likely when there is allowance
for self-interest. When lessons focus on adult civic rights and responsibilities, or
on the plight and needs of others, and when students are admonished to avoid
certain behaviors, there is no room for self-interest. Self-interest promotes engagement and increases the likelihood that what is learned will be integrated
into developing identity. Self-interest is an especially important component of
human rights education. The reasons have been explained well by Diane Goodman.[44] Her essential thesis is that support and action for democratic ideals is
motivated jointly by values, empathy, and self-interest. This latter item generally
has not been included in human rights education because self-interest tends to
be understood as selfishness. However, as Goodman explains, self-interest is not
a zero-sum game. Rather, self-interest can be inclusive and involve a consideration of others—particularly those with whom the adolescent can empathize.

There are two key benefits of engaging the interest of the students by linking the issues under discussion to their own rights and their own interests. One
is that when there is engagement in an issue, the student becomes exposed to
perspectives and information in ways so meaningful that they have the potential
to change attitudes and subsequent behavior. The second is that self-interest facilitates understanding and empathy of the other's situation. Empathy is aroused
when there is a sense of connectedness with the situation and with the feelings
of others. At this time, developments in information technology have increased
the potential connectedness of adolescents across cultures. Globally, urban adolescents demonstrate similar brand preferences and consumption patterns in
music, videos, t-shirts and soft drinks.[45] Communication through e-mail and
surfing the internet are activities as popular among Arab as among European,
North American, and Latin American adolescents.[46] While some may deplore

the homogenization of adolescence, there clearly are benefits for the teaching of global human rights.

A related advantage of acknowledging the importance of self-interest, as identified by Goodman, is that a focus on benefits for self as well as others should mitigate against beliefs that tend to confuse social justice for others with charity. Rights-promoting action is more likely to occur if students' self-focused concerns and interests are legitimized. To allow for self-interest, and thereby engagement, curriculum content and pedagogy should be relevant to the experiences and interests of the adolescent.

Teaching children's rights means that students learn their current rights. Consistent with article 42 of the convention, children must be explicitly taught the "principles and provisions" of the convention. This will be of much greater interest and relevance to students than learning about their adult citizenship rights and responsibilities.[47] The research shows that when concepts such as rights are linked with children's current realities, they are understood better and they are more likely to engage the student.[48] The relevance to self is highlighted by learning that all children have the same rights, not because they have earned them or have otherwise proven themselves worthy, but unconditionally, simply because they are children. And they learn that the purpose of these rights is to maximize their developmental potential and to make sure they are well cared for by their families and by their state. In turn, this teaching allows for self-interest and is expected to evoke a sense of interconnectedness with other children, and thereby to promote empathy, rather than sympathy, for them. The commonality of rights promised to all children cultivates a sense of global interconnectedness among children. Thus, many of the difficulties faced by children, locally or globally, can be understood as systemic rights violations, rather than attributable to individual weaknesses or failures. In turn, such empathy-based understanding encourages and empowers social action to counter perceived injustices.[49]

It is particularly important that the developmental needs of the adolescent are reflected in pedagogy. At this time, pedagogy commonly tends to be more authoritarian than participatory and quite inconsistent with children's rights. The impact has been to reduce students' engagement in school and their motivations for rights-respecting action, and to increase their cynicism and the likelihood of negative self-perceptions.

Jacquelynne Eccles and her colleagues have developed stage-environment fit theory to provide a cogent explanation of this impact.[50] The theory holds that behavior, motivation, and psychological well-being are influenced by the fit between the characteristics of individuals and those of their social environment. A poor fit predicts decreases in motivation, interest, performance, and behavior. When this theory is applied to the characteristics of adolescence and typical schools, it sheds light on underlying reasons for the lack of human rights education programs. The salience of identity issues in adolescence, the self-focus, the desire for increased participation and self-determination, peer orientation, and the capacity for hypothetical and abstract thinking, imply a classroom more like that found in a typical kindergarten than a middle or high school. Opportunities for student decision making, choice, and self-management should increase from childhood to adolescence, but, on the contrary, research informs us that they decrease.[51] Likewise, opportunities for cooperative small group learning and peer interaction should increase. They too decrease as grade level increases, with increasing emphasis on individualism and competition. Opportunities for critical thinking, disagreement, and debate should increase; they, too, decrease as there is more emphasis on rote learning. The overall result is a poor fit between the developmental needs of the adolescent and the educational environment. It is a fit that constrains the provision of effective human rights education. And it is in sharp contrast to the education goals and promises of the UN Convention on the Rights of the Child.

RIGHTS EDUCATION IN EARLY ADULTHOOD

The age of majority and full citizenship status are achieved by young adulthood. At this time there is general awareness of the basic rights of citizenship including the right to vote, to freedom of speech, to due process of law, to privacy, and to equality of opportunity without discrimination. However, there is no evidence to indicate that such knowledge is related to the sense of social responsibility that accompanies rights and to rights-respecting behavior. Rather, the evidence suggests that few young adults think about or exercise their human rights or have a strong sense of social responsibility in support of the rights of others.[52]

By adulthood, most youth have formulated an initial sense of self including the moral self and guiding values.[53] Nonetheless, that sense of identity remains flexible throughout the young adult years and there is some evidence to suggest that learning about children's rights, even after one is no longer a child, increases rights awareness and rights support. But the increase is quite limited.

Participating in a university-level credit course on children's rights has been shown to change the way young adults perceive children and their rights.[54] Compared with their preexisting rights-related knowledge and attitudes, students who completed a course with a focus on children's rights and the Convention on the Rights of the Child showed a significant increase in their knowledge of the importance of children's rights and in respect and support for the rights of children. They also showed a significant decrease in the perception of children as parental property. Thus rights education, provided as a standard university-level course, has the potential to increase an understanding and respect for rights among young adults. However, the university students did not indicate increased respect for adults' rights. That is, the increases in rights-respecting attitudes did not generalize beyond children to adult minorities.

It appears that adolescence is a critical period for the development of respect for human rights. When those in the midst of identity formation receive rights education, they incorporate ideas about rights and about values associated with rights into their emerging moral identities. In the words of Dale Snauwaert, the "I can't" (infringe upon the rights of others) and "I must" (act in a rights-respecting manner) become the guiding values of action.[55] After this initial period of identity formation, we can assume that identity is not readily reworked to incorporate new information that is of little immediate personal salience. In contrast, new information is more likely to be limited in its impact to changing schema (existing conceptions) rather than the core sense of self. This study highlights the importance of adolescence as the focal period for human rights education.

To increase the prospects of human rights education in adulthood becoming more effective, more than simple teaching in a formal setting is required. The approach that may hold the most promise is experiential, where human rights are taught through demonstrating their positive impact. This may be achieved with the following considerations in mind.

As noted earlier, adults frequently are concerned that allowing children to exercise their rights, or even allowing knowledge of them, will create a situation of anarchy and selfish and excessive demands among children. This concern may be overcome by demonstrating, in incremental fashion, the nature of children's rights and the rights-respecting outcomes associated with children's rights education. Within the community, such a demonstration may be accomplished through providing the opportunity for children's participation rights. Typically, adults are reluctant to share power with children or have children sit as equal partners on community committees.[56] However, where this has been allowed, adults have quickly learned of the benefits. Consider the following example. An inner-city play area was being designed for four- and five-year-olds. The local officials planned to put down grass. But the children wanted concrete. The children explained that grass made it difficult to see broken glass and discarded needles. The officials had not thought of this important piece of information.[57]

Also revealing is research evidence from a study of teachers who were asked to teach children about their rights.[58] A group of middle school (grade 8) teachers were asked to participate in a pilot study of rights education. They were provided the necessary information and curriculum materials, and their exist-ing attitudes and support for rights were assessed. At the end of the school year, their compliance with the program and their attitudes about children's rights were again assessed. The teachers differed widely in their a priori beliefs about rights. Interestingly, these differences did not affect compliance with use of the rights curriculum provided. However, by the end of the year, the extent of use of the curriculum predicted attitudes toward rights. The more teachers had used the rights curriculum with their students, the more supportive the teachers became of rights. One explanation is that teachers' possible misperceptions about rights may have been overcome with experience. A second is that the curriculum re-quired that teachers respect and model the rights about which they were teach-ing. Perhaps as teachers responded to their students as rights bearers, they were persuaded of the benefits of rights. A third and particularly compelling explana-tion is that the teachers' observations of the positive effect of rights education on their students had an effect on the teachers' understanding of rights. In contrast to their initial expectations, teachers noted that the more their students learned about rights, the more they behaved in rights-respecting ways.

In summary, human rights education has the potential to be a powerful tool for social justice when provided to adolescents in ways that respect and model the rights that the young people are learning about. When provided in an age-appropriate manner with appropriate pedagogy and content of interest to adolescents, there is a heightened probability of rights respect being incor-porated into the emerging moral identity of the learner.

NOTES

1.   K. Covell and R. B. Howe, "Moral Education Through the 3 Rs: Rights, Respect, and Responsibility," *Journal of Moral Education* 30 (2001): 31-42; K. Covell and R. B. Howe, "The Impact of Children's Rights Education: A Canadian Study," *International Journal of Children's Rights* 7 (1999): 171-83; J. Decoene and R. De Cock, "The Children's Rights Project in the Primary School 'De Vrijdag-markt' in Bruges," in *Monitoring Children's Rights*, ed. E. Verhellen, 627-36 (The Hague: Martinus Nijhoff, 1996).

2.   T. Hammarberg, "The UN Convention on the Rights of the Child-And How to Make it Work," *Human Rights Quarterly* 12 (1990): 97-105.

3.   G. Pike and D. Selby, *Human Rights: An Activity File* (Nepean, ON: Bacon and Hughes, 1997).

4.   E. Verhellen, *Convention on the Rights of the Child* (Kessel-Lo, Belgium: Garant, 1994).

5.   G. Melton, "Starting a New Generation of Research," in *Children, Social Science and the Law*, ed. B. Bottoms, M. Kovera, and B. McAulifff, 449-53 (Cambridge: Cambridge University Press, 2002). However, the implications of signing remain controversial in international law. See C. A. Bradley, "Unratified Treaties, Domestic Politics, and the US Constitution, *Harvard International Law Journal* 48, no. 2 (2007), accessed December 31, 2009, http://www.harvardilj.org/print/117. 48_2_Bradley[1].pdf.

6.   T. Hammarberg, "A School for Children with Rights," *Innocenti Lectures* 2 (Florence: UNICEF, 1997).

7.   P. David, "Implementing the Rights of the Child. Six Reasons Why the Human Rights of Children Remain a Constant Challenge," *International Review of Education* 48, nos. 3-4 (2002): 259-63.

8.   K. E. Knutsson, *Children: Noble Causes or Worthy Citizens?* (Florence: UNICEF, 1997).

9.   Ibid.

10.   Covell and Howe, "The Impact of Children's Rights Education," 171-83; Decoene and De Cock, "The Children's Rights Project," 627-36.

11.   P. Alderson, "Human Rights and Democracy in Schools: Do They Mean More than 'Picking up Litter and Not Killing Whales'?" *International Journal of Children's Rights* 7 (1999): 85-205; J. Torney-Purta, J. Schwille, and J. Amadeo, eds., *Education across Countries: Twenty-Four National Case Studies from the IEA Civic Education Project* (Wellington, NZ: Becky Bliss, 1999).

12.   R. Ludbrook, "Children's Rights in School Education," in *Citizen Child: Australian Law and Children's Rights*, ed. Kathleen Funder, 84-112 (Melbourne: Australian Institute of Family Studies, 1996).

13.   K. Bickmore, "Teaching Conflict and Conflict Resolution in the School: (Extra-) Curricular Considerations," in *How Children Understand War and Peace*, ed. A. Raviv, L. Oppenheimer, and D. Bar-Tal, 233-59 (San Francisco: Jossey-Bass, 1999).

14.   K. Covell and R. B. Howe, "Children's Rights Education: Implementing Article 42," in *Advocating for Children: International Perspectives on Children's Rights*, ed. A.B. Smith, M. Gollop, K. Marshall and K. Nairn, 42-50 (Otago, NZ: University of Otago Press, 2000).

15.   J. Dewey, *How We Think* (Buffalo, NY: Prometheus Books, 1993); C. R. Rodgers, "Voices Inside Schools. Seeing Student Learning: Teacher Change and the Role of Reflection," *Harvard Educational Review* 72, no. 2 (2002), 230-53.

16.   Ibid.

17.   J. Rudduck and J. Flutter, "Pupil Participation and Pupil Perspective: Carving a New Order of Experience," *Cambridge Journal of Education* 30, no.1 (2002): 75-90.

18. Alderson, "Human Rights and Democracy in Schools," 85-205.

19. P. Alderson and S. Arnold, *School Students' Views on Schools, Councils and Daily Life at School* (London: Institute of Education, University of London, 1999).

20. Alderson, "Human Rights and Democracy in Schools," 85-205.

21. P. Payne, "Identity and Environmental Education," *Environmental Education Research* 7, no. 1 (2000): 67-88.

22. F. Tibbits, "Understanding What We Do: Emerging Models for Human Rights Education," *International Review of Education* 48, nos. 3-4 (2002): 159-71.

23. Council of Europe Committee of Ministers, "On Teaching and Learning about Human Rights in Schools," Recommendation No. R (85) 7 of the Committee of Ministers to Member States on Teaching and Learning about Human Rights in Schools, adopted May 14, 1985; M. Abdallah-Pretceille, "Human Rights Education in Pre-Primary Schools," *Report of the Fortieth Council of Europe Teachers' Seminar, Donaueschingen* (Strasbourg: Council of Europe, June 20-25, 1989); H. Starkey, "The Council of Europe Recommendation on the Teaching and Learning of Human Rights in Schools," in *The Challenge of Human Rights Education*, ed. H. Starkey, 21-38 (London: Cassell, 1991).

24. J. Humphrey, epilogue to *Human Rights and Education*, ed. N. Tarrow, 235-36 (Oxford: Pergamon Press, 1987).

25. J. Torney-Purta, "Socialization and Human Rights Research: Implications for Teachers," in *International Human Rights, Society and the Schools*, ed. M.S. Branson and J. Torney-Purta, 35-48 (Washington, D.C.: National Council for the Social Studies, 1982).

26. D. Schmidt-Sinns, "How Can We Teach Human Rights?" *International Journal of Political Education* 3 (1980): 177-85.

27. C. Helwig, "The Role of Agent and Social Context in Judgments of Freedom of Speech and Religion," *Child Development* 68 (1997): 484-95.

28. R. C. Wade, "Conceptual Change in Elementary Social Studies: A Case Study of Fourth Graders' Understanding of Human Rights," *Theory and Research in Social Education* 22 no. 1 (1994): 74-95.

29. Ibid.

30. J. Torney-Purta, "Human Rights," in *Teaching for International Understanding, Peace, and Human Rights*, ed. N.J. Graves, O.J. Dunlop, and J. Torney-Purta, 59-84 (Paris: UNESCO, 1984).

31. J. Piaget, *The Origins of Intelligence in Children* (New York: International Universities Press, 1952).

32. E. D. Neimark, "Adolescent Thought: Transition to Formal Operations," in *Handbook of Developmental Psychology*, ed. B. B. Wolman, 486-502 (Engle-

wood Cliffs: Prentice-Hall, 1982); R. L. Selman, *The Growth of Interpersonal Understanding: Development and Clinical Analysis* (New York: Academic Press, 1980); I. Cherney and N. W. Perry, "Children's Attitudes Toward Their Rights," in *Monitoring Children's Rights*, ed. E. Verhellen, 241-50 (The Hague: Martinus Nijhoff, 1996).

33. R. L. Selman, *The Growth of Interpersonal Understanding: Development and Clinical Analysis* (New York: Academic Press, 1980).

34. M. L. Hoffman, "Empathy, Its Limitations, and Its Role in a Comprehensive Moral Theory," in *Morality, Moral Behavior and Moral Development*, ed. W. Kurtines and J. Gewirtz, 283-302 (New York: Wiley, 1984).

35. S. Berman, *Children's Social Consciousness and the Development of Social Responsibility* (Albany: SUNY Press, 1997), 112.

36. E. Erikson, *Identity: Youth and Crisis* (New York: Norton, 1968); M. Nisan, "Personal Identity and Education for the Desirable," *Journal of Moral Education* 25, no. 1 (1996): 75-84.

37. R. F. Baumeister and M. Muraven, "Identity as Adaptation to Social, Cultural and Historical Context," *Journal of Adolescence* 19 (1996): 405-16.

38. Ibid.

39. C. Holden, "Keen at 11, Cynical at 18? Encouraging Pupil Participation in School and Community," in *Children as Citizens: Education for Participation*, ed. C. Holden and N. Clough, 46-62 (London: Jessica Kingsley, 1998).

40. Ibid.

41. Payne, "Identity and Environmental Education," 67-88.

42. Holden and Clough, *Children as Citizens*.

43. Berman, *Children's Social Consciousness*.

44. D. Goodman, "Motivating People From Privileged Groups to Support Social Justice," *Teachers College Record* 102, no. 6 (2000): 1061-86.

45. J. J. Arnett, "The Psychology of Globalization," *American Psychologist* 57, no. 10 (2002): 774-83; S. Hornberg, "Human Rights Education as an Integral Part of General Education," *International Review of Education* 57, nos. 3-4 (2002): 187-98.

46. M. Booth, "Arab Adolescents Facing the Future: Enduring Ideals and Pressures for Change," in *The World's Youth: Adolescence in Eight Regions of the Globe*, ed. B. B. Brown, R. Larson and T. S. Saraswathi, 207-42 (New York: Cambridge University Press, 2002); C. Welti, "Adolescents in Latin America: Facing the Future with Skepticism," in *The World's Youth: Adolescence in Eight Regions of the Globe*, ed. B. B.Brown, R. Larson, and T. S. Saraswathi, 276-306 (New York: Cambridge University Press, 2002).

47. R. Barrett, "Middle Schooling: A Challenge for Policy and Curriculum," *Education Horizons* 5, no. 3 (1999): 6-9.

48. J. Beane, *Affect in the Curriculum: Towards Democracy, Dignity and Diversity* (New York: Teachers College Press, 1990); M. Griffiths and L. Davies, *In Fairness to Children: Working for Social Justice in the Primary School* (London: David Fulton, 1995); Holden and Clough, *Children as Citizens.*

49. C. D. Batson, M. Polyarpou, E. Harmon-Jones, H. Imhoff, E. Mitchner, L. Bednar, T. Klein, and L. Highberger, "Empathy and Attitudes: Can Feeling for a Member of a Stigmatized Group Improve Feelings Toward the Group?" *Journal of Personality and Social Psychology* 71, no. 1 (1997): 105-18.

50. J. S. Eccles, C. Midgley, A. Wigfield, C. M. Buchanan, D. Reuman, C. Flanagan, and D. MacIver, "Development during Adolescence. The Impact of Stage-Environment Fit Theory on Young Adolescents' Experiences in Schools and in Families," *American Psychologist* 48, no. 2 (1993): 90-101.

51. Ibid.

52. J. Torney-Purta, "Patterns in the Civic Knowledge, Engagement and Attitudes of European Adolescents: The IEA Civic Education Study," *European Journal of Education* 37, no. 2 (2002): 129-41; Berman, *Children's Social Consciousness.*

53. W. Damon and D. Hart, *Self-Understanding in Childhood and Adolescence* (New York: Cambridge University Press, 1988).

54. K. M. Campbell and K. Covell, "Children's Rights Education at the University Level: An Effective Means of Promoting Rights Knowledge and Rights-Based Attitudes," *International Journal of Children's Rights* 9 (2001): 123-35.

55. D. T. Snauwaert, "Human Rights as Claims and a Moral Capabilities Approach to Human Rights Education," Paper presented at Conference on Children's Rights, IPFW Human Rights Institute, Fort Wayne, Indiana, April 21, 2006

56. Bickmore, "Teaching Conflict and Conflict Resolution," 233-59.

57. G. Lansdown, *Promoting Children's Participation in Democratic Decision Making* (Florence, Italy: UNICEF, for the Innocenti Centre, 2001).

58. K. Covell, J. L. O'Leary, and R. B. Howe, "Introducing a New Grade 8 Curriculum in Children's Rights," *The Alberta Journal of Educational Research* 48, no. 4 (2002): 302-13.

Four

Introducing Critical Thinking and Dialogue in Preschool

⌖ Marie-France Daniel ⌖

In most industrialized societies, violence is a cause of increasing concern. Violence is observed and condemned in secondary schools, and even in elementary schools. It is the school's responsibility to promote programs oriented toward the prevention of violence. My position, based on the values of the Convention on the Rights of the Child, is that prevention must first begin with stimulation of competencies on the cognitive (critical thinking) and discursive (dialogue among peers) levels. Furthermore, I assert that this stimulation must begin as early as preschool. To this end, the instrument I favor is the Philosophy for Children (P4C) approach, which finds its essence in philosophical dialogue within a community of inquiry.

In this text, I first present the problem of violence and violence prevention. I then introduce P4C. Subsequently, I present research results regarding preschool children's learning process with respect to dialogue and critical thinking. Finally, I discuss the relationships between P4C and the Convention on the Rights of the Child (CRC).

Violence and Prevention

The Quebec Ministry of Education defines violence as "use of power (physical, hierarchical, psychological, moral, or social) in a manner that is open or concealed, spontaneous or deliberate, motivated or not, through the behavior or structures

73

of an individual or a group and that has the effect of compelling or destroying, partially or totally, by physical, psychological, moral, or social means, an object (material goods, persons, symbols) so as to ensure a response to a legitimate need or to react to this unfulfilled need."[1] Violence is therefore an abuse of power that denies a person's liberty and rights and presupposes behaviors that transgress generally accepted norms of conduct. In this sense, violence must be fought and overcome. However, violence exists in every person; it is innate, natural, and fundamental. Under desirable conditions, it is positive, insofar as it represents a motor toward love, energy, and creativity; it is an instrument for ensuring a person's survival. It is only when violence is nonintegrated that it presupposes abuse and disorders.[2] In this text, my concern is with this nonintegrated violence.

Among the most easily observable manifestations of violence are physical (hitting, striking, etc.) and sexual abuse (fondling, harassment, attempts to commit rape, etc.). There are also invisible manifestations of violence, such as psychological and verbal violence, and neglect (abandonment, disapproval, discrimination, rejection, silence, etc.), which particularly victimize the child since they are not directly observable and therefore harder to detect and eliminate. The child victims of these types of abuse are characterized by confusion and silence. Whether violence stems from adults or peers, children do not understand what is happening to them: the causes totally escape them, and they often persuade themselves that they are responsible for the other person's violent behavior.[3] They are unable to communicate what they are experiencing. Also, they are unaware of the norms or acceptable limits with regard to fundamental rights, decent touching, acceptable words, and so on. This knowledge is necessary in order to heighten the awareness of abuse and to expose the abuser.

According to the Public Health Agency of Canada's most recent statistics, the number of reports of mistreated children doubled between 1998 and 2003, rising from 24.55 to 45.68 reports per 1000 children. Of every 100 proven cases of mistreatment, neglect (29%) and physical violence (24%) are the two most common causes reported, followed by exposure to family violence (28%), psychological violence (15%), and sexual maltreatment (3%).[4]

Schools can play a major role in violence prevention, inasmuch as they educate children starting from an early age. Prevention strategies are similar whether the violence is inflicted or suffered.[5] School violence-prevention programs are generally directed toward the development of prosocial skills, relegating the development of cognitive skills to a secondary level. These approaches are generally intended for school-aged children, ages 6 to 15.

My position is that violence prevention must first begin with the stimulation of skills on the cognitive (critical thinking)[6] and discursive (dia-logos) levels.

Indeed, to recognize manifestations of violence (within oneself or in others), to refuse and expose them, children must first learn to think critically about situations related to violence. For example, what is violence? What are the manifestations of violence? What are its causes and consequences? What is anger? What is sadness? Can a word hurt as much as being hit? Do children have rights? What does it mean to be exploited? They must also learn to think critically about concepts related to comprehension of self and of the world (identity, intimacy, equality, justice, rights, plurality, relationships, responsibilities, etc.). Moreover, I postulate that the stimulation of pupils' skills on the cognitive and dialogical levels should begin as early as preschool. First, studies have shown that violent behaviors appear very early in children, even before the age of two.[7] Second, other researchers have shown that young children's thinking, particularly concerning their emotions, can have an incidence on the quality of their social interactions.[8] Third, the Convention on the Rights of the Child, ratified by the United Nations in 1989, promotes pupils' right to free speech as well as autonomous and critical thinking: "Children must know who they are. They must have a positive sense of their own identity. They must be able to think properly and express themselves clearly. They must learn to understand the different ways people have of communicating."[9]

To operationalize my position, I worked with the Philosophy for Children (P4C) approach, which finds its essence in philosophical dialogue among peers. A number of studies have shown P4C's impact on the development of complex thinking skills and on the socialization of youngsters.[10] Furthermore, an increasing number of philosophers recognize that philosophy, when it is an experiential activity (vs. a transmitted doctrine), contributes to the improvement of youngsters' quality of life.[11]

THE PHILOSOPHY FOR CHILDREN (P4C) APPROACH

P4C was conceived by American philosopher Matthew Lipman at the beginning of the 1970s. It is now established in 50 countries, and its material has been translated into 20 languages. In the wake of John Dewey's works, the aims of P4C come within the scope of pragmatism and socioconstructivism.[12] The objective of the approach is to stimulate, in young people, skills related to complex thinking through philosophical dialogue among peers.[13]

Lipman's support material includes seven educational guides intended for teachers and seven philosophical novels intended for pupils at the elementary[14] and secondary[15] levels.[16] Within the framework of two research projects centered on violence prevention, to which I refer in this text, another philosophical support text, *Tales of Audrey-Anne*, was conceived in the Lipmanian tradition.[17] This compendium of sixteen philosophical tales, intended for pre-school children, presents scenes related to the day-to-day experiences of children aged four to six. The tales are said to be philosophical in that they question open concepts (friendship, the person, rights, justice, meanness, belonging, etc.) for which there are no single answers and upon which the children are invited to reflect as a group. The *Tales* are complemented by a teacher's guide that includes some 300 exercises and discussion plans to support the teachers in their Socratic maïeutics.[18]

In facilitating philosophical sessions, Lipman and his colleagues recommend following three steps: reading, questioning, and conducting a dialogue within a community of inquiry.[19]

Reading. From the age of six onward, pupils generally enjoy reading on their own. Reading a chapter of a philosophical novel is therefore done by the pupils, out loud and in turns (a sentence or a paragraph per child, according to their age). These two aspects are important to mark "cooperation" among peers. Indeed, sometimes shy pupils only express themselves through reading (they hardly participate, or not at all, in the following steps), however this act already constitutes a first commitment toward learning, in that the pupil is no longer a receptacle that receives narrative data, but becomes an active participant in the reading. Participating in reading is also a first-level verbal exchange with peers—an exchange that will eventually turn into a sharing of ideas.

Why use a philosophical novel as the core instrument? Several teachers do not use philosophical novels (such as those of Lipman or Daniel). Instead, they use children's literature. Based on our observations within classrooms, we consider that this type of material can be interesting, at times. However, it must respect the two following conditions:

> 1. It must not contain an explicit or even implicit moral toward which the youngsters are directed. Indeed, children's literature too often contains messages relating to "proper" behaviors. Pupils rapidly detect these messages and adjust their thinking accordingly—undoubtedly judging that if they share the author's point of view, they do not risk being poorly graded by the teacher. Nevertheless, as John Dewey would say, thinking within an author's perspective is not thinking, since thinking is thinking by oneself.

> 2. The material used (if it is not philosophical) must be centered on a dilemma and contain ambiguities or paradoxes in order to encourage youngsters to question and to doubt. In other words, the material must create cognitive conflicts in children, without which the mind will hardly become aware of the existence of a problem and, therefore, will hardly get involved in a process of inquiry (see the appendix for an example of a philosophical tale intended for children aged four to six).[20]

Questioning. The second step in the Lipmanian approach is collecting questions. After reading the chapter, the pupils are invited to formulate questions that intrigue them and which they would like to discuss. This second step presupposes that they put sufficient effort into comprehending the text so that they question the situations described. Comprehension not only requires knowledge of words, but a global understanding of the text and of the context. This step encourages the child to embark on a process of inquiry, which is at the root of all critical thinking.

According to the majority of research in pedagogy, although wondering and questioning belong to childhood, they are no longer spontaneous mental acts for children when they reach grade three and onwards at school, where they have learned to receive information rather passively. Fostering pupils' wondering is a pedagogical objective that is not valued in traditional pedagogy, in which the power and the right to ask questions belong to teachers. However, (re)learning to question is fundamental, in that it stimulates autonomous and critical thinking in youngsters. Furthermore, this second step of P4C gives pupils a sense of responsibility and places them at the forefront of their own learning experience since, through their questions, the pupils (not the adults) elaborate the discussion agenda for the following weeks. In so doing, question collection ensures philosophical sessions rooted in intrinsic motivation.

The second step presupposes that pupils learn not only to formulate a question, but to formulate a philosophical question. In general, a question carries philosophical meaning when it:

- concerns the *why* rather than the *how*;
- questions concepts;
- develops around the origin, cause, consequences, and relationships between concepts and situations;
- questions, knowledge, traditions, prejudices, etc.

- In sum, learning to formulate a philosophical question stimulates pupils' critical thinking, creativity, and autonomy.

PHILOSOPHICAL DIALOGUE WITHIN A COMMUNITY OF INQUIRY

Philosophical dialogue among peers is intended to provide youngsters with elements of answers to the questions they formulated during the previous step. A philosophical dialogue is dialogical and critical; it is not merely a conversation.[21] Its apprenticeship is a complex process, going from simple to complex exchanges, as illustrated in a recent study conducted in Australia, Mexico, and Quebec, which brought to light five types of exchanges among pupils aged ten to twelve as they experimented with P4C through the school year.[22] We named the different modes of exchange as follows: anecdotal, monological, noncritical dialogical, semicritical dialogical, and critical dialogical.

An exchange is considered *anecdotal*, when youngsters speak of personal situations in an unstructured manner. In this case, pupils are not in a process of inquiry, they are not working at identifying a common goal, and they are little or not at all influenced by peer interventions. Furthermore, they do not justify their points of view and their opinions are presented as conclusions.

An exchange is considered *monological* to the extent that pupils begin to enter a process of inquiry, but one that is essentially oriented toward searching for "the" correct answer. Each pupil intervention is independent from the others. Pupils have trouble justifying their opinions.

An exchange is considered *dialogical* when pupils begin to form a community of inquiry, in other words, when they construct their interventions based on those of their peers and actively participate in reflection, at the same time as they are motivated by solving a common problem. The experiment conducted with Australian, Mexican, and Quebec pupils enabled us to realize that a dialogical type of exchange is not philosophical or critical per se. Three types of dialogical exchange emerged from the study:

Noncritical, in which pupils aged ten to twelve were perfectly capable of holding a dialogue, but not capable of evaluating the points of view or perspectives at stake, nor the validity, usefulness, or viability of the statements or criteria. At this level, pupils respect differences of opinion; they construct their points of view based on those of their peers; they begin to justify their statements.

Semicritical, in which, within a context of interdependence, some pupils are sufficiently critical to question peer statements, but not enough to be cognitively influenced by criticism, so that this criticism does not lead to improving the point of view or perspective.

Critical presupposes the following criteria: explicit interdependence among pupils; research centered on construction of meaning (vs. searching for truth); pupils are aware of the complexity of peer points of view; they search for divergence and they consider that uncertainty is a positive cognitive state; criticism is sought for its own sake, as an instrument to further comprehension; pupils spontaneously justify their points of view coherently and in an original manner; their interventions show an ethical preoccupation; their statements are expressed as hypotheses to be verified rather than closed conclusions. As a result, the initial perspective of the group is not only improved, but it also is modified.

One of the fundamental conditions for philosophical or critical dialogue to occur is a climate of cooperation. In Dewey's wake, Lipman considers that the class group must transform into a community of inquiry (CI).[23] According to Lipman, a true CI is manifested when dialogue among peers is characterized by confidence, pluralism, reciprocity, and tolerance.[24]

Forming a CI is a long-term process, since it presupposes learning on multiple levels: personal, social, affective, moral, and cognitive.[25] Indeed, the fact that pupils use the P4C approach and its philosophical material does not mean that the class group (aggregation of individuals) automatically transforms into a community of inquiry. Pupils must first learn to manage the new rights that are granted to them and which fall into the category of philosophizing (to question, to think autonomously, to express themselves, etc.).

Given the power to manage themselves, the pupils then become aware of the possibilities of the CI and work toward transformation of the class into a microsociety. In other words, they then become aware of their social responsibilities (commitment toward solving a common problem, mutual help, respect for divergences in points of view, etc.) to diminish normal tensions among pupils in the classroom and to create a climate of confidence. Observations indicate that when competition yields to cooperation, pupils become more confident in their judgment and more certain of their points of view; they develop self-esteem.[26] Thinking skills become more complex.

Finally, the pupils' development at the affective, social, and personal levels gives them the necessary impulse to transform the classroom microsociety they have created into a true philosophical CI. At this point, the pupils no longer conceive criticism as a rhetorical means intended to ensure personal victory, but as a dialogical instrument that enables them to solve the question they share. Intersubjectivity is then considered superior to intrasubjectivity.

In short, the third step in the Lipmanian approach stimulates critical dialogue among peers as well as fundamental values of the CI, such as equality of rights and opportunities among members, individual and social responsibility, active participation in solving a common question, and critical reflection for a common good.

The question that concerns us now is whether philosophical dialogue within a CI is accessible to five-year-old children. Fostering critical dialogue and thinking, opening minds to otherness and to difference, and developing behaviors of tolerance and respect are elements that should be taken into consideration when teaching children thought speech, with the intention of fostering coexistence among citizens and preventing violence.[27]

LEARNING TO PHILOSOPHIZE AT AGE FIVE

Between 2001 and 2004, a research project[28] was conducted to study the ability of five-year-old children to dialogue in a critical manner. During a full school year

(October to May), groups of five-year-old preschool children experimented with *The Tales of Audrey-Anne* on a weekly basis. We recorded five of their exchanges at various points during the year. We applied the typology described in the previous section to the analysis of exchanges between children.[29]

In the following pages, we will see that children's evolution on a discursive level is connected to learning on an epistemological level.

Anecdotal Exchange. At the beginning of the school year, before the philosophical praxis, we recorded the children's first exchange. Analyses showed that the groups of children involved in the research project exchanged in an anecdotal manner, in other words they "spoke" (vs. dialogued) egocentrically ("I," "my", etc.). The following is an example:

> Teacher: What difference is there between a doll and a person?
> Ch:The other day, my friend had a doll. It walked. It even had a little fork and it could eat. . . . You pushed on a button on the bowl and lots of glop came out. . . . Then her dog went into her room, it took the doll and threw it on the floor and broke it.
> Lv: My doll talks.
> Ab: I've seen a doll that could pee.

Monological Exchange. After a few weeks of philosophical praxis (variable according to the group), the exchange was considered monological. Pupils' answers were brief and the answers were independent from each other, as though each person was pursuing an internal monologue. The following is an example:

> Teacher: Why do children get diseases?
> AA: Because sometimes they don't get vaccinated.
> Ch: Because sometimes they go outside without a scarf.
> W: . . . I know why you catch diseases in hospitals, it's because people are sick and they drop germs around.

Noncritical Dialogical Exchange. After several months of P4C praxis, most groups of children involved in the research project were able to exchange in a noncritical dialogical manner. Pupils respected differences of opinion, constructed their points of view based on those of their peers, and began to justify their statements. In this type of exchange, the pupils did not consider evaluation of peers' points of view as fundamental for the evolution of the exchange. The following is an example:

> Teacher: On the blackboard, I am going to draw two circles that cross each other (Venn diagram). In the first circle, we will write actions that help your body heal, in the second circle, actions that harm your health, and

in the center, actions that can either help or harm your health.

AA: If you eat lots of vegetables, it helps your body grow.

Mel: Wearing gloves.

PL: Why gloves?

Mel: Gloves so you don't catch a disease in the hospital.

PL: Gloves are also useful to keep you from hurting your hands with splinters when you work.

Br: There's something else. In winter, you protect yourself with mittens.

Semicritical Dialogical Exchange. At the end of the school year, we recorded the last of the children's exchanges. The results of the analysis revealed that certain groups of children expressed themselves in a semicritical dialogical[30] manner; that is, some pupils were sufficiently critical to question peers' statements, but those whose statements were questioned were not sufficiently critical to be cognitively influenced by the criticism provided, so that this criticism did not lead to modification of the point of view or perspective. The following is an example:

Teacher: Let's do another game to think about our solutions. Here is the situation: Jojo doesn't like the candy her aunt gave her, but she eats it anyway because she doesn't want to disappoint her aunt. According to you, is this a good solution?

Ca: I think it's a good idea . . . because she won't be sad.

Teacher: Does anyone agree or disagree with Ca?

Mel: I don't agree . . . I would take the candy and drop it in the garbage and say I finished the candy. . . . because I don't want to eat mints I don't like. . . . This way, she won't know I didn't eat them.

Teacher: Do you agree with the ideas that were just said?

LS: I don't agree with Mel because if my aunt gave me some candy I don't like and I threw it away, when she throws something away, she will look in the garbage and see the candy and she would be angry with me.

Mel: If we put them way, way, way down in the bottom and put some stuff over them and then close the lid . . .

AA: Well, I would eat them even if I don't like them. If I really, really, don't like them, I'll give them back to my aunt without telling her I don't like them.

LS: I have another idea. All you have to do is tell your aunt, "could you change the candies?"

On the epistemological level, analysis of the transcripts of the exchanges indicated that at the beginning of the year, egocentricity[31] predominated, as each child brought forth a perspective that was not only concrete, but that was also particular to that child ("My friend had a doll," "My doll talks," "I've seen a doll that could pee"). The egocentric perspective was the most spontaneous among five-year-olds whose beliefs, opinions, and interests were anchored in concrete observation, or anchored in those of the adults that surrounded them (parents, teachers, media, etc.). At this age, the children are not aware that they are able to formulate their own judgments and to act accordingly. They spontaneously believe that there is a single way of looking at the world—that which they were taught and which they must master—and that the evidence for this is so plausible that there is no need to justify the belief.

On the other hand, in the final transcript of the year, the majority of children had evolved toward what we refer to as relativism. The relativistic exchange shows decentering with regard to the object of discussion and to the self; beliefs are no longer conjugated in the singular, but in the plural form; "truth" is modifiable according to context; each pupil has a different point of view; pupils' justifications presuppose a capacity to link the senses' concrete observations to abstractions in the form of reasoning; justifications are developed but only to prove that one is right. Relativism is related to intrasubjectivity. If, on the one hand, relativism should be transcended by ten- to twelve-year-olds for the enrichment of the individual and social experience, on the other hand, the attainment of relativism at five years of age requires rigorous and continuous stimulation from the teacher.

One more interesting fact: in the final transcript for the year, we also noted that some children had a tendency toward intersubjectivity. Intersubjectivity presupposes that pupils are, to a certain extent, aware that they need their peers in order to transcend their own beliefs and concepts, to increase coherence in their judgments, and to construct their comprehension of the world. The perspective related to intersubjectivity implies pupils' ability to justify their beliefs and to use complex thinking skills to interpret and solve a common problem. It also implies pupils' ability not to represent the solutions as grounded in certainty or "truth," but rather as evidence that must be placed into context, nuanced, and questioned. In the final transcript (see the example previously presented), we observed that the interventions of some children reflected complex thinking skills and attitudes (justifying their points of view, listening actively, using logical reasoning, taking into account peer points of view to construct their own, evaluating the relevance of peer points of view and criticizing them). As a corollary, the children's solutions became more nuanced and refined as the exchange took place: the starting point was situated in disrespect of self (eating candies you don't like so as not to hurt your aunt's feelings) or in disrespect of the other (throwing the candy in the garbage to fool the aunt), whereas the end of the exchange was oriented toward a compromise that stemmed from reflection ("If I really, really, don't like them, I'll give them back to my aunt without telling her I don't like them") and toward communication (All you have to do is tell your aunt, "could you change the candies?"). In a specific manner, we speak of a tendency toward intersubjectivity (vs. rooted in perspective) since at age five, children do not have a high degree of awareness regarding what is happening in the CI. Furthermore, at this age, although the children use complex thinking skills, they do not master the critical attitudes that accompany these skills in older children.

In a perspective of violence prevention, my hypothesis is the following: inasmuch as children's thinking is situated in relativism, their behavior should be more inclusive and tinged with awareness of others; their behavior should be more in keeping with the social norms of the environment and therefore less violent. Inasmuch as children's thinking is oriented toward intersubjectivity, they should have a greater tendency to replace instinct with reflection and to replace "the truth" with a coconstruction of a temporarily satisfactory reality. In this regard, a recent study on children's representations of violence shows that children whose discourse was oriented toward intersubjectivity were inclined to nuance their interpretations of reality, to question prejudices, and to go beyond incomprehension by asking questions or for precisions.[32] A current research project (SSHRC 2005-2008) studies the potential relationships between the evolution of children's exchanges (anecdotal, monological, noncritical, semicritical, and critical dialogical), epistemological perspectives (egocentrism, relativism, and intersubjectivity) and behaviors (competition, individualism, collaboration, and cooperation) during the P4C sessions and outside (classroom, schoolyard, etc.).[33]

THE CONVENTION ON THE RIGHTS OF THE CHILD AND P4C

The values implicitly contained in the philosophical CI and in the critical dialogue are similar: respect of self and of others, communication, rights, critical reflection, responsibilities, involvement in the community. I maintain that these values converge toward those recommended by the Convention on the Rights of the Child (CRC). As mentioned previously, the CRC, adopted by the United Nations General Assembly in November 1989, promotes, for the first time in history, children's right to autonomous and critical speech, in particular in articles 12 to 15 and article 17.[34]

Articles 12 to 15 of the CRC explicitly promote children's right to autonomous, critical, and responsible thought. In these articles, the CRC recognizes that children must have freedom of choice and expression to become persons in their own right; in other words, to fulfill their social role as children, pupils, workers, friends, and citizens, and to be able to face the challenges of daily life.

In submitting these articles, the CRC establishes, on the one hand, the status of children as persons in their own right and, on the other hand, children's right to speak. In so doing, the signatories of the CRC recognize that children think, that they think in a critical manner, and that they have information to convey, experiences to share, and ideas to communicate.

Furthermore, in article 17, it is recommended that children be given the right to information. Through this article, the CRC promotes the development of youngsters' awareness. To be aware means to be open, to show objectiveness, and to be realistic. To be aware means not only to appreciate beauty, but also to see ugliness. Water that cools, birds that sing, the rising sun, the smile that illuminates a face, a positive word that has the power to stimulate self-esteem, these are manifestations of what we refer to as beauty. Homeless people who suffer rejection, children who are indoctrinated and who lose the capacity to think by themselves, words that hurt and make others feel insignificant, looks that emphasize differences and prejudices, blows that hurt and kill, these are manifestations of what we refer to as ugliness. Too often, the mind attaches itself to beauty and represses ugliness. However, in a violence-prevention perspective, being aware of beauty as well as ugliness is fundamental. For it is in awareness of reality (beautiful or ugly) that involvement is born; that the need to dialogue, to cooperate, and to condemn violence is born.

Appropriately, the CRC specifies (in several articles, including 5 and 29) that the development of children's autonomy and rights must not take place to the detriment of their security: adults remain responsible for children's education and protection. Furthermore, protection does not go hand-in-hand with domination, paternalism, or overprotection, which can lead to children's feelings of inferiority, marginalization, and exclusion. "The notion of citizenship and how active one is, or is allowed to be, is an issue of power and in the context of children and adults, children certainly have the less powerful stance and are thus limited in the contributions they can make because of this powerful 'dominance' adults have over them."[35]

With regard to articles 12 to 15 and article 17, fundamental relationships between P4C and the CRC emerge. First, they emerge regarding the representation of the concept of "child" which is rooted in the notion of "person in their own right," and then regarding values that underlie this representation and highlight the validity of cooperation, involvement, equality, rights, and responsibilities. This representation presupposes that maturity, particularly on the cognitive and discursive levels, is acquired through praxis. In contrast to negative prejudices that are conveyed in society and in education, and in agreement with Lipman, I maintain that the capacity to judge develops through the practice of judgment, and that the sense of responsibility is acquired through the exercise of responsibilities.[36] This is why I argue for the need to provide preschool children with the opportunity to reflect with their peers on situations and concepts related to the world and to violence, and to practice the values advocated by P4C and the CRC through the CI, rather than waiting for children to acquire the required maturity before beginning.[37] Four- and five-year-old children take lessons in violin, classical ballet, and skating, and the relevance of such teachings is not questioned. Why then should children not exercise their ability to think and to dialogue within a CI as early as preschool? My argument is all the more significant since research results indicate that when stimulated, five-year-old children are able to think and dialogue in a semicritical manner. In addition, from the perspective of prevention, it has been shown that early interventions are more effective than late interventions.

The second relationship I noted between the CRC and P4C is that both subscribe to the same socioconstructivist vision of education: not telling children what to think, but teaching them how to think. Telling children what to think can have a certain impact in the short term, but if education does not stimulate young people to define problems on their own, to explore with others the causes and consequences of behaviors, to search for viable hypotheses, to verify their conclusions using criteria, and so on, then in the long term it can be feared that the impact of such apprenticeships will be not be significant.[38]

In terms of nuances between P4C and the CRC, I note that the CRC is a theoretical convention, whereas P4C is a pedagogical approach that actualizes its aims with regard to the cognitive, discursive, and social development of children. The impact of the philosophical approach on the development of critical dialogue and thought in a CI is even more relevant to the quality of citizen education, since rights and values are not static; they should be interpreted differently as society evolves, as contexts change, and as new facts are integrated into the fundamental principles.[39] In the pragmatist and socioconstructivist perspective, citizen action is not only a matter of knowledge and strict (blind) application of norms; it presupposes the capacity to reason and to use rules wisely to prevent potential social crises and to better circumscribe them if they occur. Indeed, the essence of existence is not situated in the repetition of a previous choice, but in a succession of increasingly appropriate individual choices, and of experiences that become increasingly meaningful.[40]

Conclusion

The framework for this paper concerns violence prevention among children. To this effect, my first argument concerned the fact that it is crucial for schools to invest in the development of critical thinking in pupils. Indeed, on the one hand, critical thinking enables one to access a true comprehension of events instead of upholding a simplified vision of these events and, on the other hand, critical thinking can contribute to the construction of a culture of nonviolence by replacing blows with words among aggressive children, and by giving victimized children the power to refuse and to condemn violence.[41] The pedagogical instrument I chose for our experiments was P4C because this approach is recognized as stimulating critical dialogue in elementary school pupils.

My second argument was that violence-prevention work (through critical thinking and dialogue within a philosophical CI) should include preschool children, since, at this age, children are curious and certainly able to learn to reflect on ethical dilemmas.

Results from a recent research project indicated that five-year-old children who "philosophized" through a full school year were able to engage in semicritical thought and dialogue. Also, results have shown that philosophical praxis enabled these children to refine epistemological perspectives, which progressed from egocentrism to relativism, and even to intersubjectivity in some of them. A recent research project (2005-2008) involving children from Quebec, Toronto, France, Belgium, and England has pursued the systematic study of these elements with regard to prevention of violence.

Appendix

Philosophical Tale. The Injured Butterfly (Daniel, 2002)

Philip and Audrey-Anne are out on a school outing. They are chasing butterflies. Not to catch them! Not to kill them! Simply to get a closer look at them. A tiny light yellow butterfly settles on a flower near Phillip's net. The butterfly appears to be comfortable on the back of the flower. The flower is dark yellow, almost orange. Philip wants to tame the little butterfly. Softly he whispers to it: "Hello. What is your name? How old are you? You are so small!" The little butterfly is afraid to be caught. It flies away, but soon comes back. Philip tries to tame it again: "My name is Philip. I am small, just like you." The butterfly does not answer but its antennas are moving very fast. "Do butterflies talk by moving their antennas?" wonders Philip. Then, the butterfly's wings start moving too. They do not move as fast as the antennas. Their movement is slow and regular. They look like little lace fans. Audrey-Anne and Philip watch them move. They laugh. They are happy. Suddenly, they notice something: the butterfly's wings are not the same. One of them is torn. Audrey-Anne is worried by this difference: "Little butterfly, does your wing hurt? How did you tear it? Was it an accident or did another butterfly hurt you on purpose?" The little butterfly does not answer. Audrey-Anne continues: "Tell me, in Butterfly Land, are there stronger butterflies that like to hurt the smaller ones?" The little butterfly flaps its wings. Audrey-Anne worries: "Did you stand up for yourself? What did you do to protect yourself, little butterfly?"

Notes

1. *Prévenir et contrer la violence à l'école* (Quebec City: Bibliothèque Nationale du Québec, 1990).

2. J. Bergeret, "La violence fondamentale," in *Violences*, ed. P. Mazet and S. Lebovici, cahier no. 49, 1-18 (Bobigny: UFR de Médecine de Bobigny, 1999).

3. M. Erkohen-Marküs and P-A Doudin, "Le devenir de l'enfant violenté et sa scolarité," in *Violences à l'école. Fatalité ou défi?*, ed. M. Erkohen-Marküs and P.-A. Doudin, 17-47 (Brussels: Les Presses de l'Université De Boeck, 2000).

4. M.-R. Sauvé, "Y a-t-il plus d'enfants maltraités au Québec?," lecture, Le Forum, Université de Montréal, October 10, 2006.

5. J. Pransky, "A Conceptual Framework for Prevention," in *Prevention: The Critical Need*, ed. J. Pransky, 14-33 (Springfield, MO: Burrell Foundation and Paradigm Press 1991).

6. Researchers have not reached a consensus regarding the concept of critical thinking, and this is at the core of our argument. There are at least three views: 1. Critical thinking may be viewed as a product whose development is a technique intended to enhance control of the environment according to predefined standards. The rhetoric of critical thinking is then becomes mechanically applied. It presupposes cognitive skills almost exclusively, most often occurs in a context of competition, and is sometimes a means of achieving undesirable ends. 2. Critical thinking may be understood as a practice which develops through comprehension of the social environment; it is part of an intrasubjective perspective in which where each justification, each meaning, each interpretation is simply accepted. 3. Critical thinking may be distinguished as a praxis whose development is realized through critical awareness, leading to emancipation and autonomy of the person and of the community. The purpose, which is the enhancement of individual and social experience, is realized through knowledge of the children's own constructions rather than through merely transmitted knowledge. Critical thinking here is dialogical or, in other words, cooperative rather than chiefly competitive. It presupposes social skills and ethical attitudes in addition to know-how. We adhere to this third orientation.

7.   F. Dodson, *Tout se joue avant 6 ans* (Paris: Robert Laffont, 1972); J. Dumas, *L'enfant violent: le connaître, l'aider, l'aimer* (Paris: Bayard, 2000).

8.   F. Pons, P. Harris, P.-A. Doudin, "Teaching Emotion Understanding," *European Journal of Psychology of Education* 17, no. 3 (2003): 293-304; F. Pons, P. Harris, and M. de Rosnay, "Emotion Comprehension Between 3 and 11 Years: Developmental Periods and Hierarchical Organizations," *European Journal of Developmental Psychology* 9, no. 2 (2003): 127-52; F. Pons, J. Lawson, P. Harris, and M. de Rosnay, "Individual Differences in Children's Emotion Understanding: Effects of Age and Language," *Scandinavian Journal of Psychology* 44, no. 4 (2003): 345-51; L. Villanueva, R. Clemente, and F. Garcia, "Theory of Mind and Peer Rejection at School," *Social Development* 9 (2000): 271-83.

9.   J. Garbarino, "The Child's Evolving Capacities," in *Children's Rights in America: UN Convention on the Rights of the Child Compared with United States Law*, ed. C. Price Cohen and H. Davidson, 19-32 (N.p.: American Bar Association Center on Children and the Law, 1990).

10.   D. Camhy and G. Iberer, "Philosophy for Children: A Research Project for Further Mental and Personality Development of Primary and Secondary School Pupils," *Thinking* 7, no. 4 (1988): 18-26; D. Cannon, "Good Reasoning: A Reconsideration Drawn from Experience with Philosophy for Children," *Analytic Teaching* 8, no. 1 (1987): 30-35; D. Cannon and M. Weinstein, "Reasoning Skills: An Overview," *Thinking* 6. no. 1 (1985): 29-33; M.-F. Daniel, ed. *Philosophie et Pensée chez l'Enfant* (Montreal: Agence d'Arc, 1990); Daniel, L. Splitter, C. Slade, L. Lafortune, R. Pallascio, and P. Mongeau, "Are the Philosophical Exchanges of Pupils Aged 10 to 12 Relativistic or Inter-subjective?," *Critical and Creative Thinking* 10, no. 2 (2002): 1-19; M.-F. Daniel, L. Lafortune, R. Pallascio, L. Splitter, C. Slade, and T. De la Garza, "Modeling the Development Process of Dialogical Critical Thinking in Pupils Aged 10 to 12 Years," *Communication Education* 54, no. 4 (2005): 334-54; A. Gazzard, "Thinking Skills in Science and Philosophy for Children," *Thinking* 7, no. 3 (2008): 32-41; J. C. Lago-Bernstein, "The Community of Inquiry and the Development of Self-Esteem," *Thinking* 9, no. 1 (2009): 12-17; N. R. Lane and S. A. Lane, "Rationality, Self-Esteem and Autonomy through Collaborative Enquiry," *Oxford Review of Education* 12 (1986): 263-75; M. Schleifer, M.-F. Daniel, L. Lafortune, and R. Pallascio, "Concepts of Cooperation in the Classroom," *Païdeusis* 12, no. 2 (1999): 45-56; M. Schleifer, M.-F. Daniel, E. Auriac, and S. Lecompte, "The Impact of Philosophical Discussions on Moral Autonomy, Judgment, Empathy and the Recognition of Emotion in 5 Year Olds," *Thinking* 16, no. 4 (2003): 4-13.

11.   F. Galichet, "Pratique de la philosophie à l'école et citoyenneté," in *Quelle formation pour l'enseignement de l'éthique à l'école?*, ed. F. Ouellet, 23-55 (Quebec

City: Les Presses de l'Université Laval, 2006); L. Marcil-Lacoste, "Y a-t-il un âge pour philosopher?," in *La philosophie pour enfants. L'Expérience Lipman*, ed. L. Marcil-Lacoste, 3-19 (Quebec City: Le Griffon d'Argile, 1990); R. Paul, "Critical and Reflective Thinking: A Philosophical Perspective," in *Dimensions of Thinking and Cognitive Instruction*, ed. B. F. Jones and L. Idol, 445-95 (Hillsdale, NJ: Lawrence Erlbaum Associates Publishers, 1990); R. Paul, *Critical Thinking: What Every Person Needs to Survive in a Rapidly Changing World* (Santa Rosa, CA: Foundation for Critical Thinking, 1993).

12. M.-F. Daniel, "Présupposés philosophiques et pédagogiques de Matthew Lipman et leurs applications," in *La Philosophie pour enfants: Le modèle de Lipman en discussion*, ed. C. Leleux, 25-47 (Brussels: Les Presses de l'Université De Boeck, 2005).

13. M. Lipman, *Thinking in Education* (Cambridge: Cambridge University Press, 2003).

14. Among the novels Lipman conceived for elementary school pupils, *Elfie* (for ages 6-7) is about a child's questions upon starting school; *Kio and Augustine* (for ages 7-8) is centered on environmental questions; *Pixie* (for ages 8-10) centers on relationships of language; and *Harry Stottlemeier's Discovery* (for ages 11-12) centers on relationships of logic.

15. Among the novels Lipman conceived for secondary school pupils, *Lisa* (for ages 13-14) deals with ethical questions; *Suki* (for ages 14-15) deals with aesthetic questions; and *Mark* (for ages 15-16) deals with social questions.

16. See also Gareth Matthew's philosophical stories published in *Thinking, The Journal of Philosophy for Children*, 1979-2005.

17. M.-F. Daniel, *Les Contes d'Audrey-Anne* (Quebec City: Le Loup de Gouttière, 2002).

18. M.-F. Daniel, *Dialoguer sur le corps et la violence: Un pas vers la prévention* (Quebec City: Le Loup de Gouttière, 2003).

19. The following section is taken from: M.-F. Daniel, *Pour l'Apprentissage d'une pensée critique au primaire* (Quebec City, Les Presses de l'Université du Québec, 2005); M. Lipman, A. M. Sharp, and F. S. Oscanyan, *Philosophy in the Classroom* (Philadelphia: Temple University Press, 1980).

20. J. Dewey, *The Quest for Certainty: A Study of the Relation Between Knowledge and Action* (New York: Capricorn Books, 1960).

21. L. Splitter, and A. M. Sharp, *Teaching for Better Thinking* (Melbourne, Australia, ACER, 1995).

22. The research was conducted under the direction of M.-F. Daniel, in collaboration with L. Lafortune, R. Pallascio, P. Mongeau, L. Splitter, C. Slade, and T. de la Garza. A grant from the Social Sciences and Humanities Research

Council (SSHRC) of Canada between 1998 and 2001 made this research possible. For more detail, see M.-F. Daniel and A. Delsol, "Learning to Dialogue in Kindergarten. A Case Study," *Analytic Teaching* 25, no. 3 (2005): 23-52; Daniel et al., "Are the Philosophical Exchanges"; Daniel et al., "Modeling the Development Process."

23. Dewey, *The Quest for Certainty*; J. Dewey, *Theory of the Moral Life* (New York: Irvington Publishers, 1980); J. Dewey, *Moral Principles in Education* (New York: Greenwood Press, 1969).

24. M. Lipman, *Thinking in Education*, 2nd ed. (Cambridge: Cambridge University Press, 2003).

25. M.-F. Daniel, L. Lafortune, R. Pallascio, and M. Schleifer, "La Formation philosophique des jeunes du primaire dans l'apprentissage des mathématiques et son influence sur le développement de leurs habiletés de pensée complexes et de leurs comportements coopératifs," in *Enseigner et comprendre le développement d'une pensée critique*, ed. L. Guilbert, J. Boisvert, and N. Ferguson, 212-37 (Quebec City: Les Presses de l'Université Laval, 1999).

26. J. C. Lago-Bernstein, "The Community of Inquiry and the Development of Self-Esteem," *Thinking* 9, no. 1 (1990): 12-17.

27. C. McCall, "Young Children Generate Philosophical Ideas," in *Thinking Children and Education*, ed. M. Lipman, 569-93 (Dubuque, Iowa: Kendall/Hunt Publishing, 1993).

28. The research project was subsidized, between 2001 and 2004, by the Social Sciences and Humanities Research Council (SSHRC) of Canada. Head of research: M.-F. Daniel; coresearchers: M. Schleifer and C. Garnier (Quebec), E. Auriac (France).

29. M.-F. Daniel and A. Delsol, "Learning to Dialogue in Kindergarten. A Case Study," *Analytic Teaching* 25, no. 3 (2005): 23-52.

30. In the exchanges between five-year-old children that we have collected to date, semicritical dialogue is the most sophisticated type of exchange to which we had access.

31. For more information concerning the epistemological model used here, see Daniel et al., "Modeling the Development Process" of dialogical critical thinking in pupils aged 10 to 12. *Communication Education* 54, no. 4 (2005): 334-54.

32. M.-F. Daniel, P.-A. Doudin, and F. Pons, "Children's Social Representations of Violence. Epistemology and Moral Development," *Journal of Peace Education* 3, no. 2 (2006): 209-34.

33. Head of research: M.-F. Daniel; coresearchers: M. Schleifer and C. Martiny (Quebec), E. Auriac (France), F. Pons (Denmark), and M.-P. d'Outrelepont (Belgium).

34. C. Price-Cohen and H. Davidson, eds. *Children's Rights in America: UN Convention on the Rights of the Child Compared with the United States Law* (Chicago: American Bar Association, 1990), 19-32.

35. C. Cassidy, "Child and Community of Philosophical Inquiry," paper presented at Glasgow Electronic Privacy Information Center, International Conference, June 2006, 11.

36. M. Lipman, *Thinking in Education.*

37. It should be noted that although P4C was conceived over thirty-five years ago it is still not a part of very many school programs in Canada and the United States. Adults that manage schools are opposed to it on the pretext that children are too young to think critically. These critics are supported by professional philosophers who claim that philosophy cannot be exercised before a person has reached adult-aged maturity, that is, not before college or the university.

38. M.-F. Daniel, *La Philosophie et les enfants. Les Modèles de Lipman et de Dewey* (Brussels: Les Presses de l'Université de Boeck, 1997).

39. C. Cassidy, "Child and Community of Philosophical Inquiry"; M. Lipman, *Philosophy Goes to School* (Philadelphia: Temple University Press, 1988).

40. J. Dewey, *Moral Principles in Education* (New York: Greenwood Press, 1969); Dewey, *Theory of the Moral Life.*

41. *L'Education, un trésor est caché dedans* (Paris: Odile Jacob, 1996). Report to UNESCO from the International Commission on Education for the Twenty-first Century.

PART 2

THE OPPOSITION

Five

Nannies with Blue Berets

The UN Convention and the Invasion of National and Family Sovereignty

⤺ MICHAEL P. FARRIS ⤻

A number of philosophical principles central to the American founding are implicated by the UN Convention on the Rights of the Child (CRC). The chief motivation driving American independence from Britain was a record of parliamentary invasions of long-standing principles of self-government. Many of the specific allegations against King George enumerated in the Declaration of Independence illustrate the Americans' commitment to govern themselves. When King George gave his assent to parliamentary laws "suspending our own legislatures, and declaring [the parliamentary laws] invested with power to legislate for us in all cases whatsoever," the Americans claimed a violation of their inalienable rights. In the Americans' view, established practice prohibited the Parliament in London from legislating for people in Boston, or Richmond, or Philadelphia. Ignoring this limitation constituted a tyrannical usurpation. Self-government was considered a fundamental human right.

The Americans endeavored to protect the right of self-determination by two means: through a written constitution and through the structure of government. The concept of a written constitution was an American innovation, since the British had no written constitution then—or now, for that matter. Nonetheless, the American colonialists regularly asserted that the actions of London were "unconstitutional." In context, this meant that the challenged practice was contrary to the established legal practice. It was much like the modern concept of customary international law, which requires both established practice and *opinio juris*. The American colonial experience established the inadequacy of a constitution of custom. A written constitution was essential to preserve self-government.

The Founders were also convinced that for government to stay within the delegated allocation of powers to which the governed had consented, structures were needed to carefully balance and limit government powers. The familiar principles of separation of powers and federalism emerged from this fundamental conviction. Key federalists, including James Madison and Alexander Hamilton, were convinced that the balances contained in the structure of the federal government were sufficient to protect liberty. Accordingly, they contended that a bill of rights was unnecessary. Antifederalists, like George Mason and Patrick Henry, strongly opposed the Constitution because of the absence of a bill of rights and other claimed deficiencies. Their objections were successful to the extent that Madison found it necessary to promise that Congress would take the steps to add a bill of rights after ratification. Thus, the government of the United States was founded on a twin commitment to self-government and human rights.

The Founders' emphasis on the importance of self-government was magnified by the location of this rule in the Constitution. Article I, section 1 of the Constitution states that all legislative power in the United States is vested in Congress. Neither the president nor the judiciary can make law. It would have been unthinkable in the extreme to suggest that a foreign parliament or a group of nations would be allowed to make law for the United States. As I intimated at the outset, these fundamental principles of self-government and liberty would be unacceptably compromised if the Convention on the Rights of the Child became binding in the United States—either by ratification or in a piecemeal fashion by judicial adoption of certain components of the CRC as binding rules of customary international law. Many advocates of the CRC point to all the "good" things the CRC might accomplish. And indeed, there are several discrete provisions of the CRC that I could embrace as good policy if presented as domestic legislation. It should be against the law to sexually exploit children, steal a child, commit child sacrifice, or abuse or neglect a child. (And, of course, all of these things are currently illegal throughout the United States.) These are just a few of the concepts in the CRC that should be the law in any nation that wishes to be considered civilized. Even if the CRC were limited to such unquestionable provisions—which is most certainly not the case—there remains the underlying question of who has the authority to make such rules.

The CRC purports to establish comprehensive rules for children that touch every aspect of their life. The convention touches the civil, political, social, economic, and cultural rights of the child, which are deemed interdependent and indivisible. Every institution in society, including the family, is under the rules established by this treaty. While the state is the guarantor of the rights, the CRC establishes rights that touch every child and every person or institution who deals with children. It claims to enact a plenary regime for children.

If an agency of government has plenary authority over children, then it not only has the power to make rules about the sexual exploitation of children but also has the power to dictate their school curriculum. Plenary power may be used to ban child stealing but also includes the power to interfere with religious education. Such power may punish child abuse but plenary power includes the authority to define "child abuse"—and it is in the definitions where disagreements over child-rearing practices quickly emerge.

The regime established by the CRC is quite different from the current legal practices of the United States. Currently, each of the fifty states possesses plenary power over children's issues. They are limited only by the state and federal bills of rights—and any limitations on grants of legislative authority contained in the state constitutions. If the United States becomes a party to the CRC all of this changes.

Under the principle of *pact sunt servanda*, the United States would enter into a binding international legal obligation to implement every provision contained in the CRC upon accession. It is the national government that would be the party to the CRC and it is the national government which would have the responsibility to implement its terms. The accepted theory of international human rights law is that such treaties are living instruments, which means that the meanings of the terms of the treaty migrate over time. The Committee on the Rights of the Child claims the authority to be the authoritative voice in explicating the meaning of the treaty in both the normal interpretative sense and in the living instrument sense. The committee does this through both its concluding observations and its general comments.

Congress then has the duty to implement the CRC as it has been authoritatively interpreted by the CRC committee. As Clark Butler has argued in this volume, this arrangement is not an interference with sovereignty; sovereignty is exercised by acceding to the treaty. After that, the policy choices of the nation are circumscribed by the nation's legal obligation to obey and implement the provisions of the treaty.

Thus, Congress would be under an international law mandate to implement the treaty in good faith. Since the national government has acceded to the treaty and is the sole agency allowed to become a party to the treaty, all responsibility for obedience to and implementation of the CRC committee's interpretations falls upon the Congress. Under the Necessary and Proper Clause, Congress has all the authority it needs to implement all provisions of the treaty. Accordingly, no longer is plenary power over children's issues a state law matter. Plenary power resides in Congress—subject to the mandates flowing from the CRC text and the authoritative interpretations of the CRC committee.

I hope it is self-evident that it would violate important principles of human rights for the legislature of Nebraska to pass rules for the public schools and families of France. Simply put, every nation should be able to decide for itself the particulars of its public policy toward children. See article 1 of both the UN Covenant on Civil and Political Rights and the Covenant on Economic, Social, and Cultural Rights. Any other form of government is unjust. Even the important goal of protecting children should not be achieved in a manner that contravenes the principle of self-government. American self-government has established the best set of laws in the world for the benefit of children. Even if there remain lacunae in the necessary protections for children, there is no evidence that democracy is such a discredited form of government that we need to abandon it to accomplish any legitimate aims contained in the CRC.

I aim to demonstrate:

1. That the UNCRC violates the fundamental principle of self-government as applied to the United States because of the unique provisions in the Supremacy Clause of the Constitution;
2. That it would be improper both as a matter of policy and law to bind the United States to the UNCRC through the judicial application of the doctrine of customary international law; and
3. That the UNCRC improperly invades the decision-making role of every parent, particularly in regard to education.

The Unique Difficulties Posed by the Supremacy Clause

Most of the nations in the world have formally approved the Convention on the Rights of the Child, with the United States and Somalia as the only exceptions. Nonetheless, it is fair to conclude that CRC is not viewed as binding domestic law by most party nations.

First, the ratifications of the nations are riddled with reservations and declarations. Afghanistan, Algeria, Brunei Darussalam, Djibouti, Iran, Iraq, Jordan, Kuwait, Maldives, Mauritania, Morocco, Qatar, Saudi Arabia, Syrian Arab Republic, and the United Arab Emirates all declare that the UNCRC shall not be interpreted or applied in a way to violate Islamic law.[1] Maldives's is especially interesting. One of its reservations declares: "The Government of the Republic of Maldives expresses its reservation to paragraph 1 of article 14 of the said Convention on the Rights of the Child, since the Constitution and the Laws of the Republic of Maldives stipulate that all Maldivians should be Muslims."[2]

Numerous other nations declare that the CRC shall either be interpreted in accordance with the nation's traditional law and practices, or be simply inapplicable to domestic law. For example, the Cook Islands stated upon acceptance: "Domestically, the convention does not apply directly. It establishes state obligations under international law that the Cook Islands fulfills in accordance with its national law."[3] Similarly, Indonesia made a declaration stating:

> The 1945 Constitution of the Republic of Indonesia guarantees the fundamental rights of the child irrespective of their sex, ethnicity or race. The Constitution prescribes those rights to be implemented by national laws and regulations. The ratification of the Convention on the Rights of the Child by the Republic of Indonesia does not imply the acceptance of obligations going beyond the Constitutional limits nor the acceptance of any obligation to introduce any right beyond those prescribed under the Constitution.[4]

France declares that its ratification shall not be interpreted to interfere with the right of abortion.[5] And Denmark declares that its consent to the Optional Protocol to the Convention on the Rights of the Child on the sale of children, child prostitution, and child pornography shall not be interpreted to apply to children who voluntarily appear in pornographic depictions if they have completed their fifteenth year.[6] One has to wonder how such a reservation is consistent with object and purposes of the treaty. Reservations incompatible with the object and purposes are supposedly "not permitted" by article 51.

In terms of actual practice, even the most cursory reading of the numerous concluding observations from the Committee on the Rights of the Child clearly reveals that virtually every nation is far from compliant with its obligations under the treaty. Absolutely no nation is fully compliant. Many nations routinely fail even the most rudimentary form of compliance since they fail to file the periodic report mandated under the terms of the treaty.

When this happens, the committee's response is noteworthy only as an illustration of the impotent nature of the entire system of international human rights. Consider this anemic response to Saint Lucia: "The Committee welcomes the submission of the initial report of the State party, which was prepared in conformity with the Committee's guidelines, and the written replies to its list of issues. . . . However, the Committee regrets that the report was submitted almost 10 years after the date it should have been submitted."[7]

In contrast to the vast majority of the rest of the world, if the United States becomes a party to the CRC, there would be a rigorous method for enforcing its provisions. To the extent that the CRC is deemed to be a self-executing treaty, all courts in the United States, both state and federal, would be bound to immediately enforce the treaty in any litigation which affects children. This rule of law is stated expressly in the second paragraph of article 6 of the Constitution provides: "This Constitution, and the Laws of the United States which shall be made in Pursuance thereof; and all Treaties made, or which shall be made, under the Authority of the United States, shall be the supreme Law of the Land; and the Judges in every State shall be bound thereby, any Thing in the Constitution or Laws of any State to the Contrary notwithstanding." If ratified, the CRC would thus be accorded by article 6 the status of "the supreme law of the land" in the United States. State laws and constitutions would be entirely subjugated to the CRC—that is the unambiguous meaning of the final phrase of this clause. It is also important to note that virtually all law in this country that relates to the treatment of children is state law. Thus, the CRC would trump any inconsistent provisions in American state law upon its ratification.

As stated, the immediacy of this result is dependent upon the view of American courts concerning the self-executing nature of the treaty. The most knowledgeable of the pro-CRC legal experts admit that the children's treaty has a mix of self-executing and nonself-executing provisions.[8] And it will be up to our own courts to determine which is based upon the court's view of the intent of the Senate and the plain language of the convention.[9] If Congress passes broad implementing legislation, there would be no doubt that such enactments would override state law. If there are the votes to ratify a treaty by a two-thirds margin in the Senate, it is easy to foresee that a simple majority could be mustered in each house to enact enabling legislation which would provide some form of a federal directive to the states, that is, "the several states shall take immediate action to implement the provisions of the treaty."

The provisions of the treaty that would be the most likely to be deemed nonself-executing would be those arising in the sector of economic, social, and cultural rights. These so-called positive rights flow from the CRC's mandate to create a massive welfare state that ensures that the needs of every child are fully met by the American taxpayer.

The Supreme Court has already employed article 37's provisions in two important juvenile justice cases. In *Roper v. Simmons*, 543 U.S. 551 (2005) the court used the CRC's ban of the juvenile death penalty as a guiding, albeit nonbinding, precedent to rule juvenile executions to be unconstitutional.[10] In a similar vein, the court used article 37 to hold that sentencing juveniles in nonhomicide cases to life in prison without parole was also unconstitutional.[10] If article 37 wields this much weight in the Supreme Court when we are not even a party to the treaty, then it takes no imagination to conclude that article 37's ban of corporal punishment would be held to be judicially enforceable as a self-executing provision of the CRC.

A recent Zogby poll revealed that 85.1% of the American public agreed with the right of parents to administer a modest spanking to their children. It is little wonder, then, that there is not the political will to ban normal spankings through the American political process. But, those who disagree see international law as a means of achieving a political objective that would simply be impossible through straightforward legislation.

Even among the tiny minority of those who want to ban spanking in America, the love of democracy is hopefully sufficient for them to conclude that the ends do not justify the means. Surely some antispanking advocates believe that international law should not supplant democracy even if they like this particular policy outcome. Article 37 does not explicitly ban spanking. But, the committee has issued both a general comment and countless concluding observations that make it plain that it believes that the article's prohibitions on torture and cruelty include a blanket prohibition of all forms of spanking by any person including a parent. If the United States had become a party to this treaty before any of these interpretations were issued, perhaps there would be some room for American courts to adopt a different meaning for article 37. But, after twenty years of consistent interpretation by the CRC committee and other adjudicatory bodies, there is no longer room for the United States to claim that we did not understand the meaning of this article at this late date. Article 37 has a settled meaning and we would be stuck with it and our courts would enforce it according to the mountain of interpretative material that has been issued.

Allowing a committee of experts to interpret the treaty and thereby establish the meaning of binding law in the United States should be especially troubling when it is understood that two members of this committee are from nations that have proclaimed they will not interpret the CRC to have any meaning inconsistent with the Sharia law of Islam. It is possible, of course, for the United States to ratify the CRC with a reservation that robs it of any meaning, just as all of the Islamic states have done. Of course, any American court would have the prerogative to invalidate such a reservation under article 51 of the convention, which prohibits reservations that are contrary to the object and purpose of the treaty. Moreover, membership on the UN Human Rights Commission is conditioned on a nation's commitment to the UN human rights regime. Removal of broad reservations is one of the factors to be considered in evaluating eligibility for membership. The United States would be under enormous pressure to remove any reservations to the CRC—especially one as broad in scope as the Sharia exceptions. Ratifying with such reservations is completely contrary to the asserted need for the United States to ratify the treaty. We are repeatedly told that we need to be seen as a world leader in protecting human rights if we are to influence those nations who continue to permit the atrocities of sex trafficking and female genital mutilation despite being a party to the CRC. We would gain no moral leadership in the rest of the world if we accede to the treaty only in form and not in substance. The United States should truly lead the world by demonstrating absolutely faithful compliance with all our treaty obligations. We should keep our word if we give it. And if we have no intention of fully complying with the CRC, then we should simply not ratify it cheaply with a series of reservations that turn it into a sham.

In sum, if the CRC were ratified as indicated, policy decisions now made by each of the fifty states would be overridden by treaty provisions as interpreted by a structurally nondemocratic body of advocates, not impartial judges, but advocates. Congress, not the states, would be charged with the responsibility of implementing the CRC's provisions. Principles of democracy, one-person, one-vote, federalism, and the most fundamental assumptions of our Constitution would be forfeited. Americans and only Americans should make the rules for America.

THE UN CONVENTION ON THE RIGHTS OF THE CHILD AND CUSTOMARY INTERNATIONAL LAW

The CRC is finding its way into an ever-growing number of federal court decisions despite the fact that the treaty has never been sent to the Senate for ratification. The repeated claim is made that the United States is already bound to the treaty because provisions within the treaty have become customary international law. In international law, any rule of customary international law is binding on all nations whether or not they consent. This rule has been fashioned into a formal definition by the highly influential International Law Association.

> i. A rule of customary international law is one which is created and sustained by the constant and uniform practice of States and other subjects of international law in or impinging upon their international legal relations, in circumstances which give rise to a legitimate expectation of similar conduct in the future.
> ii. If a sufficiently extensive and representative number of States participate in such a practice in a consistent manner, the resulting rule is one of "general customary international law". . . . Such a rule is binding on all States.

iii. Where a rule of general customary international law exists, for any particular State to be bound by that rule it is not necessary to prove either that State's consent to it or its belief in the rule's obligatory or (as the case may be) permissive character.[11]

There are two recognized elements to establish a rule of customary international law—consistent practice and *opinio juris. Opinio juris* refers to the subjective element of the rule. Not only must there be a widely shared practice, there must be a widely shared belief that the practice is legally required and not a mere matter of courtesy. A growing number of federal court litigants have asserted that the provisions of the Convention on the Rights of the Child are binding on the United States under this theory. Adoption of this treaty is nearly universal; every nation has become a party to the treaty save for the United States and Somalia.

Widespread adoption of a treaty does not automatically satisfy the standards for the creation of a rule of customary international law (CIL). First, it is the practice of nations, not the promises of nations that matters for the creation of a rule of CIL. The actual practice of nations is far from compliant with the wide-ranging dictates of the CRC. Second, there is a significant difference between a creating a rule of international law as opposed to a rule of domestic law. The vast majority of nations do not treat the CRC as automatically binding in domestic law. Accordingly, if few state parties treat the provisions of the CRC as automatically binding in domestic courts, then it should be simple for the courts of a nonparty—that is, the United States—to reject its purported domestic application.

Only one court to date has affirmed the theory that the CRC is binding as a rule of customary international law; many have rejected this theory. Jack B. Weinstein of the Eastern District of New York has aggressively applied this theory of the domestic applicability of international law in two separate cases. The first was *Beharry v. Reno*, 183 F. Supp. 2d 584 (E.D.N.Y. 2002), a deportation case involving an illegal alien parent whose child was born in the United States. The essence of the claim—which has become a familiar theme in a number of deportation cases—was that the child's CRC rights were violated by being forced to choose to between his native country and living with his parent. There is certainly some emotional and logical resonance to such a claim.

The issue in Beharry was the proper interpretation of a federal deportation statute. Judge Weinstein contended that the statute should be interpreted to comply with binding international law if at all possible. He held that the CRC's nearly universal ratification was a sufficient basis for holding that its provisions were binding on the United States as customary international law. He was reversed on other grounds by the Second Circuit which expressly disclaimed, but did not reverse, his international law contentions.[12]

A number of other circuits have been required to deal with similar arguments based on the CRC in deportation cases where the illegal alien parents had given birth to children who were American citizens. All such challenges have failed to date. See, e.g., *Cabrera-Alvarez v. Gonzales*, 423 F. 3rd 1006 (9th Cir. 2005) in which the CRC was cited favorably in dissent by Judge Pregerson, who believed that the parent's deportation implicated protectable rights.

While the claim that the CRC is formally binding is having trouble gaining traction, the Supreme Court has twice given substantial credence to this child's rights treaty as a supporting authority in the course of constitutional interpretation.

In *Roper v. Simmons*, 543 U.S. 551 (2005) the court focused on two aspects of international practice in reaching its decision that execution of juvenile murderers was an unconstitutionally cruel and unusual punishment. First, the court noted the near-universal ratification of the CRC. Second, the court bought the claims of the defendants and their amici that the United States was the only nation on the planet that actually executed juvenile murderers and that all nations providing for the possibility of juvenile executions had made commitments to repeal such provisions. Subsequent findings by the Committee on the Rights of the Child reveal that such claims were naïve. The CRC committee has chided the following countries for juvenile death penalty violations after Roper was decided: Niger,[13] Bangladesh,[14] Burkina Faso,[15] Gambia,[16] Guatemala,[17] Liberia,[18] Kenya,[19] and Saudi Arabia.[20]

Buttressed by the successful introduction of the CRC in Roper, an even more aggressive form of the customary international law argument was advanced in *Sullivan v. Graham*, 130 S. Ct. 2011 (2010). The issue in Sullivan was the constitutionality of sentencing a juvenile to life in prison without the possibility of parole (LWOP) in a nonhomicide prosecution. The defendants claimed that the prohibition of sentencing juveniles to life imprisonment contained in article 37 of the CRC was a binding rule of customary international law. Amnesty International and a group of international human rights organizations went even farther. These amici claimed that the prohibition of LWOP was a principle of *jus cogens*—the highest level of international human rights law. Amnesty International relied on article 53 of the Vienna Convention on the Law of Treaties (VCLT) for recognition of the principle of *jus cogens*—a preemptory norm of international law from which no derogation is permitted.

The author of this chapter submitted an amicus brief in direct opposition to the Amnesty International brief on behalf of sixteen members of Congress.[21]

This brief noted that article 53 of the VCLT did not purport to create a rule of domestic law. Rather, the nonderogation rule simply prohibited any treaty from adopting a rule which violates a rule of *jus cogens*. Moreover, this amicus brief gave the court the full record of the Committee of the Rights of the Child which clearly disproved the claim that the United States is the only nation on the earth that permits and implements the LWOP sentence. Amnesty cited emails from lawyers and a law review article that relied on research by Amnesty to bolster its claim that the United States was alone in its LWOP practice. Ultimately, the Supreme Court accepted Amnesty's assertions and emails and ignored the evidence revealed by the findings of the official UN committee to conclude that the United States was the only nation implementing LWOP.

Although the Court cited the amicus brief submitted by the members of Congress, it did so to reject the brief's core argument that international law had no applicability in a case where the task was to interpret the text of the United States Constitution.[22]

Given this repeated use of the CRC as a supporting and interpretative authority, the Supreme Court has opened the door for increasing use of the CRC as an "interpretative" aid. Advocates like Amnesty International have to be encouraged by this gradual approach. The CRC is being used as a soft precedent for now. There is little doubt that the efforts to solidify its domestic applicability will continue despite the fact that the United States is not a party to this treaty.

THE CRC IMPROPERLY INVADES THE DECISION-MAKING ROLE OF EVERY PARENT

The two central provisions of the CRC are the "best interest" standard contained in article 3 and the right of the child to be heard, contained in article 12. University of London professor Geraldine Van Bueren, author of the leading legal treatise on the CRC, explains these two standards and the impact on the traditional rights of parents: "Best interests provides decision and policy makers with the authority to substitute their own decisions for either the child's or the parents', providing it is based on considerations of the best interests of the child. Thus, the Convention challenges the concept that family life is always in the best interests of children and that parents are always capable of deciding what is best for children."[23] Van Bueren further asserts that:

> State parties are obliged to "assure" to children who are capable of forming views the rights to express those views "in all matters affecting the child" and to give those views "due weight in accordance with the age and maturity of the child." By incorporating a reference to "all matters affecting the child" there is no longer a traditional area of exclusive parental or family decision making.[24]

International law is therefore establishing boundaries within which states are under a duty to ensure that parental power is properly exercised and within limits. . . . The international protection of children's civil rights now touches the core of family life.[25]

Washington's legislature enacted these two core principles—best interest and child's wishes—into a state law which has subsequently been radically modified. I litigated a case under this original statute which perfectly illustrates how these two legal standards would work in American courts if they become binding through the CRC. A thirteen-year-old boy objected to the fact that his parents wanted him to attend church with them for services on Sunday morning, Sunday evening, and the Wednesday night prayer meeting. He was willing to attend Sunday morning, and that was all. Washington state law allowed the state social services agency to intervene in any family where there was conflict between the wishes of the child and those of his parent. It also obliged the judiciary to employ the best interest standard in resolving the dispute.

Social workers had done an emergency removal of the boy because Sunday was coming and they deemed it a sufficiently urgent matter to remove him without a prior hearing. This resulted in a mandatory hearing the following week to test the legality of the removal of the child. There was no issue before the court except for church attendance. There was no allegation of abuse or neglect by the parents.

The trial judge determined that one time a week was enough in church for a thirteen-year-old boy. The judge instructed the parents that they would only be allowed to regain custody of their son if they agreed to limit his church attendance to once a week. The judge simply substituted his personal view about the proper amount of church attendance for that of the parents. While the best interest standard has a long and appropriate history in the dispositional stage of family and child welfare litigation, it is invoked only after there is a showing that the family is broken (in divorce, for example) or that the parents have harmed their child through abuse or neglect. Employing the best interest standard without a prior showing of harm is akin to sentencing a person to prison prior to a trial court determination of guilt.

The net effect of separating the best interest standard from the necessity to establish a predicate showing of harm is that all American parents would be in the same legal position as parents who had been convicted of abuse or neglect.

Van Bueren is not the only pro-CRC expert who believes that the application of the CRC invades the core of family life. The CRC committee has made it abundantly clear that the treaty creates legal criteria applicable to the family and the ability of parents to make decisions for their children.

In the 2005 and 2006 country reviews, several nations were criticized by the CRC committee because their legal structures and societal attitudes failed to adhere to the standards of the CRC. Consider these two examples regarding the applicability of the CRC to family decision making.

> Saudi Arabia: "[The committee] is concerned that traditional attitudes towards children in society, in particular toward girls, limit the right to express their views and to have them taken into account, especially within the family, schools and media."[26]
> Trinidad and Tobago: "The committee is concerned that the views of child are not given sufficient consideration in all areas of children's lives and that the provisions of article 12 of the convention are not fully integrated into the State party's legislation. . . . The committee recommends that the State party . . . promote and facilitate respect for the views of children and ensure their participation in all matters affect them. . . . particularly in the family . . . in accordance with article 12 of the convention."[27]

Similar comments can be found concerning failures of the following nations to have appropriate protections for the right of the children to have their viewpoint considered in the context of families: Peru, Lithuania, Hungary, Ghana, Uganda, Russian Federation, Algeria, Yemen, Bosnia and Herzegovina, Costa Rica, Ecuador, Mongolia, Nepal, Nicaragua, and the Philippines, inter alia.[28] In a great number of these CRC committee's concluding observations, traditional attitudes in society were criticized for violating the right of the child to have his wishes considered in every situation.

Homeschooling parents are particularly concerned about a prior determination of the committee relative to article 12. In the 1995 report on the United Kingdom's compliance with the CRC, the nation was criticized for allowing parents to make decisions to remove their child from participation in sex education classes in government schools without adequate measures to ensure that the child's viewpoints were considered and weighed appropriately.[29] It is noteworthy that no criticism was leveled against the UK schools for failing to consider the child's viewpoint when parents enrolled the child in the government schools in the first instance. Nor were the schools criticized for failing to ask the child whether or not he wanted to attend the sex education classes. The net lesson from the committee appears to be that the child's wishes must be considered any time the decision goes against the substantive views of this body of UN experts on how children should be raised. Children need not be consulted when the CRC committee approves the underlying decision.

As it turns out, children's rights are not about the wishes of the child in the final analysis. This treaty ensures that children will be required to do that which the UN and their cooperating governments believe is best for children. Remember the words of Professor Van Bueren: "Best interests provides decision and policy makers with the authority to substitute their own decisions for either the child's or the parents', providing it is based on considerations of the best interests of the child."[30]

There are other decisions of the committee relative to education that are troubling to those who believe in home and private education. In the 2005 report on Norway, there is a criticism of that nation's public school system for including a course entitled "Christian Knowledge and Religious and Ethical Education."[31] Americans tend to think that such a course would violate the separate of church and state. We forget that the American Establishment Clause is not binding on the whole world. More to the point, there is nothing like the Establishment Clause in the CRC. It applies equally to all children in all forms of schools—public, private, religious, and home schools. Every state party is required to guarantee that all children in all schools are treated in accord with the CRC's version of the requirement of religious freedom. Thus, when the CRC committee determines that it is improper to teach the Christian knowledge course in Norway's public schools, it is logical to conclude that even American Christian schools would be prohibited from teaching such a course—at least as a mandatory offering.

Indeed, the American Bar Association (ABA)—an organization that fully endorses the ratification of the CRC in the United States—has discussed the application of the CRC in the context of private Christian schools, and has found that certain religious teachings within those schools would violate the rights of the child under this convention.[32] The ABA says that it is not certain what the outcome of such a case would be if the Supreme Court had to make a decision in the face of a First Amendment challenge. Nonetheless, the ABA interprets the CRC to conclude that it bans intolerant religious instruction—that is, any religious instruction that claims to have a corner on truth.

A brief review of a few other concluding observations reveals the radically nontraditional requirements contained in the CRC. The UK violates articles 3, 19, and 37 by allowing parents to exercise "reasonable [physical] chastisement,"[33] and the committee has objected to an article of the Civil Code in Spain which permits parents to "administer punishment to their children reasonably and in moderation."[34] Any nation which permits spanking, allows spanking to be "socially acceptable," or fails to aggressively prosecute spanking is held to have violated the treaty. Nations cited include Belize,[35] Canada,[36] Belgium,[37] Yemen,[38] Spain,[39] and Poland.[40] Belize was criticized because "persons under 18 years are not allowed to have any medical counseling, including counseling on reproductive health, without parental consent."[41] Pakistan was likewise cited for lacking an "organized system of reproductive health counseling and services" and "family life education for adolescents."[42] Canada, Belize, and a number of other nations were criticized for their failure to have a proper system for data collection concerning children.[43] Austria,[44] Australia,[45] Denmark,[46] the UK,[47] and others were criticized for failing to spend enough tax dollars on social welfare for children. Government workers were ordered to receive better training on the content and principles of the UN Convention in almost all nations.

It is certainly true that the committee has pointed out some problems that deserve condemnation. Uganda is justly criticized for the prevalence of child sacrifice in that nation.[48] Yet Mr. Awich Pollar, from Uganda, serves on the Committee for the Rights of the Child with full decisional authority over the meaning of the treaty and the compliance of other nations with its provisions.

Several nations are appropriately criticized for the high incidence of child prostitution, child pornography, and sex trafficking of children. These include Ghana, Lithuania, Thailand, and Mauritius.[49] There is utterly no indication that the presence of the CRC or UN observers has made any material improvement in any of these situations. The Ghana report indicates that "sex tourism is growing in the country and that many girls and boys at a very young age are engaged in commercial sexual exploitation."[50] Ghana became a party to the treaty in 1990, yet sex trafficking was found to be still increasing in 2006.

The whole world may have signed a piece of paper relative to the rights of children, but a careful reading of the record of the concluding observations leads to the inevitable conclusion that it is only a piece of paper for the vast majority of the nations on earth.

Ratification by the United States Senate would not change the legal or social situation for any child outside our national jurisdiction. We would become bound to a drastically flawed convention that treats all American parents the same way our current juvenile justice system treats parents who have been convicted of abuse or neglect. As an aspirational statement the CRC is a mixed bag—many good principles, some bad principles—depending on one's parenting philosophy. As a statement of binding international law it is a tyrannical disaster waiting in the wings.

Notes

1. Declarations and Reservations to the Convention on the Rights of the Child, *United Nations Office of the High Commissioner for Human Rights,* accessed March 2, 2006, http://www.ohchr.org/english/countries/ratification/11. htm#reservations.

2. Maldives, reservation upon signature (21 August 1990) and upon ratification (11 February 1991), *United Nations Office of the High Commissioner for Human Rights,* accessed March 6, 2006, http://www.ohchr.org/english/countries/ratification/11.htm#reservations.

3. Cook Islands, declaration upon acceptance (6 June 1997), *United Nations Office of the High Commissioner for Human Rights,* accessed March, 6, 2006, http://www.ohchr.org/english/countries/ratification/11.htm#reservations.

4. Indonesia, reservation upon ratification (5 September 1990), *United Nations Office of the High Commissioner for Human Rights,* accesses March 2, 2006, http://www.ohchr.org/english/countries/ratification/11.htm#reservations.

5. France, declaration and reservation made upon signature (January 26, 1990) and confirmed upon ratification (August 7, 1990), *United Nations Office of the High Commissioner for Human Rights,* accessed March 2, 2006, http://www. ohchr.org/english/countries/ratification/11.htm#reservations.

6. Denmark, declaration upon ratification (July 24, 2003), *United Nations Office of the High Commissioner for Human Rights,* accessed March 6, 2006, http:// www.ohchr.org/english/countries/ratification/11_c.htm#reservations.

7. Paragraph 2, *Concluding Observations of the Committee on the Rights of the Child: Saint Lucia,* Committee on the Rights of the Child, 39th sess., UN Doc. CRC/C/15/Add.258 (2005).

8. Arlene Andrews, Director of the Division of Family Policy at the University of South Carolina, writes that "the Convention is generally regarded as having two classes of rights for the purposes of self-execution, one class that is self-executing and one that is not self-executing." Quoted in Robin Kimbrough, "Entitlement to 'Adequacy': Application of Article 27 to US Law," in *Implementing the UN Convention on the Rights of the Child: A Standard of Living Adequate for Development,* ed. Arlene Bowers Andrews and Natalie Hevener Kaufman (Westport, CT: Prager, 1999), 167, 171.

9. See Medellin v. Texas, 552 U.S. 491 (2008).

10. See Sullivan v. Graham, 130 S.Ct. 2011 (2010).

11. Committee on the Formation of Customary (General) International Law, International Law Association, London (2000), 8 (Working Definitions).

12. Beharry v. Ashcroft, 329 F.3d 51, 62 (2d Cir. 2003); "Nothing in our decision to reverse on other grounds the judgment of the district court should

be seen as an endorsement of the district court's holding that interpretation of the INA in this case is influenced or controlled by international law."

13. Committee on the Rights of the Child, Consideration of Reports Submitted by States Parties Under Article 44 of the Convention, Concluding Observations: Niger, CRC/C/NER/CO/2, 18 June 2009, para. 81. (All such reports hereafter cited as CRC Report.)

14. CRC Report: Bangladesh, CRC/C/BGD/CO/4, 26 June2009, para. 92.

15. CRC Report: Burkina Faso, CRC/C/15/Add.193, 9 October 2002, para. 60.

16. CRC Report: Gambia, CRC/C/15/Add.165, November 2001, para. 68.

17. CRC Report: Guatemala, CRC/C/15/Add.58, 7 June 1996, para. 47. Guatemala's most recent report in 2001 reads: "The Committee expresses its serious concern that its previousrecommendation encouraging the reform of the juvenile justice system to ensure full compatibility with the principles and provisions of the Convention has not been implemented."CRC/C/15/Add.154, 9 July 2001, para. 56.

18. CRC Report: Liberia, CRC/C/15/Add.236, 1 July 2004, para. 68.

19. CRC Report: Kenya, CRC/C/KEN/CO/2, 19 June2007, para. 32.

20. CRC Report: Saudi Arabia, CRC/C/SAU/CO/2 17, March 2006, para. 32.

21. See Brief of Sixteen Members of the United States House of Representatives as Amicus Curiae. In Support Of Respondent, 2009 WL 3023518.

22. 130 S.Ct. 2011, 2034 (2010).

23. G. Van Bueren, *The International Law on the Rights of the Child* (The Hague: Kluwer International, 1998), 46.

24. Ibid., 137 (quoting CRC, article 12).

25. Ibid., 73.

27. Paragraph 36, *Concluding Observations of the Committee on the Rights of the Child: Saudi Arabia,* unedited version, Committee on the Rights of the Child, 41st sess., UN Doc. CRC/C/SAU/CO/2 (2006).

28. Paragraphs 33 and 34, *Concluding Observations of the Committee on the Rights of the Child: Trinidad and Tobago,* unedited version, Committee on the Rights of the Child, 41st sess., UN Doc. CRC/C/TTO/CO/2 (2006).

29. See *Concluding Observations of the Committee on the Rights of the Child* for Peru (Paragraph 31, 41st sess., 2006), Lithuania (Paragraph 31, 41st sess., 2006, unedited version), Hungary (Paragraph 24, 41st sess., 2006, unedited version), Ghana (Paragraph 30, 41st sess., 2006, unedited version), Uganda (Paragraph 35, 40th sess., 2005), Russian Federation (Paragraph 30, 40th sess., 2005), Algeria (Paragraph 33, 40th sess., 2005), Yemen (Paragraph 37, 39th sess., 2005), Bosnia and Herzegovina (Paragraph 30, 39th sess., 2005), Costa Rica (Paragraph 21, 39th sess., 2005), Ecuador (Paragraph 33, 39th sess., 2005), Mongolia

(Paragraph 25, 39th sess., 2005), Nepal (Paragraphs 39 and 40, 39th sess., 2005), Nicaragua (Paragraph 30, 39th sess., 2005), and the Philippines (Paragraphs 29 and 30, 39th sess., 2005).

30. *Concluding Observations of the Committee on the Rights of the Child: United Kingdom of Great Britain and Northern Ireland,* Committee on the Rights of the Child, 8th sess., UN Doc. CRC/C/15/Add.34 (1995).

31. Paragraph 20, *Concluding Observations of the Committee on the Rights of the Child: Norway,* Committee on the Rights of the Child, 39th sess., UN Doc. CRC/C/15/Add.263 (2005).

32. C. Price Cohen and H. Davidson, *Children's Rights in America: UN Convention on the Rights of the Child Compared with United States Law* (Chicago: ABA, 1990), 182.

33. Paragraph 36, *Concluding Observations of the Committee on the Rights of the Child: United Kingdom of Great Britain and Northern Ireland,* Committee on the Rights of the Child, 31st sess., UN Doc CRC/C/15/Add.188 (2002); see also *Concluding Observations,* 8th sess., CRC/C/15/Add.34 (1995).

34. Paragraph 30, *Concluding Observations of the Committee on the Rights of the Child: Spain,* Committee on the Rights of the Child, 30th sess., CRC/C/15/Add.185 (2002).

35. Paragraph 40, *Concluding Observations of the Committee on the Rights of the Child: Belize,* Committee on the Rights of the Child, 38th sess., UN Doc. CRC/C/15/Add.252 (2005); see also *Concluding Observations,* 20th sess., CRC/C/15/Add.99 (1999).

36. Paragraph 32, *Concluding Observations of the Committee on the Rights of the Child: Canada,* Committee on the Rights of the Child, 34th sess., UN Doc. CRC/C/15/Add.215 (2003); see also *Concluding Observations,* 9th sess., CRC/C/15/Add.37 (1995).

37. Paragraph 23, *Concluding Observations of the Committee on the Rights of the Child: Belgium,* Committee on the Rights of the Child, 30th sess., UN Doc. CRC/C/15/Add.178 (2002); see also *Concluding Observations,* 9th sess., CRC/C/15/Add.38 (1995).

38. Paragraph 41, *Concluding Observations of the Committee on the Rights of the Child: Yemen,* Committee on the Rights of the Child, 39th sess., CRC/C/15/Add.267 (2005); see also *Concluding Observations,* 20th sess., CRC/C/15/Add.102 (1999).

39. Paragraph 30, *Concluding Observations: Spain* (2002); see also *Concluding Observations,* 7th sess., CRC/C/15/Add.28 (1994).

40. Paragraph 34, *Concluding Observations of the Committee on the Rights of the Child: Poland,* Committee on the Rights of the Child, 31st sess., CRC/C/15/

Add.194 (2002); see also *Concluding Observations*, 8th sess., CRC/C/15/Add.31 (1995).

41. Paragraph 23, *Concluding Observations: Belize* (2005).

42. Paragraph 54, *Concluding Observations of the Committee on the Rights of the Child: Pakistan,* Committee on the Rights of the Child, 34th sess., UN Doc. CRC/C/15/Add.217 (2003).

43. Paragraphs 19 and 20, *Concluding Observations: Canada* (2003); Paragraphs 17 and 18, *Concluding Observations: Belize* (2005).

44. Paragraph 46, *Concluding Observations of the Committee on the Rights of the Child: Austria,* Committee on the Rights of the Child, 38th sess., UN Doc. CRC/C/15/Add.251 (2005).

45. Paragraph 17 and 18, *Concluding Observations of the Committee on the Rights of the Child: Australia,* Committee on the Rights of the Child, 40th sess., UN Doc. CRC/C/15/Add.268 (2005).

46. Paragraphs 18 and 19, *Concluding Observations of the Committee on the Rights of the Child: Denmark,* Committee on the Rights of the Child, 40th sess., UN Doc. CRC/C/DNK/CO/3 (2005).

47. Paragraph 10, *Concluding Observations: UK* (2002).

48. Paragraph 33, *Concluding Observations of the Committee on the Rights of the Child: Uganda,* Committee on the Rights of the Child, 40th sess., UN Doc. CRC/C/UGA/CO/2 (2005).

49. Paragraphs 67-70, *Concluding Observations of the Committee on the Rights of the Child: Ghana,* unedited version, Committee on the Rights of the Child, 41st sess., UN Doc. CRC/C/GHA/CO/2 (2006); Paragraphs 64-67, *Concluding Observations of the Committee on the Rights of the Child: Lithuania,* unedited version, Committee on the Rights of the Child, 41st sess., UN Doc. CRC/C/LTU/CO/2 (2006); Paragraphs 72-75, *Concluding Observations on the Rights of the Child: Thailand,* unedited version, Committee on the Rights of the Child, 41st sess., UN Doc. CRC/C/THA/CO/2 (2006); Paragraphs 64 and 65, *Committee on the Rights of the Child: Republic of Mauritius,* unedited version, Committee on the Rights of the Child, 41st sess., UN Doc. CRC/C/MUS/CO/2 (2006).

50. Paragraph 67, *Concluding Observations: Ghana* (2006).

Six

Educational Freedom and Human Rights

Exploring the Tensions between the Interests and Rights of Parents, Children, and the State

⇌ PERRY L. GLANZER ⇌

When discussing human rights and education, a tension always exists between the educational rights and freedoms of parents and children and the role of the state with regard to both groups.[1] If one looks to the United Nations' rights declarations and treaties for help resolving this tension, one will not find a clear answer. On the one hand, the original Universal Declaration of Human Rights appears to give parents the priority in this balancing act. It states, "Parents have a prior right to choose the kind of education that shall be given to their children."[2] School choice proponents such as Charles Glenn and Jan de Groof argue that this statement provides a clear standard according to which states should recognize the educational freedom of parents.[3]

On the other hand, the UN Convention on the Rights of the Child (CRC) affirms that "States Parties shall respect and ensure the rights set forth in the present convention to each child within their jurisdiction." These rights the state shall interpret and enforce include the right to compulsory education, freedom of thought, conscience, and religion and the right to freedom of association.[4] In this case, the state, as a definer and protector of the child's interests, appears to be given priority in educational decisions.

One might hope to find further clarification in the CRC's two extensive articles covering education, articles 28 and 29. Article 28, however, largely deals with the responsibilities of the state with regard to a child's right to education.[5] Article 29 then stipulates some particular ends of education upon which it claims all state parties agree.[6] Neither article mentions the role parents should actually play in determining the form or substance of the education offered. Interestingly, a general comment on article 29, clause 1 only mentions that states should be in consultation with parents about how to measure progress toward the educational ends listed but not about the actual educational ends which were determined by state parties.[7] Only in *Interim Report, Senate Standing Committee Report on Human Rights*, article 3, clause 2, does the article acknowledge that when states consider the well-being of a child, they must also take "into account the rights and duties of his or her parents,"[8] but what this caveat entails for parental educational rights remains unclear.

The convention's lack of clarity about the role of parents' educational rights in relation to their children and the state raises concerns for homeschooling parents and groups who believe the state may use this language to limit parental rights in the name of protecting children's rights. For example, the Home School Legal Defense Association (HSLDA) claims the convention is "the most dangerous attack on parents' rights in the history of the United States."[9] The leader of HSLDA, Michael Farris, argues that the United States is the only major government in the world with a constitutional stipulation "that makes a provision of a treaty automatically part of the 'highest law of the land.'"[10] Consequently, "if this treaty becomes binding, all parents would have the same legal status as abusive parents, because the government would have the right to override every parental decision if it deemed the parent's choice contrary to the child's best interest."[11] With regard to homeschooling, he claims,

> children would be required to be taught in a religiously "tolerant manner." (The American Bar Association, which supports the treaty, has already opined that teaching children that Jesus is the only way to God violates the spirit and meaning of the CRC.) The ability to homeschool one's children would become not a right, but a UN-supervised activity that could be overturned if social services personnel believed that it would be "best for your child to receive another form of education." These are not idle speculations, but the proven result of the UN's own interpretation of the treaty as they have reviewed other nations' compliance with the treaty's provisions.[12]

To prove this point, HSLDA cites the controversial 2009 *Report to the Secretary of State on the Review of Elective Home Education in England* by Graham Badman.[13] Badman argues, "there has to be a balance between the rights of the parents and the rights of the child. I believe the balance is not achieved through current legislation or guidance, and the imbalance must be addressed."[14] To justify the increased regulation of homeschooling based on the CRC, Badman's argument relies upon article 12. He writes:

> The United Nations Convention on the Rights of the Child (CRC) gives children and young people over forty substantive rights which include the right to express their views freely, the right to be heard in any legal or administrative matters that affect them and the right to seek, receive and impart information and ideas. Article 12 makes clear the responsibility of signatories to give children a voice: "Parties shall assure to the child who is capable of forming his or her own views the right to express those views freely in all matters affecting the child, the views of the child being given due weight in accordance with the age and maturity of the child."[15]

Yet under the current legislation and guidance, local authorities have no right of access to the child to determine or ascertain such views.

Badman's solution is to ensure that local authority officers "have the right of access to the home" and "have the right to speak with each child alone."[16] Badman also argues that local authorities should be given extensive powers to monitor the effectiveness of homeschooling and to determine which curriculum should be used. He refers to the CRC to justify this state intervention, particularly article 29, which stipulates five ends of education state parties should include in a child's education.[17] Badman's report was submitted and accepted in full by the British Secretary of State for Children, Schools, and Families. Understandably, HSLDA views the report as evidence of their concern over how the CRC will be used in regards to homeschooling.

Since some may consider this example unique to England, it appears reasonable to ask whether a basis exists for HSLDA's concerns in recent North American scholarship. The goal of this paper is to show that the HSLDA, in light of recent scholarship in this area, certainly has good reason to be concerned about how the convention might be used to influence policy regarding the educational rights of parents. In the first part of this paper I show the validity of HSLDA's concerns by describing the views of three prominent scholars who justify extensive state intervention and control over children's education at the expense of parental rights and interests. After describing the arguments used to justify greater state intervention and regulation of the parental role in education, I will attempt to point out the problematic aspects of these arguments.

LIBERAL REGULATORS OF PARENTAL EDUCATIONAL FREEDOM

In the growing scholarly literature addressing the relationship between parents, children, and the state in education, there is an increasing number of scholars who want either to eliminate other options outside public schools altogether or to increase dramatically state regulation of such options.[18] In other words, most of these authors want to increase the amount of restrictions governing the educational choices and freedom of parents. In particular, this paper focuses on the proposals suggested by James Dwyer, Marcia Levinson, and Robert Reich because of certain commonalities in their arguments. All three of these thinkers acknowledge that parents, children, and the state have educational interests and that we should consider all of these interests when formulating theory and policy.[19] As Robert Reich notes, "a theory of educational authority that claimed only the interests of one party mattered could potentially establish a kind of parental despotism, state authoritarianism, or child despotism."[20] The key questions are: 1. Where do we draw the lines between parental authority and the interests of the child? 2. What should be the limits of parental interests?

In general Dwyer, Levinson, and Reich argue that in the current American situation, children's and the state's educational interests and the protection of human rights would best be achieved by strengthening the state's comprehensive educational system and highly regulating (or even outlawing) other educational options parents might choose, such as homeschooling and private schooling. The major threats to both the good of the children and basic human rights, according to these authors, are illiberal or incompetent parents and communities. Thus, they place the burden on parents or the elements of civil society running nonstate educational institutions to demonstrate why they should be allowed to educate children or make educational choices for them. The following section outlines the philosophical basis and practical public policy implications of their arguments.

MEIRA LEVINSON

The Basis. In *The Demands of Liberal Education*, Meira Levinson argues that the liberal state "must adopt autonomy as its political ideal for human beings."[21] Levinson defines autonomy as "a substantive (as opposed to formal or procedural) notion of higher-order preference formation within a context of plural constitutive values and beliefs, openness to others' evaluations of oneself, and a broadly developed moral, spiritual, or aesthetic, intellectual, and emotional personality. It is substantive in that it denies that individuals whose volitions involve completely subsuming their will to another can be autonomous."[22] Since she believes the liberal state must adopt this ideal, she also insists the state must force it upon children. As Levinson herself words the implications, "the liberal ideal of autonomy not merely permits but requires the intrusion of the state into the child's life, specifically in the form of compulsory liberal schooling."[23]

Public Policy Application for Private and Home Schooling. Levinson clearly asserts that the implications of the state promoting her understanding of autonomy, ironically, will result in decreased parental power and choice in every area of schooling. She claims: "All schools must be structured as autonomy-promoting communities which are 'detached' from local and parental control. Although significant forms of parent involvement in their children's education should be encouraged, parents and other groups should not be able to control schools' curricula, ethos or aims."[24] What is intriguing is how Levinson appears willing to abandon the role of democratically elected local school boards as well as parental involvement in helping choose such boards if they do not promote this end. She does note that although parents should not control a school's curricula, ethos, or aims, the state should provide parental choices when it comes to the size, learning styles, or pedagogy of schools. The ends of public education, however, are not up for choice.

Levinson acknowledges that her vision would result in a tremendous increase in state or federal control of education, especially with regard to nonpublic options.

> Private schools would be subject to the same requirements and regulations as state schools: they have to be common (i.e., open to all children) and adopt the aim of educating for autonomy. . . . In the service of the former goal private school fees should be restricted by state law to no more than the maximum amount provided by the state, in the form of a voucher, tax credit, or assisted places scheme, to low income families in order to meet the cost of schooling.[25]

To those asking what would make private schools any different from public schools, Levinson gives a clear answer, "All told, therefore, there would in practice be little if anything to distinguish private schools from state schools—which is exactly the way it should be."[26] In fact, she even admits that in light of her regulations few individuals and organizations would possess an incentive to open private schools. Although Levinson does not mention homeschooling, her vision clearly involves outlawing homeschooling. She writes, "Bad schools are ones which are not common, are not detached [from children's home communities], and do not help children develop their capacities for autonomy . . . one thing it means is that schools should not reflect fundamental or socially divisive conceptions of the good."[27] Her theory also entails outlawing religious schools since, "because of religion's status as both a fundamental and a socially divisive conception of the good, religious schools would violate the liberal educative aims of commonality, autonomy, and citizenship."[28]

Finally, Levinson argues for exactly what some in this book promote and what others fear. In the United States, she advocates embedding "children's rights to an autonomy-producing education" in the Constitution as well as reversing US Supreme Court decisions that have promoted parental educational freedom such as *Pierce v. Society of Sisters* (1925) and *Wisconsin v. Yoder*.[29] She reiterates this point by arguing that children's' rights trump the UN Declaration cited above that "parents have a prior right to choose the kind of education that shall be given to their children." By contrast, she claims a parental right to govern a child's education "is insupportable within liberal theory, and is not an acceptable ground on which to deny children their right to autonomy-focused schooling."[30]

JAMES DWYER

The Basis. James Dwyer also believes that in the conflict of interests between the state, parents, and children, children's interest should clearly triumph.[31] He argues, "A legitimate political theory of children's education must recognize and give full effect to the distinct personhood of children. Children must not be subsumed under the identity of parents, and it should not be assumed that children's interests coincide with those of parents."[32] What this means, according to Dwyer, is that in a liberal democracy the burden must rest on parents to prove why they should possess any educational control over a child's education. He writes: "But if as a general matter we believe it neither necessary nor appropriate to attribute to anyone a right to determine how other persons live, a proper respect for the personhood of children demands that we not attribute such rights in connection with child rearing, absent a convincing demonstration, grounded in sound general principles, that child rearing should be treated anomalously."[33] What this would mean for education is that children's developmental interests would be treated as more important than adult or state interests.

Dwyer admits that figuring out what those developmental interests are is not easy since we cannot directly ask children. He suggests one possible approach involves using Rawls's original position. Adults could picture themselves in the original position as children and imagine what children are owed as a matter of justice. He claims this activity would lead us to grant to children the same liberties in the US Constitution: "freedom of the person (i.e., physical freedom, freedom of association, freedom of thought and expression, freedom of religion, and basic political rights, e.g., to vote and hold office)."[34] A second approach would involve comparing these results to the results of asking adults what they resent or regret in adulthood about their childhood. He suggests that few adults would likely regret or resent an education that taught critical thinking or what he calls intellectual autonomy. Perhaps a third approach would entail surveying "the empirical literature on the extent to which people experience happiness or a sense of fulfillment in different sorts of lives—lives that appear to involve critical thinking and those that do not."[35] Dwyer clearly places great confidence in the ability of adults (versus parents), especially those in political power, to find out exactly what is good for a child's welfare.

Dwyer demonstrates little concern with the fact that his approach would disturb parents. "That some parents will be upset, feel affront, fear for their children's salvation, and/or become dismayed at the prospect of their children rejecting their beliefs and way of life in and of itself has no bearing," he writes. "Children's interests trump. That some religious conservatives object to a liberal education out of fear that it might undermine their efforts to ensure their children think as they do is, in and of itself, unimportant."[36]

Policy Implications. Dwyer welcomes the fact that his view has radical consequences for nonpublic forms of education. Any private form of education that fails to provide an adequate secular education, he believes, should be shut down. Nonetheless, the state should give private schools that do provide a good secular education vouchers. The state would then need to regulate these schools to ensure that the money went only to secular instruction. In addition, it would need to heavily regulate the curriculum to ensure particular secular academic outcomes. Dwyer remains unconcerned about the implications for various private Christian schools (and likely would believe the same about homeschools). He writes, "The changes would certainly be radical for Fundamentalist schools and substantial for most Catholic schools. That Fundamentalist and Catholic schooling as presently constituted would no longer exist should not, however, be cause for mourning, at least not for anyone who respects the personhood of children. It should rather be cause for celebration."[37]

ROBERT REICH

The Basis. In *Bridging Liberalism and Multiculturalism in America*, Robert Reich presents a position that is slightly modified from Levinson's and Dwyer's.[38] For example, instead of promoting autonomy, he proposes that the key educational end in a liberal democracy should be "minimalist autonomy." Nonetheless, Reich's understanding of minimalist autonomy is similar to Levinson's understanding of autonomy. He defines it as "a person's ability to reflect independently and critically upon basic commitments, values, desires and beliefs, be they chosen or unchosen, and to enjoy a range of meaningful life options from which to choose, upon which to act, and around which to orient and pursue one's life projects."[39] The two parts of this definition of minimalist autonomy are equally important.

First, Reich contends that to be autonomous is to be able to separate oneself from one's particular social and institutional environment. Reich distinguishes this minimalist understanding from a Kantian version that defines autonomy more as self-creation or authorship. Instead, he believes his concept of minimalist autonomy as "sovereignty or self-determination"[40] is much more realistic. He cites the following as one example: "It is possible for my proselytizing parents to compel me to devote myself to God. But we would not say that the person who unhesitatingly and unthinkingly followed the exhortations of others was autonomous."[41] Reich wants to note here, however, that he does not mean to exclude certain kinds of lives (e.g., a follower of the Catholic tradition). Instead, he suggests, "What matters for minimalist autonomy is that the decision to lead a life of any sort—liberal or traditionalist, agnostic or devoted, cosmopolitan or parochial—be reached without compulsion from others and always be potentially subject to review, or critical scrutiny, should the person conclude that such a life is no longer worth living."[42]

Second, Reich notes that possessing the ability to perform "critical and independent second-order reflection on first-order commitments, values, desires and beliefs" does not fully constitute minimalist autonomy. Autonomy does not merely mean being knowledgeable about different views of the good life. It must involve "sustained intellectual engagement with diverse values and beliefs"[43] and the possibility of choosing other life options.

Similar to Levinson, Reich further argues that the state must not only respect autonomy but "treat autonomy as a value to be pursued and supported."[44] In fact, "nurturing the capacity for and exercise of autonomy must come *before* we respect it." The logical conclusion is that the state must make the development of autonomy in children a fundamental educational aim. Moreover, Reich provocatively claims, "The state should violate respect for autonomy in efforts to foster its exercise."[45] In other words, the state interest in minimalist autonomy should always trump parental authority. When a parent fails to fulfill this interest, the state should intervene.

Thus, with regard to parental authority Reich writes: "By my account, parental authority must end when its exercise compromises the development of their children into adults capable of independent functioning or when it disables or retards the development of minimalist autonomy in children. . . . If parental authority over education does not foster the self-sufficiency and independence of children, the state must step in and ensure such outcomes."[46] In the end, Reich admits that his argument shares much in common with Levinson's and Dwyer's views.[47] Like Levinson, he defends an education that promotes a form of autonomy, and like Dwyer, he advocates placing children's interests (from the perspective of the state) in a primary position in any consideration of how to weigh different educational interests.

Policy Implications. To outline what his views would mean in practice, Reich uses the concrete example of homeschooling. When it comes to homeschooling, the state, Reich claims, should ensure the development of homeschooled children's self-sufficiency, not by outlawing homeschooling, but by regulating it to ensure that the state's and child's interests are met.

Reich gives four specific suggestions. First, the state should require registration with local educational authorities so it can keep information about homeschoolers. Second, according to Reich, "the burden of proof that homeschools will satisfy the state's and child's interest in education must rest with the parents who express the desire to homeschool."[48] Thus, "parents must demonstrate to relevant educational officials that their particular homeschooling arrangements are up to determined educational standards."[49] Third, "the state must ensure that the school environment provides exposure to and engagement with values and beliefs other than those of a child's parents, [and] the state should require parents to use multicultural curricula that provide such exposure and engagement."[50] To satisfy this requirement, parents "could submit their curriculum for review to local school officials, they could choose curricular materials from a state-approved list, or they could allow their children to enroll in some public-school classes, or community-college courses, in which intellectual engagement with cultural diversity is a central task."[51] Finally, Reich claims the state should require homeschoolers to take annual standardized tests, and maintains that "if children repeatedly fail to make academic progress relative to their peers in public or private schools, the state should intervene and compel school attendance."[52]

Reich admits in the end that he is not merely interested in regulating a freedom to ensure it is not abused. He also hopes the regulation will persuade parents not to exercise their freedom. He writes, "in fact, finding ways to draw homeschooling families back to the public school system seems to me a necessary complement to the passage of effective regulations."[53]

SHIFTING THE BURDENS AND BOUNDARIES

A RESPONSE TO LIBERAL ARGUMENTS FOR LIMITING PARENTAL AUTHORITY

Before I respond to the above, I wish to make it clear that I accept important parts of their views. I agree that parents, children, and liberal democratic states have educational interests. I also agree that limits must be imposed on those interests and boundaries must be drawn between them. Nonetheless, I contend that how and where they draw these boundaries exhibits serious flaws. All of these theorists insist that one of the central goals of liberal education must be helping children attain what they variously label intellectual, minimalist, or liberal autonomy. Two problems emerge when using the goal of autonomy as a basis for state regulation.

WHAT WE EXPECT OF CITIZENS

First, this goal is not something for which we test immigrants when they apply to become citizens. A look at the list of what is required for a person to become a US citizen demonstrates this point. In addition to physical presence or resident requirements, future US citizens are expected to display the following: an ability to read, write, and speak English; a knowledge and understanding of US history and government; good moral character; attachment to the principles of the US Constitution; and a favorable disposition toward the United States.[54] Interestingly, what we want future adult citizens to demonstrate is not a particular type of autonomy but evidence of certain kinds of abilities and commitments. While we might agree that the ability to demonstrate an informed commitment to good moral character, attachment to the principles of the US Constitution, and a favorable disposition to the United States all require a degree of moral or political autonomy, the immigration service does not give tests to determine whether new immigrants have moral or political autonomy. They want evidence of commitment.

Moreover, what is certainly not on this list is a requirement that the person demonstrate autonomy as defined by these theorists. It does not require, in Levinson's words, "that the individual be able to challenge and reflect upon every first-order desire, including desires that are constitutive of the self."[55] In other words, nothing exists in the naturalization process that requires someone to take a philosophy of life course in which they must think through the various life philosophy options and make a choice (which seems to be what all these theorists imply should be part of becoming American). George Counts' criticism of this liberal progressive vision in 1932 still applies today:

> There is the fallacy that the great object of education is to produce the college professor, that is, the individual who adopts an agnostic attitude towards every important social issue, who can balance the pros against the cons with the skill of a juggler, who sees all sides of every question and never commits himself to any, who delays action until all the facts are in, who knows that all the facts will never come in, who consequently holds his judgment in a state of indefinite suspension, and who before the approach of middle age sees his powers of action atrophy and his social sympathies decay ... although college professors, if not too numerous, perform a valuable social function, society requires great numbers of persons who, while capable of gathering and digesting facts, are at the same time able to think in terms of life, make decisions and act. From such persons will come our real social leaders.[56]

Not surprisingly, what American citizenship requires is not autonomy concerning one's life philosophy but commitment (hopefully arrived at in an autonomous fashion) to be a certain kind of person with regard to one's moral and political life (which is much more narrow). Moreover, we expect that new citizens possess an autonomy that leads them to a significant and perhaps permanent commitment to the democratic tradition. In many ways this type of autonomy-based, high-level commitment to a particular tradition is what various religious or other communal groups hope to instill in children when they undertake home or private education. Of course, what these authors doubt is whether these groups seek to foster a long-term commitment that is arrived at autonomously. What exactly that would look like is the subject of the next section.

PROBLEMATIC GOALS AND WEAK EVIDENCE

The second problem with the goals of the authors outlined above is how exactly a school, state, or parent could ever determine when and whether a child met the goal of achieving intellectual, minimalist, or liberal autonomy. While I would agree that the ability to reflect critically about different intellectual traditions is a vitally important quality, it proves quite difficult to identify and test for such a skill. Moreover, it remains unclear how such a skill can be imparted apart from a particular tradition of rationality.[57] Yet, if these authors are going to claim that developing some particular form of autonomy is liberal democratic education's final aim, and they propose educational policies and regulations limiting parental choice of nonstate educational options based on this aim, then they should do the following: 1) provide clear standards, measures, and examples by which we can identify whether a child has at least demonstrated the appropriate developmental markers of reaching this goal; 2) use these standards to demonstrate either that forms of education such as homeschooling or religious education in general are preventing children from achieving this goal or the state public schools will meet this goal better; and 3) use these standards to show that a particular state-mandated method or curriculum will meet these interests the best. The thinkers addressed do not do any of these things when it comes to what the various types of autonomy they describe.

LEVINSON, DWYER, AND REICH FAIL TO PROVIDE CLEAR STANDARDS, MEASURES AND EXAMPLES

Not one of the above thinkers provides clear standards and measures by which one can determine whether forms of education chosen by parents such as homeschooling or religious education in general are inhibiting autonomy. What are the standards and measures? What would be the state's test to determine when a child, student, or adult lacks or possesses minimalist, intellectual, or liberal autonomy? Could we, in fact, devise an Iowa Basic Skills Test of Minimalist Autonomy for each grade level?

Reich admits that the answer to the important question of how one could measure autonomy could be subjected to this kind of empirical critique: "Given a definition of minimal autonomy, some test or evaluation might be concocted to measure its development. The test would then be administered to homeschooling children. If they did not achieve at some determined level, state intervention would then be justified." Nonetheless, Reich acknowledges that such a test is "highly unlikely" and agrees, "The empirical measurement of autonomy, especially in children, seems to me an exceptionally difficult and probably quixotic quest."[58] Amazingly, this admission does not stop Reich from believing we need to increase state regulation of home and private schooling to achieve this end.

Dwyer and Levinson appear more optimistic. Not surprisingly, Dwyer does not provide any such standards or measures but only assumes, for the sake of analysis,

> that the state can identify some components of a good secular education, that these are quite substantial—including fostering many cognitive skills such as critical and creative thinking, generating understanding of methods of inquiry in a variety of disciplines, and imparting a robust body of knowledge and that this education would, from the state's perspective (since we are talking about state decision making), be good for all children in our society, including many whose parents would object to it on religious grounds.[59]

Similar to Dwyer, Levinson merely provides a list of ideals, that she admits could go on and on, of "skills, areas of knowledge, competencies, psychological states, habits and structures of belief" that children need to achieve autonomy.[60] The ideals range from demonstrating humility when one's position is challenged to being "creative, observant, and sensitive to subtlety."[61]

Again, while I have no doubt that the goals listed are noble, I simply want to point out that the state cannot use these noble goals as a basis for regulation of education, particularly home and private education. If the state wants to use these goals as a basis for regulation it must have clear, commonly agreed upon means by which we could identity when children at different grade levels have reached these goals. Consider these authors' claim that developing autonomy involves cultivating a capacity for critical reflection and, as Reich puts it, "sustained intellectual engagement with diverse values and beliefs,"[62] or as Levinson states, the ability "to challenge and reflect upon every first-order desire, including desires that are constitutive of the self."[63] If state authorities are going to override parents' educational authority because their educational practices are impeding their children's minimalist autonomy, the state would need to answer the following questions:

1. What is the extent of exposure to and intellectual engagement with different traditions, beliefs and values that will result in the achievement of autonomy for children at various age levels?
2. In what areas of life must they be able to perform critical reflection: political ideology, religion, morals, cultural habits and norms, career, choice of club activities, choice of friends, and choice of classes?
3. What does it mean for children at different age levels to "enjoy a range of meaningful life options"?

Again, it is difficult to imagine how educational regulators in any state could answer such questions when encountering specific situations.

Consider the first question—if two Orthodox Jewish parents homeschool their daughter and always encourage her to examine other views through the critical lens of Orthodox Judaism and to chose an Orthodox Jewish life as the best life, is that a problematic limitation on the development of minimalist autonomy which the state should correct? Would our authors consider a homeschooling or a private school education largely undertaken within one religious tradition too restrictive? Since they believe autonomy is best achieved primarily by having the state control educational inputs versus examining educational outputs, they offer few clear standards by which to assess if teachers or schools are meeting their ambiguous ends.

The ambiguity of the goal of autonomy extends beyond these authors' definitions and standards to the examples or, more accurately, the lack of examples these thinkers offer of children lacking autonomy. Reich never uses actual examples of homeschooled children who might lack minimalist autonomy under his definition. For instance, when Reich argues that "some parents or cultural groups" may resist an education encouraging minimalist autonomy "because they do not wish for their children to become autonomous,"[64] Reich does not provide specific stories or instances. Yet, Reich claims to agree with Bertrand Russell's statement that "the question of home versus school is difficult to argue in the abstract."[65] In general, one can only guess about the specific groups or parents that garner Reich's concern.

Levinson offers some of the most specific examples. She argues that it would be "virtually impossible" for Sister Susan, a nun in a silent Carmelite sect, to be autonomous since she "has devoted her entire life to the service of God, shunning the establishment of an earthly family or close friends in favor of a singular focus on serving God."[66] If she challenges her beliefs, she would destroy her selfhood. The illustration breaks down, however, in numerous ways, since Sister Susan could possibly choose to leave the sect and retain important understandings of her identity (her name, her Catholic identity, her gender identity) and possibly recover old aspects of her identity (contact with her extended family, old friends). Levinson also claims that Sister Susan would need a plurality of values and desires from which to make "higher-order judgments about lower-order preferences," yet the question remains why we should believe that Sister Susan still does not wrestle with desires to marry and have children, hold a secular job, own a mansion, drive a Jaguar, or perhaps become an atheist. For some reason, Levinson imagines the decision to enter monastic life means Sister Susan once and for all cuts off past desires and thinking and no longer constantly and continually directs her desires to particular ends in light of autonomously made commitments.

AUTONOMY ADVOCATES FAIL TO PROVE THAT PUBLIC SCHOOLS ARE BETTER OR HOME OR PRIVATE SCHOOLS ARE WORSE, AS A WHOLE, AT DEVELOPING CHILDREN WITH AUTONOMY

Nowhere do these authors demonstrate that the state, through its public schools, does a better job of developing autonomy in a greater number of children on average or to a greater degree than homeschooling parents. The reason is that they cannot produce clear standards of evaluation by which we could do comparative tests of the autonomy of students at public and private schools and homeschooled children.

Instead, they offer various reasons for failing to do this straightforward comparison. Levinson admits that her decision to not include private schools in her descriptive analysis weakens her argument but she claims space and theoretical clarity do not allow it.[67] She even critiques the current American system for its failure to provide the coherence and emphasis upon one's civic or public identity required for her vision of political liberal education.[68]

Dwyer also admits that he does not provide a comparison of private with public schools when evaluating private school harms to freedom of thought and expression, since he believes the harms of private schools can speak for themselves and that the regulatory burdens placed on public schools are sufficient to prevent such harms.[69] Much of Dwyer's lack of concern stems from his belief that private and home schools cause various sorts of damage. He claims that they end up causing four major harms:

> First, these schools infringe children's basic liberties by imposing excessive restrictions on students' intellectual and physical freedom and fostering excessive repression of desires and inclinations. Second, they fail to promote, and in fact actively discourage, children's development of the generalized capacity for independent and informed critical thinking (i.e., "intellectual autonomy"). Third, they foster in students dogmatic, inflexible modes of thought and expression and, at least in the case of Fundamentalist schools, intolerance for persons who hold viewpoints different from their

own. Fourth, these schools have adverse psychological effects for many students, including diminished self-esteem, extreme anxiety, and pronounced and sometimes life-long anger and resentment.[70]

Dwyer's anger about his own private school experience appears to drive much of his agenda.

However, Dwyer's exaggerated and dogmatic generalizations about the dangers of private schools to critical thinking are difficult to believe by anyone familiar with the diverse types of private Christian schools. For example, of Fundamentalist Christian schools he writes, "Students in these schools are therefore not permitted to question what they are taught on any subject or to express any opinion contrary to the orthodox views that teachers, school administrators, and pastors aggressively impress upon them . . . absolute truths must be forced upon students without opportunity for reflection."[71] Not surprisingly, these generalizations are not footnoted.

This type of one-sided attack is unfortunate, because although such particular types of private or home education may restrict a child's autonomy, education in public schools might impede or warp the autonomy of children perhaps more than in private or home schools.[72] Pressures for drug or alcohol abuse, the threat of gang violence, sexual pressures, and peer cruelty, all of which can limit and harm a child's autonomy, may be amplified dangers in some public schools. Certainly, the authors do not offer any evidence that public schools are better at preventing children from various addictions, which invariably limit their autonomy. After all, what many public schools actually do through communal life and peer pressure is reduce a student's autonomy. Students can become servile to group interests where they are primarily exposed to the options of hedonism and crass forms of individualist utilitarianism.[73] Textbooks may also leave children with a very limited view of the various options regarding the good life.[74] Even if they do encounter other options, it is perhaps only through textbooks or other students and not in an embodied communal form.

Not surprisingly, parents who choose private schools or homeschooling recognize these possibilities. Richard J. Medlin summarizes the conclusions of nine studies that talked to actual homeschooling parents to discover their concerns about public schools:

> They describe conventional schools as rigid and authoritarian institutions where passive conformity is rewarded, where peer interactions are too often hostile or derisive or manipulative, and where children must contend with a dispiriting ideological and moral climate. Home schooling parents argue that this kind of environment can stifle children's individuality and harm their self-esteem. They say it can make children dependent, insecure,

or even antisocial. They believe it can undermine their efforts to teach their children positive values and appropriate behavior. Finally, they insist that it is unlikely to foster the kind of rewarding and supportive relationships that foster healthy personal and moral development.[75]

The initial research on homeschooling confirms some of these opinions. Medlin notes that we still need more research, but from the studies that have taken place he concludes that homeschoolers "have good self-esteem and are likely to display fewer behavior problems than do other children. They may be more socially mature and have better leadership skills than other children as well. And they appear to be functioning effectively as members of adult society."[76] In fact, scholars should study whether private or home schooled children are less likely to engage in destructive habits that reduce or impinge a child's future autonomy. The little evidence that exists actually reveals that home schooled adults are much more active in civic life than other US adults.[77] Although this evidence comes from a strong home school supporter, opponents of the homeschooling movement fail to produce research or analysis that counters this evidence or proves their point. Instead, they are content to argue that the state must be vigilant against private or parental failure and abuse with regard to civic engagement while giving little attention to state schools' failure and abuse in these matters. They also, as will be discussed in the next section, believe they can produce the ambiguous goal of autonomy by state-mandated means (instead of looking at outcomes).

THESE AUTONOMY ADVOCATES DO NOT PROVE THAT A PARTICULAR REGULATORY APPROACH FOR DEVELOPING AUTONOMY WOULD WORK BEST

Despite the fact that Dwyer, Levinson, and Reich cannot supply a concrete outcome measure of minimalist autonomy, they have no problem making a case for the extensive regulation of private and home schools. In other words, they claim to know the curriculum and methods everyone *must* use to achieve their immeasurable ends. Using this logic, one could argue that since we want all children to be moral and we know we cannot agree what "moral" means, we should still require all children to recite and study the Ten Commandments. Perhaps this method and curriculum may, on the surface, appear to make children moral, but it also clearly reduces the variety of approaches one might use for reaching that end. It also enforces only one particular and contested means for achieving this goal. Finally, it makes the assumption that the method and curriculum works but provides no evidence that it does.

The approach of these theorists overlooks the fact that a variety of ways to develop autonomy may exist. Indeed, one might argue that parents who choose private schools or homeschooling show a greater value for autonomy by example than most parents who "unthinkingly and unhesitantly" follow the crowd and send their children to public schools instead of "intellectually engaging" with the diverse educational traditions available. These parents may value autonomy in their children but believe in different ways to achieve that end. Some might believe that a child must first of all be initiated into a particular home, a particular language, a particular culture, a particular set of beliefs, before he or she can begin to analyze critically other cultures and beliefs. In other words, children must first understand their own identity and tradition and the stories associated with them before they can adequately understand and critically examine other traditions.[78] Just as I am not free to play Mozart on the piano because I never subjected myself to the required training to enjoy such a freedom, children must first endure the necessary training to enjoy the autonomy they describe. In other words, parents may merely take Reich's view that "the state should violate respect for autonomy in efforts to foster its exercise" and apply it to themselves. Parents must also initially violate respect for autonomy in order to foster its later exercise.

Moreover, parents might argue that by first understanding their own story and identity, children also gain a sense of place, confidence, and self-esteem. As certain advocates of multiculturalism note, we gain a sense of our identity through the stories we are told. Parents may want to tell stories they believe their children need to sustain themselves, their confidence, and their identity. For example, one characteristic of African American homeschooling families is their belief that public schools support institutionalized racism and that homeschooling allows their children to develop a secure cultural and ethnic identity.[79]

Parents who choose private schools or homeschooling may also believe that exposure to and engagement with different beliefs and values tend to be comparable to engaging in casual sex. Such approaches want students to have intellectual intimacy with various philosophical, religious, and cultural traditions without contemplation of commitment. In such cases, the examination of beliefs and values is treated as trivial instead of as an important and serious process in continuing a quest for the good and truthful life. These authors would likely deny that their approach entails such a viewpoint. Yet merely requiring a certain kind of curriculum in public schools hardly guarantees serious contemplation of different views of the good life. It certainly does not involve active engagement with living traditions.

Finally, parents may also want to protect their children from the threat of a state that seeks to foster servility. Reich claims "the liberal state must regulate for autonomy by ensuring that the school, through its curriculum and pedagogy, does not aim solely to replicate and reinforce the worldview of the parents or cultural groups of the children who attend the school."[80] One could easily argue the reverse: parents must protect their children's "autonomy by ensuring that the [public] school, through its curriculum and pedagogy, does not aim solely to replicate and reinforce the worldview of the" state.[81]

Of course, these authors downplay the threat the regulatory state poses to children's and parents' autonomy. Levinson claims such views derive "from some combination of unexamined cultural and historical biases, fuzzy thinking, careless policy analysis, political theorizing that ignores children, and/or indifference to the influence of certain forms of political, educational, and familial structures on children's development."[82] In reality, it is highly centralized political states, often communist or totalitarian (e.g., China, Vietnam, Cuba, Saudi Arabia, or Iran), where home and private schooling are outlawed and public school attendance mandated for all. In fact, the emergence of young forms of democracy actually resulted in the emergence of homeschooling (e.g., in Bulgaria, Czech Republic, Poland, Romania and Ukraine)[83] and private schooling.[84] In illiberal states, one finds a centralized government that uses the public school system to indoctrinate the populace. Past and present communist regimes especially demonstrate this point, as do other totalitarian or fascist governments. In these situations, the regulatory state clearly poses the biggest and most important threat to the minimalist autonomy of parents, children, and families as a whole. It employs public education to reduce autonomy. Levinson never explains why educational systems that allow for and encourage private and homeschooling, as well as diverse ways of developing autonomy, are more respectful of human rights such as freedom of thought, conscience, and religion.

CONCLUSION

It is clear that for Dwyer, Levinson, and Reich, parental choice of a child's education is not a freedom to be celebrated in liberal democracies but a freedom to be feared. Fear of the abuse of freedom leads them to restrict the freedom of parents even more. Unfortunately, it is not clear whether the concern for failure of children to develop autonomy is deeper than the concern with the substantive religious views taught to children. The reality may be that the current individuals and groups promoting parental choice, while not a proven danger to the liberal state or the rights of children, are more of a danger to the worldviews these authors prize.[85] Dwyer is actually quite transparent about his concern with parents' religious worldviews and his belief that parents have no interests to protect. He writes that his view "means that the state must ultimately decide what the interests of children individually or collectively are; the state cannot decide that a child's interests are whatever his or her parent's religion says they are."[86] In the end, these thinkers support a liberalism aptly described by Stephen Carter, one that "tends toward hegemony. Not content to serve as a theory of organization of the state, it has grown into a theory of organization of private institutions in the state."[87] In this respect, I believe the concerns of HSLDA or other parental rights defenders with how the UN Convention on the Rights of the Child could be used have a valid point. Although states already regulate homeschooling in various ways,[88] many critics of homeschooling regulation, such as these scholars, argue for more extensive regulation, and in some cases, the abolition of this right. Thus, it would not be surprising if the growing number of scholars and educators in favor of the arguments above, as well as government regulatory bodies empowered by such arguments, seized upon the convention to advance their agenda of promoting children's autonomy and state restrictions of parental freedom in education. In other words, it is likely they may use the CRC to argue for regulations that severely reduce the educational freedoms homeschoolers in America now enjoy.

These proponents of the rights of children should be careful, however, that their visions do not undermine the very freedom and protections they want to promote. Their proposed state regulation of home and private schooling too quickly takes away, through government regulation, a freedom liberal democracies should respect. In the name of the liberal end of freedom, they envision aiding children imprisoned by ideology. In contrast, I suggest that their suggestions for using state power to limit parental freedom could enslave both parents and their children to other narrow views of freedom. Therefore, one of the best defenses against the abuses of freedom of thought, conscience, and religion is a robust civil society that allows for a variety of educational options and choices, including private education and homeschooling. The more a society respects humanity and human rights, the more it will seek to empower parents to direct their child's education and civil society to furnish a variety of educational options with various visions of what it means to be fully human.

NOTES

1.   See for example *UNICEF: A Human Rights-Based Approach to Education for All* (New York: United Nations Children's Fund, 2007), 20-21.

2.   *The Universal Declaration of Human Rights* (1948), article 3, accessed March 2, 2009, http://www.un.org/en/documents/udhr/index.shtml.

3.   C. Glenn and J. de Groof, *Finding the Right Balance: Freedom, Autonomy and Accountability in Education* (Utrecht: Leema, 2002), 1:4. In contrast, some opponents deny such a right. For example, Amy Gutmann declares: "A

democrat must reject the simplest reason for sanctioning private schools—
that parents have a 'natural right' to control the education of their children."
Democratic Education (Princeton, NJ: Princeton University Press, 1987), 116.

4.   United Nations Convention on the Rights of the Child, articles 14, 15,
28. Usually, this issue is framed as a conflict between parental choice and the best
interest of the child. For example, one UNICEF publication states, "In the case
of conflict between a parental choice and the best interests of the child, however,
the child should always be the priority." *UNICEF: A Human Rights-Based Approach to Education for All* (New York: United Nations Children's Fund, 2007),
21. However, state parties must always act on the child's behalf to define and
enforce those interests in relationships to parents.

5.   Ibid., article 28.

1. States Parties recognize the right of the child to education, and
with a view to achieving this right progressively and on the basis of
equal opportunity, they shall, in particular:

(a) Make primary education compulsory and available free to all;

(b) Encourage the development of different forms of secondary
education, including general and vocational education, make them
available and accessible to every child, and take appropriate measures
such as the introduction of free education and offering financial assistance in case of need;

(c) Make higher education accessible to all on the basis of capacity by every appropriate means;

(d) Make educational and vocational information and guidance
available and accessible to all children;

(e) Take measures to encourage regular attendance at schools and
the reduction of drop-out rates.

2. States Parties shall take all appropriate measures to ensure that
school discipline is administered in a manner consistent with the
child's human dignity and in conformity with the present convention.

3. States Parties shall promote and encourage international cooperation in matters relating to education, in particular with a view to
contributing to the elimination of ignorance and illiteracy throughout
the world and facilitating access to scientific and technical knowledge
and modern teaching methods. In this regard, particular account shall
be taken of the needs of developing countries.

6.   Ibid., article 29.

1. States Parties agree that the education of the child shall be
directed to:

(a) The development of the child's personality, talents and mental and physical abilities to their fullest potential;

(b) The development of respect for human rights and fundamental freedoms, and for the principles enshrined in the Charter of the United Nations;

(c) The development of respect for the child's parents, his or her own cultural identity, language and values, for the national values of the country in which the child is living, the country from which he or she may originate, and for civilizations different from his or her own;

(d) The preparation of the child for responsible life in a free society, in the spirit of understanding, peace, tolerance, equality of sexes, and friendship among all peoples, ethnic, national and religious groups and persons of indigenous origin;

(e) The development of respect for the natural environment.

2. No part of the present article or articles shall be construed so as to interfere with the liberty of individuals and bodies to establish and direct educational institutions, subject always to the observance of the principle set forth in paragraph 1 of the present article and to the requirements that the education given in such institutions shall conform to such minimum standards as may be laid down by the State.

7.   *General Comment No. 1 on the CRC: The Aims of Education*, article 28, clause 1 (2001). Elsewhere in another general comment the CRC also gives this limited power to parents within ends chosen and specified by the convention, "The convention recognizes the rights and responsibilities of parents, or other legal guardians, to provide appropriate direction and guidance to their children (see paragraph 84 above), but underlines that this is to enable the child to exercise his or her rights and requires that direction and guidance are undertaken in a manner consistent with the evolving capacities of the child." *General Comment No. 12 on the CRC: The Right of the Child to be Heard* (2009), para. 91.

8.   Ibid., article 2.

9.   C. J. Klicka, "The UN Convention on the Rights of the Child: The Most Dangerous Attack on Parents' Rights in the History of the United States," *Home School Legal Defense Association*, November 1, 1999, accessed April 6, 2006, http://www.hslda.org/docs/nche/000000/00000020.

10.   M. Farris, "Parental Rights: Why Now Is the Time to Act," *Court Reporter* (March/April 2006), accessed March 12, 2007, http://www.hslda.org/parentalrights/default.asp.

11.   Ibid.

12.   Ibid.

13. G. Badman, *Report to the Secretary of State on the Review of Elective Home Education in England* (London: Crown Copyright, 2009). See also "UN Treaty Jeopardizes Homeschool Freedom in Britain," *Home School Legal Defense Association*, accessed April, 22, 2010, http://www.hslda.org/docs/news/200906161.asp.

14. Badman, *Report*, 3.

15. Ibid., 5.

16. *I Interim Report, Senate Standing Committee Report on Human Rights*, ibid., 18.

17. Ibid., 8.

18. For examples from the past decade see R. Reich, *Bridging Liberalism and Multiculturalism in America* (Chicago: The University of Chicago Press, 2002); S. Macedo, *Diversity and Distrust: Civic Education in a Multicultural Democracy* (Cambridge, MA: Harvard University Press, 2000); A. Gutmann, *Democratic Education* (Princeton, NJ: Princeton University Press, 1999); M. Levinson, *The Demands of Liberal Education* (Oxford: Oxford University Press, 1999); W. Feinberg, *Common Schools, Uncommon Identities* (New Haven, CT: Yale University Press, 1998); E. Callan, *Creating Citizens* (Oxford: Clarendon Press, 1997). In contrast, one finds few books defending parental rights. Exceptions come from an Australian author, B. Crittenden, *Parents, the State and the Right to Educate* (Melbourne: Melbourne University Press, 1988); a Canadian, E. Thiessen, *In Defense of Religious Schools and Colleges* (Montreal: McGill-Queen's University Press, 2002); and an American law professor, S. Gilles, "On Educating Children: A Parentalist Manifesto," *University of Chicago Law Review* 937 (1996): 937-1034.

19. The theorists often fail to note that the state is not some abstract identity that exists apart from people but that its interests overlap with others in that parents and children are citizens and parents are participants.

20. Reich, *Bridging Liberalism and Multiculturalism*, 158.

21. Levinson, *The Demands of Liberal Education*, 23.

22. Ibid., 58.

23. Ibid.

24. Ibid., 144.

25. Ibid., 145.

26. Ibid.

27. Ibid., 157.

28. Ibid., 158.

29. Ibid., 162.

30. Ibid., 163.

31. Dwyer's recent works include J. Dwyer, *The Relationship Rights of Chil-*

dren (New York: Cambridge University Press, 2006); J. Dwyer, "Changing the Conversation about Children's Education," in *Moral and Political Education*, ed. S. Macedo and Y. Tamir, 314-58 (New York: New York University Press, 2002); J. Dwyer, *Vouchers within Reason: A Child-Centered Approach to Education Reform* (Ithaca, NY: Cornell University Press, 2002); J. Dwyer, *Religious Schools v. Children's Rights* (Ithaca, NY: Cornell University Press, 1998).

32. Dwyer, "Changing the Conversation," 329.

33. Ibid., 330-31.

34. Dwyer, *Religious Schools*, 155.

35. Dwyer, "Changing the Conversation," 333.

36. Ibid., 334.

37. Dwyer, *Religious Schools*, 180.

38. Portions of my summary of Robert Reich's position as well as my analysis of his views originally appeared in P. L. Glanzer, "Rethinking the Boundaries and Burdens of Parental Authority over Education: A Response to Robert Reich's Case-Study of Homeschooling," *Educational Theory* 58, no. 1 (2008): 1-16.

39. Reich, *Bridging Liberalism and Multiculturalism*, 92.

40. Ibid., 98.

41. Ibid., 102.

42. Ibid.

43. Ibid., 161-62.

44. Ibid., 108.

45. Ibid., 108.

46. Ibid., 160.

47. Ibid., 192.

48. Ibid., 169.

49. Ibid.

50. Ibid.

51. Ibid., 169-70.

52. Ibid., 170.

53. Ibid., 172.

54. US Citizenship and Immigration Services, *A Guide to Naturalization* (Washington, DC: US Government Printing Office, 2007) Publication M-476, 18.

55. Levinson, *The Demands of Liberal Education*, 32.

56. G. Counts, *Dare the School Build a New Social Order?* (Carbondale, IL: Southern Illinois University Press, 1978), 18.

57. A. MacIntyre, *Whose Justice? Which Rationality?* (Notre Dame, IN: Notre Dame University Press, 1988).

58. Ibid., 161.

59. Dwyer, "Changing the Conversation," 335.

60. Levinson, *The Demands of Liberal Education*, 60.

61. Ibid.

62. Reich, *Bridging Liberalism and Multiculturalism*, 161-62.

63. Levinson, *The Demands of Liberal Education*, 32.

64. Ibid., 156.

65. Ibid., 253.

66. Levinson, *The Demands of Liberal Education*, 33.

67. Ibid., 110.

68. Ibid, 120-22.

69. Dwyer. *Religious Schools*, 7-15.

70. Ibid., 14-15.

71. Ibid., 24.

72. I should note that Dwyer acknowledges this point and notes, "undoubtedly many public schools also violate one or more of their students' liberties, and they should be taken to task for it." Ibid., 162.

73. J. D. Hunter, *The Death of Character* (New York: Basic Books, 2000).

74. See, for example, W. Nord's evaluation of US textbooks in *Religion and American Education: Rethinking a National Dilemma* (Chapel Hill, NC: University of North Carolina Press, 1995), 138-59.

75. R. G. Medlin, "Home Schooling and the Question of Socialization," *Peabody Journal of Education*, 75 (2000) 109.

76. Ibid., 119.

77. B. Ray, *Home Educated and New Adults: Their Community and Civic Involvement, Views about Homeschooling and Other Traits* (Salem, OR: NHERI Publications, 2004), 5-54.

78. This line of argument is set forth in E. Thiessen's books, *In Defense of Religious Schools and Colleges* (Montreal: McGill-Queen's University Press, 2002) and *Teaching for Commitment: Liberal Education, Indoctrination and Christian Nurture* (Montreal: McGill-Queen's University Press, 1993). The idea that we learn practical rationality by participating in a particular tradition has also been robustly defended in a variety of recent scholarly works such as those by Alasdair Macintyre. See A. MacIntyre, *After Virtue: A Study in Moral Theory.* (Notre Dame, IN: University of Notre Dame Press, 1984); and *Three Rival Versions of Moral Enquiry: Encyclopedia, Genealogy and Tradition* (Notre Dame, IN: University of Notre Dame Press, 1990).

79. S. McDowell, A. Sanchez, and S. Jones, "Participation and Perception: Looking at Home Schooling through a Multicultural Lens," *Peabody Journal of Education*, 75 (2000): 124-46.

80. Reich, *Bridging Liberalism and Multiculturalism*, 197.

81. Ibid. One could also argue that Reich's approach to education for minimalist autonomy raises an important question at this point: "Are women [or men] who have been forcibly re-educated, or brainwashed, or systematically conditioned from infancy to value autonomy really autonomous?" Thiessen, *Teaching for Commitment*, 133.

82. Levinson, *The Demands of Liberal Education*, 1.

83. It is intriguing to glance through the countries that do allow some form of homeschooling: Australia, Brazil, Bulgaria, Canada, Chile, Czech Republic, France, Hungary, Japan, Ireland, Kenya, Mexico, Netherlands, New Zealand, Poland, Romania, South Africa, Switzerland, Taiwan, Ukraine, United Kingdom, and United States. Home Schooling—International, *HSLDA*, accessed March 4, 2009, http://www.hslda.org/hs/international/default.asp. For a discussion of home education law in Europe, see L. A. Taylor and A. Petrie, "Home Education Regulations in Europe and Recent UK Research," *Peabody Journal of Education*, 75 (2000): 49-70.

84. C. Glenn, *Educational Freedom in Eastern Europe* (Washington, D.C.: Cato Institute, 1995).

85. See, for example, H. Rosin, "God and Country," *The New Yorker* 81, no. 18 (2005): 44-49.

86. Dwyer, "Changing the Conversation," 335.

87. S. Carter, *God's Name in Vain: The Wrongs and Rights of Religion in Politics* (New York: Basic Books, 2000), 26.

88. C. Klicka, *The Right to Home School: A Guide to the Law on Parents' Rights in Education* (Durham, NC: Carolina Academic Press, 2002).

Seven

Implementing the Convention on the Rights of the Child in Canada

A Question of Commitment

⇌ R. BRIAN HOWE ⇌

There is no question about Canada's official commitment. In 1991, with the approval of the provinces, with the exception of Alberta, the Government of Canada ratified the United Nations Convention on the Rights of the Child (CRC), committing governments at all levels in Canada to a policy of ensuring that Canadian laws, policies, and practices are consistent with the rights of the child as described in the CRC. Alberta initially was hesitant, but in 1999 it too gave its support.[1]

Official commitment, however, is not the same thing as actual commitment. Official commitment is when a government makes a pledge to pursue a particular course of action. In Canada, upon ratifying the CRC, the federal and provincial governments made a pledge to implementing the rights of the child. Actual commitment is when a government follows through on a pledge through undertaking measures to put the pledge into effect, whether in the form of laws, policies, or programs. This is done despite whatever obstacles stand in its way. Based on an examination and analysis of developments in Canada during the 1990s and 2000s, this article will assess the level of the commitment by Canadian governments to the rights of the child.

As with an individual person, the commitment of a government is not an all-or-nothing affair. It varies in degree and may be described in an ascending

141

order of strength. First is symbolic commitment, where government support for a particular course of action is at a low level. Commitment may be real but it is shallow, as reflected in no or very limited efforts and in much reliance on symbolism, where words are used as substitutes for deeds.[2] Second is wavering commitment, where political authorities are ambivalent about a course of action, supportive and positive at one time but hesitant or vacillating at another. This is reflected in government efforts that occur in spurts and where there are forward and backward developments without clear signs of progress. Third and finally is deep commitment, where government authorities sustain a high level of commitment to a course of action as shown in strong and determined efforts to overcome obstacles. Efforts ultimately are successful and are recognized as such.

I propose to assess the level of Canada's commitment and to explain what level the country has reached and why. The first part of the paper will set the stage by providing a brief background discussion of the significance of the convention and obstacles to implementation. The second part will look at Canada's record since 1991 and provide evidence of its wavering commitment. The final part will account for why Canada has wavered in its commitment and will discuss prospects for change. I argue that this wavering is due in large part to a lack of unified public support for the principle of children's rights.

Obstacles to Implementation

It is impressive that apart from the United States and Somalia, 192 countries have ratified the CRC, making it the most widely and most quickly ratified international treaty in world history. It also is impressive that these countries have agreed to the general meaning of children's rights outlined in the the so-called three Ps in the CRC: rights of provision (provision of health care, education, economic welfare), rights of protection (protection from abuse, neglect, violence, exploitation), and rights of participation (a voice in decisions affecting the child).[3] And it is impressive that they have agreed to the convention's three guiding principles: nondiscrimination, where children are to be protected from all forms of discrimination; the best interests of the child, where a primary consideration in all actions concerning children is their best interests; and participation, where children have the right to be heard and their views given weight in accord with their age and maturity.[4] With such widespread international agreement, it is virtually impossible for countries to defend themselves against failure to act on the basis that they do not support the concept of children's rights. They might try to defend themselves by saying that they have done more than that suggested by critics or that shortcomings and failures are due to unforeseen circumstances. But they cannot deny their official support of the convention. This is an advance.

The CRC is a significant document because it is a legally binding piece of international law.[5] By ratifying the CRC, a state party has agreed to implement the articles of the CRC (if not already implemented) and to ensure that its laws, policies, and practices are in compliance with the convention. A country may choose not to act immediately, but nevertheless, it is obligated to do so over time. This may not be a system of "hard law" in the sense that rights in the CRC are capable of immediate enforcement through a court of law. Rather, it is generally a system of "soft law" in which the law is enforced indirectly and over time through a reporting system and on the basis of public opinion and national and international peer pressure.[6] Under the CRC, a state party makes a report to an expert committee—the UN Committee on the Rights of the Child—every five years. The country documents how well it has been complying and what measures it has taken to implement the articles of the CRC. The committee then reviews the report and makes its own report—called concluding observations—where it notes progress and shortcomings. On the basis of the concluding observations, a country is expected to improve its performance, though it is not legally obligated to act on the committee's recommendations. The CRC ultimately is enforced through the court of public opinion and on the basis of moral and political pressure. A state party typically does not want to be embarrassed by criticism. Although the CRC may not be hard law, it is significant because it is legally binding. A country cannot respond to criticism simply by saying that it is not bound by the CRC. Inadequate though it might be, there is pressure to demonstrate progress.

With ratification in 1991, Canada officially became committed to ensuring the implementation of the rights of the child.[7] As required by the convention's article 4, Canada was obligated to "undertake all appropriate legislative, administrative, and other measures for the implementation of the rights recognized in the present convention." It was to do so through a reporting and monitoring system where Canada would send reports to the UN committee for review (it sent reports in 1994, 2001, and 2009) and to make the reports widely available to the public. However, that was the easy part. The more difficult part was (and is) to demonstrate that Canada's commitment was real. The real test of Canada's commitment was (and is) to overcome the obstacles and to translate the provision, protection, and participation rights of the child into practice.

There are three chief obstacles to Canada's implementation of the rights of the child. The first is Canada's complicated and sometimes difficult system of federalism.[8] Under Canada's constitution, the federal government has the authority

to sign and ratify international treaties or conventions, but not the sole authority to implement them.[9] If a subject matter falls under provincial jurisdiction, it
is the provinces and territories that have responsibility for implementation. A
problem may be that a particular province or group of provinces is resistant to
implementing change in a particular area for ideological or other reasons. It may
also be the case that jurisdiction is unclear or contentious. A further problem is
that although the federal government has responsibility for certain child-related
matters—criminal law, matters of divorce, aboriginal affairs—the provinces and
territories have the lion's share of responsibility, including in the areas of health
care, education, child protection, child care, and the enforcement of child support. The system poses problems because although the provinces and territories
have major child-related responsibilities, they often do not have the financial resources to fulfill them. Most are highly dependent on the federal government for
fiscal transfers. Given these complications, a major challenge for implementing
the CRC is to gain federal, provincial, and territorial cooperation in coordinating efforts. This is no easy task.

A second obstacle, then, is the availability of financial resources.[10] Implementing the rights of children, especially those dealing with issues such as child
poverty and child care, requires a sizable allocation of financial resources. Apart
from the problem of an imbalance of resources between the federal and provincial governments, a more general problem is that Canadian governments, like
governments elsewhere, can claim that economic difficulties preclude public
expenditures on children. Indeed, the decade following Canada's ratification
was an era of major fiscal restraint by both federal and provincial governments.
That this was a possible excuse for inaction was foreseen as Canada and other
countries were preparing to ratify the CRC in the early 1990s. In 1990, at the
World Summit for Children, attention was given to the issue of children's basic
needs and to the possibility of governments giving children low priority in their
budgets despite their official commitment to children. It was agreed, therefore,
that there be a global plan of action to provide for the basic needs of children.
Within this global plan, it was further agreed that individual countries were to
design their own plans, provide the necessary financial resources, and abide by
the principle of "first call for children."[11] According to this principle, the needs
of children should be given first priority in a nation's budget during hard economic times as well as good. The challenge for Canada and other countries was
to take this principle seriously.

A third obstacle is the lack of public pressure for implementation. In Canada, as elsewhere, government action is highly influenced by political pressure.[12]
However, in the area of children's rights, little pressure comes from the chief

stakeholders—Canada's children. They do not vote, they have little money and resources, and they seldom are involved in organizational and lobbying activity. To make up for this, children depend on pressures on government from child advocacy organizations and the public. But pressure from child advocacy organizations is made difficult because they are relatively few in number and without the resources and membership for sustained lobbying and influence. Pressure on the basis of public opinion in support of children is made difficult because, thanks to a lack of public education on the CRC, most Canadians have little knowledge about the rights of the child and little understanding of the importance of implementing the convention.[13]

To some degree, public pressure does emanate from the notion that children are not to be blamed for misfortunes such as poverty and abuse. This allows child advocates a basis for mobilizing public support to address particular problems such as child poverty and child abuse. However, for the most part, the pressure is based on sympathy rather than on support for principle of rights, which makes it less compelling. This leaves implementation largely dependent on the political will of governments. This is a challenge because amidst the multiple claims and demands on government, it is easy for issues of children's rights to become ignored or squeezed out by other issues. Because the CRC is soft law rather than hard law, without sustained public pressure, it may be attractive for politicians to take the path of least resistance and delay or forego implementation.

What the Record Shows

In order for Canadian governments to demonstrate their commitment to the rights of children, they would have had to do three things during the 1990s and 2000s. First, as in countries such as Norway and Belgium, they would have incorporated the convention into Canadian law and into the goals of child-related public policy. New legislation and new policy initiatives would have referenced and reflected the relevant articles of the convention. Second, as in countries such as Sweden and Iceland, a national children's commissioner or ombudsman office would have been established to monitor developments and advocate on behalf of children. As children lack power and resources, an agency is required to hear their voices, and a commissioner would fulfill that role. Third and most important, Canadian governments would have translated the provision, protection, and participation rights of the child into practice.

The record shows that Canada has failed in all of these areas. Canada has failed, first of all, to incorporate the convention into its domestic law.[14] It perhaps is understandable that, upon ratification, the CRC would not be automatically incorporated into Canadian law. Unlike countries such as Belgium that subscribe to the doctrine of monism, where international treaties have automatic legal application upon ratification, Canada operates on the basis of dualism where, although it is legally bound by an international treaty, a treaty is not yet part of domestic law and has no internal effect until it has been incorporated through the enactment of legislation. Under a system of dualism, the convention has to become incorporated statute by statute. However, unlike other dualist countries such as Norway, Canada has chosen not to incorporate the CRC into domestic law. The federal government has operated under the assumption that the CRC already has been incorporated into domestic law by means of the Charter of Rights, federal and provincial human rights legislation, and other federal and provincial legislation.[15] The position of the federal government has been that prior to ratifying the CRC, it consulted with the provinces and made the determination that Canadian laws already were in conformity with the convention. This was necessary to do because issues of children's rights cut across all jurisdictions and because of the complexity of the federal system. Thus, from the federal government's point of view, there has been no need for the incorporation of the convention after 1991. This is highly dubious. If a government were confident about its commitment to the rights of children, why would it not make its commitment explicit through incorporation after 1991, as dualist countries such as Norway have done?

Canadian governments have chosen not even to make reference to the convention in most child-related legislation enacted after ratification. A review of federal, provincial, and territorial legislation since 1991 shows that there has been no mention of the CRC apart from the federal Youth Criminal Justice Act (where the CRC is referred to only in the preamble, where it has no legal effect), provincial adoption acts dealing with international adoptions, and the Northwest Territories Child Protection Act.[16] Thus the convention has little direct legal application in Canada. Moreover, because the convention has little or no effect, Canadian judges have seldom made reference to it in decisions except in a limited number of legal cases.[17] At best, the convention has been deemed to have "persuasive force" in Canadian courts but not "obligatory force."[18]

Canada also has failed to establish a special institution for the rights of the child at the national level.[19] A major effort was made by child advocates in the late 1990s to create a new national office for children called the children's commissioner.[20] But this effort ultimately fell on deaf ears. Possible reasons included the lack of sufficient pressure by child advocates, a belief by federal officials that such an office was not required as the needs of Canada's children were well taken care of, and a fear that an independent office might cause the federal government political embarrassment, just as other independent offices did in the past.[21] The failure of this effort does not mean that there are no official offices for children in Canada. At the provincial level, most provinces have established what are called child advocacy or child ombudsman offices. However, these do not exist in all provinces—there is yet to be one in Prince Edward Island—and not in the three northern territories.[22] Where they do exist, while they do perform very important tasks, their mandates are limited to a particular area or areas of children's rights, usually in the fields of child protection and care or youth justice. Their mandates do not include monitoring the implementation of the convention or promoting the convention rights of the child in their jurisdiction.

Finally, Canada has failed to make substantial progress in all or most areas of children's rights. On the one hand, progress has been made in some areas. In the area of provision rights, child benefits for low income families have been steadily increased to counter child poverty, and spaces for child care have been expanded through greater financial support by federal and provincial governments. In the area of protection rights, stronger criminal laws have been developed to protect children from sexual abuse and exploitation, and a new federal Youth Criminal Justice Act has been enacted, with a greater focus than before on rehabilitation through community and treatment programs. And in the area of participation rights, governments have made greater efforts than before in providing an opportunity for youth voices in decision making through representation in committees and boards. But on the other hand, since the ratification of the CRC, child poverty has not been significantly reduced in Canada, nor has the child care system been substantially improved.[23] Laws to protect children from abuse and neglect have continued to vary across jurisdictions with insufficient resources for prevention programs.[24] The new Youth Criminal Justice Act has the major shortcoming of allowing for the wider use of adult sentences for youth in conflict with the law.[25] Participation rights have not been provided for on a comprehensive and legislative basis.[26] And because education on the rights of the child has not been provided for in schools, very few children in Canada—as well as in most other countries—are even aware of their basic human rights.[27]

What Canada's record indicates is wavering commitment to the rights of the child. That Canada has taken modest steps to provide for children's rights suggests that the level of commitment is beyond symbolic. But that there are major shortcomings and failures suggests that commitment is certainly not deep. At best, Canada's commitment to children's rights is wavering. This begs the question of why.

Why Canada's Wavering Commitment?

The obvious place to look in searching for an answer to Canada's wavering commitment is in the obstacles to implementation. Canada's system of federalism, cited above, is a possible explanation. Without question, federalism does pose problems. Given the fact that many child-related matters are in the provincial jurisdiction, successful implementation of the rights of the child requires a high degree of intergovernmental collaboration and cooperation. Difficulties occur because of the complexities and uncertainties of jurisdiction and because different jurisdictions have different priorities and different resources. Furthermore, it is questionable whether the federal government has the constitutional authority to compel the provinces to implement an international convention.[28] However, although federalism is an obstacle, it does not fully explain Canada's wavering commitment. Some matters are largely in the federal jurisdiction (e.g., youth justice) and some largely in the provincial (e.g., education). Here, there is no legitimate jurisdictional excuse for inaction. In areas of shared responsibility, as shown in the history of the delivery of health care and postsecondary education, cooperation and agreements can be achieved despite quarrels and conflict. Moreover, under international law (specifically, the Vienna Convention on the Law of Treaties, to which Canada is bound), lack of federal jurisdiction is not as valid an excuse for failure in implementing an international convention.[29] Federalism is not a legitimate legal excuse for failing to implement the CRC.

Another possible explanation, also cited above, is the shortage of financial resources. On the one hand, it is true that Canadian governments were highly concerned about budgetary issues in the period following ratification. Beginning in the late 1980s and increasingly during the 1990s, governments at all levels became preoccupied with deficits and debts. In varying degrees and with considerable public support, these governments pursued policies of deficit and debt reduction and cuts or restraint on government spending. In such an environment, spending on matters related to children became difficult. But on the other hand, while fiscal restraint was a factor, it does not in itself fully explain Canada's wavering commitment. Not all areas of children's rights involve high costs. Participation rights, for example, involve adjustments to legislation and policies, not major expenditure. Moreover, with budgetary surpluses in the late 1990s and early 2000s, the financial situation of the federal government improved substantially, increasing the fiscal capacity of the federal government to act on its own or support the provinces and territories in child-related expenditure. Thus, it was not simply a matter of finances.

A third possible reason for Canada's wavering commitment is the lack of public and political pressure for action which we have noted. This, perhaps, is most persuasive. Because children lack political power and resources, they are dependent on pressures from child advocacy organizations and from the public to protect and advance their interests. Child advocacy organizations, however, have limited influence. Within government, provincial child advocacy offices do not have the mandate to advocate for the implementation of the CRC. Outside of government, child advocacy groups are too few in number and not sufficiently organized to mount a strong and sustained campaign to implement the CRC. This leaves the advance of children's rights dependent on pressure from the Canadian public. However, there is little public pressure because despite Canada's obligation under the convention (article 42) to spread awareness of the rights of the child, the Canadian public has remained uninformed. Without an agency such as a national children's commissioner to spread awareness, and without comprehensive and effective education on the rights of children in schools and through the media, the lack of public education and thus the lack of public pressure is not surprising.

But there is another and deeper problem. Although most Canadians remain uninformed and uneducated about the rights of the child as described in the convention, most do have general views about children and about children's rights. On the one hand, most support the notion that children have basic human rights. They do not believe, for example, that parents have absolute rights in the raising of their children, or that police and justice officials should be able to use their discretionary power to override due process rights in dealing with youth in conflict with the law. Children have rights against parental abuse and arbitrary police treatment. But on the other hand, many Canadians also subscribe to the belief that children's rights must be balanced against or subordinate to the rights of parents and adults in positions of authority over children. For example, contrary to the CRC, many citizens (as well as political and judicial authorities) believe that parents have fundamental rights in relation to children (rather than obligations) and these rights deserve to be respected.[30] Such a belief means that when a claim is made on the basis of the fundamental rights of children, there will be considerable reluctance to support such a claim as it spells the loss of parental rights and unwanted state intrusion into the affairs of the family.

Concern about parental rights has been reflected not only in public debate on issues involving children but also in political decisions and court cases. It was reflected, for example, in Alberta's conditional approval of the convention. As in the United States, citizens and politicians in Alberta initially were reluctant to agree to the convention for fear that children's rights would undermine parental rights and adult authority. Thus, unlike other provinces which approved the CRC in 1991, Alberta refused to approve it until 1999. When Alberta finally endorsed it, it expressed its support "based on the understanding that the UN convention does not usurp or override the authority of parents."[31]

Concern about parental rights also has been reflected in court cases dealing with the issue of the physical punishment of children. During the early 2000s, courts in Ontario and the Supreme Court of Canada were called on to decide whether the legal defense of the physical punishment of children (permitted under section 43 of Canada's Criminal Code) was unconstitutional and contrary to the rights of children under the Canadian Charter of Rights and the CRC.[32] The main legal argument of those challenging the law was that the law violated the rights of children to security of person and to equality without discrimination under the Charter and the principle of the best interests of the child under the CRC. In defending the law, the federal government and interest groups representing parents and teachers argued that the existing law did not violate the constitutional rights of children. They argued that parents (and teachers in the role of parents) have a basic right and responsibility to use reasonable force, including physical force, for the correction of the child. This is required, they said, because it is part of a "protected sphere" of decision making necessary for parents in raising their children. Furthermore, they argued that parental rights did not unduly compromise the rights and welfare of children, including the principle of the best interests of the child. Rather, the parental right to make decisions concerning children, including decisions about discipline and, if necessary, corporal discipline, is a central part of the best interests of the child. It is parents who generally know best about the best interests of their children. About 50 percent of the Canadian public agreed with the federal government's position.[33]

To a large extent, the courts also agreed. The Supreme Court of Canada, in a 6-3 decision, ruled that the existing law allowing for physical punishment does not violate the constitutional rights of children. Rather, it recognizes their developmental needs and their best interests. However, the court did define a zone of the acceptable use of physical punishment: it is to be administered by a parent (not a teacher); the child is to be between the ages of 3 and 12 years; the child is to be capable of learning from it; it constitutes "minor corrective force of a transitory and trifling nature"; it does not involve the use of objects or blows or slaps to the head; it is not degrading, inhuman, or harmful; and it is for corrective purposes (not out of a parent's frustration or loss of temper or abusive personality). Within this zone, said the court, the parental practice of physical punishment is legally permissible. Parents have the basic right to a protected sphere in which to raise their children and to use violence in the name of the best interests of the child.

Illustrated in this case and in Alberta's reluctance to endorse the convention is the fact that Canadian public opinion and the views of judicial and political authorities are somewhat divided on the question of children's rights. At the very least, many Canadians are suspicious of a strong concept of children's rights and believe that the rights of children should be subordinate to or balanced against the rights of parents and adults. This makes it difficult for child advocates to mobilize public opinion on the side of a fuller implementation of children's rights. Public opinion can be a significant force in the making of public policy if it is solidly on one side of an issue and the issue is salient to citizens.[34] If public opinion is unified and strong, it is in the political interests of governments to respond. But if public opinion is divided, as is the case of opinion on children's rights in Canada, it is a major challenge to spread public awareness and to increase public pressure on behalf of children's rights and the CRC.

PROSPECTS FOR CHANGE

In 2004, the Senate of Canada authorized the Standing Senate Committee on Human Rights to examine and report on Canada's progress in implementing the UN Convention on the Rights of the Child. The Senate Committee subsequently studied the issue, held hearings, and presented an interim report in 2005 and a final report in 2006.[35] The analysis and recommendations in the report provides some glimmer of hope that Canada can move forward from wavering to an increasing if not deep commitment to the rights of the child.

In its final report, the committee did not shy away from criticizing Canada's lack of progress on children's rights. It pointed out several problems, including the inadequate incorporation of the CRC into Canadian law, the inefficiency of the reporting system, the difficulties of federalism and the lack of uniform national standards on children's rights, the lack of public and governmental awareness of the convention, and the lack of public and parliamentary input into the implementation process. The committee also pointed to a number of substantive shortcomings in Canada's record, including inadequate measures to combat child poverty, improve the child care system, improve laws and programs in the field of child protection and alternative care, provide opportunities for youth participation, and educate children, adults, and government officials on the rights of the child. The committee urged that Canada undertake more vigorous action to implement the convention, including incorporating the CRC into Canadian law. It recommended also that a national children's commissioner be established for the objective of monitoring and spreading awareness of children's rights and

that a new system be developed to facilitate greater collaboration and cooperation among different levels of government and a much fuller implementation
of the convention.

The test of Canada's future commitment to children will be in its response
to the Senate committee's recommendations. In the short term, the prospects
for a positive response are not great. Given the fact that children continue to
lack resources and political power, that child advocacy organizations lack significant influence, that the Canadian public lacks awareness, and that governments respond mainly to those who have influence and resources, the chances
of Canadian governments listening to and acting on the committee's recommendations are minimal. A movement for change is further dampened by the
ambivalent or divided views that Canadians have of children and children's
rights. But over the longer term, the prospects are better. Canada's political
culture has been evolving in the direction of greater human rights consciousness and wider public appreciation of the need to overcome obstacles to participation and inclusion.

Canadians increasingly are becoming what Rhoda Howard-Hassmann
has referred to as "compassionate Canadians," conscious of the need to give
support to historically disadvantaged or marginalized groups, including ethno-
cultural minorities, women, persons with disabilities, aboriginals, and sexual
minorities.[36] In such an evolving political culture, there is reason to think that
child advocates would have an easier time in mobilizing the Canadian public on
behalf of children, downsizing the ambivalence and elevating the importance of
the rights of the child, and pressuring governments into a more vigorous implementation of the convention.

There is an evolving logic that says that if adult minority members and
women are to be as citizens with rights, children should be treated in the same
way and barriers to their participation removed. Movement in this direction
has already begun. Most Canadians no longer think of children as the property of their parents. Many believe that children are a vulnerable class of persons in need of special protection and care, if not by parents, then by the state.
It is true that many Canadians do not yet regard children as bearers of rights
and as full citizens, as the Government of Canada officially does through its
ratification of the CRC. But a long-term change in public consciousness in
the direction of conceiving children as bearers of rights is quite possible with
expanded children's rights education in schools and society. Building on the
cultural change that already has been going on, and building on programs of
children's rights education that already exist, child-friendly educators and child
advocates are a position to develop comprehensive and robust programs of hu-

man rights education in which children learn about their rights and responsibilities. Children are the adult citizens, child advocates, and policy makers of the future. Imbued with children's rights consciousness, they will be in a position to make a difference.

Notes

1. Support was in the form of letter from Premier Klein to Prime Minister Chretien in 1999.

2. The classic work on the role of symbolism in politics is M. Edelman, *The Symbolic Uses of Politics* (Urbana, IL: University of Illinois Press, 1964).

3. T. Hammarberg, "The UN Convention on the Rights of the Child, and How to Make it Work," *Human Rights Quarterly* 12 (1990): 97-105.

4. M. Hill and K. Tisdall, *Children and Society* (London: Addison Wesley Longman, 1997), 28-30.

5. J. Doek, "The Current Status of the United Nations Convention on the Rights of the Child," in *The United Nations Convention on the Rights of the Child*, ed. S. Detrick, 632-40 (Dordrecht: Martinus Nijhoff, 1992).

6. D. Stasiulis, "The Active Child Citizen: Lessons from Canadian Policy and the Children's Movement," *Citizenship Studies* 6, no. 4 (2002): 508; "Editorial: The UN Convention on the Rights of the Child as a Touchstone for Research on Childhoods," *Childhood* 6, no. 4 (1999): 403.

7. K. Covell and R. B. Howe, *The Challenge of Children's Rights for Canada* (Waterloo: Wilfrid Laurier University Press, 2001), 22-32; S. Toope, "The Convention on the Rights of the Child: Implications for Canada," in *Children's Rights: A Comparative Perspective*, ed. M. Freeman, 33-64 (Aldershot: Dartmouth Publishing, 1996).

8. R. Andreychuk and L. Pearson, *Who's In Charge Here? Effective Implementation of Canada's International Obligations with Respect to the Rights of Children*. Interim Report, Senate Standing Committee Report on Human Rights (Ottawa, 2005), 59-68, accessed December 1, 2008, http://www.parl.gc.ca/38/1/parlbus/commbus/senate/com-e/rep-e/rep19nov05-e.pdf.

9. P. Hogg, *Constitutional Law of Canada* (Toronto: Carswell, 1992), 281-99.

10. S. Toope, "The Convention on the Rights of the Child: Implications for Canada," in *Children's Rights: A Comparative Perspective*, ed. Michael Freeman, 51-52 (Aldershot: Dartmouth Publishing, 1996).

11. K. Covell and R. B. Howe, *The Challenge of Children's Rights for Canada* (Waterloo: Wilfrid Laurier University Press, 2001), 38.

12. Most theories of the formation of public policy are society centered in that pressures or interests in society are believed to be of primary influence. However, in state-centered theory and institutionalism, it is assumed that the structure of the state and autonomous state actors have a central role. See S. Brooks, *Public Policy in Canada: An Introduction* (Toronto: Oxford University Press, 2003), 22-45.

13. R. B. Howe and K. Covell, *Empowering Children: Children's Rights Education as a Pathway to Citizenship* (Toronto: University of Toronto Press, 2005), 35-42.

14. R. Joyal, J.-F. Noel, and C. Chapdelaine Felciiati, eds. *Making Children's Rights Work: National and International Perspectives* (Montreal: Les Editions Yvon Blais, 2005), 30-31; Andreychuk and Pearson, *Who's In Charge Here?*, 74-87.

15. Andreychuk and Pearson, *Who's In Charge Here?*, 46-48.

16. Database, *Canadian Legal Information Institute*, accessed December 31, 2008, http://www.canlii.org.

17. From 1991 to December 2005, the convention was referred to in only 54 cases. Database, *Canadian Legal Information Institute*, accessed December 31, 2008, http://www.canlii.org.

18. J. Brunnée and S. Toope, "A Hesitant Embrace: Baker and the Application of International Law by Canadian Courts," *The Canadian Yearbook of International Law* (Vancouver: University of British Columbia Press, 2002), 40:3-60.

19. Joyal, Noel, and Felciiati, *Making Children's Rights Work*, 23-27, 31; Andreychuk and Pearson, *Who's In Charge Here?*.

20. A leading figure in this effort was Senator Landon Pearson.

21. Examples include the Privacy Commissioner, the Commissioner of Official Languages, and, of course, the Auditor-General of Canada.

22. Some municipalities have established child advocacy offices. Toronto, for example, designates a councilor as a "children's advocate" who is responsible for issuing periodic reports.

23. R. B. Howe and K. Covell, "Child Poverty in Canada and the Rights of the Child," *Human Rights Quarterly* 25 (2003): 1067-87; G. Doherty, M. Friendly, and J. Beach, *OECD Thematic Review of Early Childhood Education and Care: Background Report for Canada* (Ottawa: Social Development Canada, 2003), published for the Organization for Economic Cooperation and Development, accessed December 1, 2008, http://www.hrsdc.gc.ca/eng/cs/sp/sdc/socpol/publications/reports/2004-002623/english.pdf.

24. R. B. Howe, "Implementing Children's Rights in a Federal State: The Case of Canada's Child Protection System," *The International Journal of Children's Rights* 9 (2001): 361-82.

25. M. Denov, "Children's Rights or Rhetoric? Assessing Canada's Youth Criminal Justice Act and Its Compliance with the UN Convention on the Rights of the Child," *The International Journal of Children's Rights* 12, no. 1 (2004): 1-20.

26. D. Stasiulis, "The Active Child Citizen: Lessons from Canadian Policy and the Children's Movement," *Citizenship Studies* 6 (2002): 4, 507-38.

27. Howe and Covell, *Empowering Children,* 35-40.

28. That the federal government apparently cannot enforce the implementation of international treaties is due the ruling of Judicial Committee of the Privy (Canada's highest court until 1949) in the *Labour Conventions* case (1937). See P. Russell, R. Knopff, and T. Morton, *Federalism and the Charter* (Ottawa: Carleton University Press, 1989), 104-10.

29. Andreychuk and Pearson, *Who's In Charge Here?,* 43-44.

30. R. B. Howe, "Do Parents Have Fundamental Rights?," *Journal of Canadian Studies,* 36, no. 1 (2001) : 61-78.

31. A. Pellatt, *United Nations Convention on the Rights of the Child: How Does Alberta's Legislation Measure Up?* (Calgary: Alberta Civil Liberties Research Centre, 1999), accessed March 8, 2006, http://www.aclrc.com.

32. The Supreme Court's decision may be viewed at http://scc.lexum.org/en/2004/2004scc4/2004scc4.html. See also J. Durrant, *Joint Statement on Physical Punishment of Children and Youth* (Ottawa: Coalition on Physical Punishment of Children and Youth, 2004); Howe, "Do Parents Have Fundamental Rights?"

33. Durrant, *Joint Statement,* 12.

34. P. Burnstein, "The Impact of Public Opinion on Public Policy: A Review and an Agenda," *Political Research Quarterly* 56 (2003) : 29-41.

35. Andreychuk and Pearson, *Who's In Charge Here?.*

36. R. Howard-Hassmann, *Compassionate Canadians* (Toronto: University of Toronto Press, 2003).

Eight

Implementing the Convention on the Rights of the Child in the UK

A Problem of Political Will

⌦ CLAIRE CASSIDY ⌫

This essay explores the difficult implementation of the United Nations Convention on the Rights of the Child in one developed industrial nation, the United Kingdom, where we might expect children to enjoy a favorable situation in relation to their rights. The 2008 report of the Committee on the Rights of the Child has documented the UK's limited success in implementing the convention. While not denying some successes, I shall summarize the funding, coordination, and other obstacles to the implementation of basic protection and provision rights as highlighted by the committee. However, from a pedagogical perspective, what is most important is that the convention adds participation to protection and provision as its third major goal. Without greater effort in this area implementation will fall short despite success in the other two areas.

The United Kingdom comprises four countries: Scotland, England, Northern Ireland, and Wales. While the devolved parliaments since 1999 have assumed responsibility for areas such as education, social services, health, and law and order, the central UK government maintains control over social security, foreign policy, monetary policy, and some legislation. Further, the three countries hold their devolved powers to a greater or lesser extent. A difficulty in enacting children's rights in the UK lies in the fact that the regulatory professional bodies in the four countries are not interconnected.[1]

157

While the Convention on the Rights of the Child (CRC) was quickly ratified by the UK in 1991—and the UK government maintains overall charge of
its implementation—the convention has not yet become part of domestic legislation. Thus the CRC does not have the force of law in the UK. There is, of
course, evidence of its articles in several pieces of legislation. It has informed,
for example, the Children's Act (2004) for England and Wales, the Childcare Act
(2006), also for England and Wales, the Children's Plan for England (2007), and
the Children (Scotland) Act 1995. An obvious manifestation of the CRC was the
creation of children's commissioners, though each country took some time to
create these positions. Wales led the UK by appointing its commissioner in 2001
with Northern Ireland and Scotland following in 2003 and 2004, respectively.
Interestingly, while it took England until 2005 to appoint its commissioner, Oxfordshire Social Services in 1997 funded a local children's rights commissioner;
the first such post in the UK.[2] The children's commissioners work to protect and
promote children's rights, including publicizing children's rights and the CRC,
consulting children, and collaborating with others with similar responsibilities.
The commissioners work to respond to the most recent United Nations' report
card on the UK's progress in meeting the articles of the CRC.[3]

UN CHILD RIGHTS COMMITTEE REPORT ON THE UK

Under article 44 of the CRC, each state must submit a report to the United Nations committee within two years of the convention being ratified by the state
and then every five years thereafter. States should report on measures they have
taken in the promotion of the CRC as well as evidencing the "progress made on
the enjoyment of those rights" (article 44). In October 2008, the United Kingdom of Great Britain and Northern Ireland received the concluding observations
from the CRC. The report reads very much that the UK could do much better.

While the committee welcomed the influence the convention had had on
policy and legislation, such as the acts mentioned above and England's creation
of the Department for Schools and Families, the creation of an Equality and Human Rights Commission, and the fact that the convention had been cited in the
UK's various domestic courts, the commission was disappointed that the convention had not yet been incorporated fully into the four nations' laws. This was
a carryover from the committee's previous recommendations. Other areas that
had not been responded to positively since the previous report were budgetary
allocations, dissemination and awareness of the convention, nondiscrimination,
corporal punishment, education, asylum seekers, refugee children, and juvenile
justice. Further, there had been little or no movement by the UK on the definition of the child, domestic violence, ill treatment, abuse, and drug and substance

abuse.[4] Some of these criticisms were directed towards some of the UK's Overseas Territories. Beyond the recommendations made by the committee in its previous report, there were now further points that the UK had to take into account. The committee encouraged development of a bill of rights in Northern Ireland and a British bill of rights incorporating a section on children's rights, although it acknowledged the difficulties inherent in devolved governments and the issues surrounding coordination. The statement suggested that a well-resourced "single, high-profile mechanism"[5] coordinate and monitor the implementation of the convention in response to the fact that each jurisdiction has power over its budgetary allocations and development priorities. This coordinating and monitoring mechanism would support "comprehensive plans of action"[6] to ensure that both the public and private sectors act to promote and protect children's rights. The committee further emphasized the need for careful attention being paid to those "children belonging to the most vulnerable groups."[7]

While the committee commended the four children's commissioners created in the UK, it questioned the independence of the commissioners and the limitations of their powers. To be fully independent and able to exercise their powers, children's commissioners should have both the human and financial resources necessary to discharge their responsibilities. Further, it states that a "child rights impact assessment should be regularly conducted to evaluate how the allocation of budget is proportionate to the realization of policy developments and the implementation of legislation."[8]

Though publicizing children's rights and the CRC is part of the commissioners' role, the committee was not satisfied that this has been done effectively. Improved child rights training for adults who work with children would likely improve matters.[9] The committee recommended inclusion of the convention in national school curricula. However, the four nations of the UK lack the same curriculum, and Scotland does not have a national curriculum. There is scope in Scotland's new "Curriculum for Excellence"[10] for teaching and learning related to children's rights and the CRC, but this is not compulsory. The duty of teaching about the convention is not merely that of teachers, however, and the committee recommended that other agencies with a responsibility for children should play a part.

Greater evidence of dissemination and training in children's rights should make it a simpler task for the UK to tackle discrimination. While the committee welcomed the forthcoming Equality Bill relating to antidiscrimination law, concern was expressed regarding specific vulnerable groups and the discrimination they experience at several levels. Roma and Irish Traveler children, asylum-seeking and refugee children, lesbian, gay, bisexual, and transgender children, and children from minority groups continue to experience institutionalized discrimination as well discrimination on a personal basis. The committee stressed the need for measures to protect such children from discrimination in all sectors of society as well as for raised public awareness of antidiscrimination legislation and practices. An additional note was made that not only should discrimination not be tolerated but that discriminatory behavior should be penalized.

One approach to dealing with discrimination towards and amongst children is to give consideration to children's views and to promote their participation in civil society. While it is acknowledged that children have been consulted during inspections to schools and in other institutional settings, and that children are encouraged to share in the development of school policies, there has been little movement in enshrining article 12 in educational policy and legislation across the UK. Children's views should, as the committee recommended, be facilitated in all areas of society: family, community, and schools, as well as in judicial and administrative proceedings. The existence of the United Kingdom Youth Parliament, Funky Dragon in Wales, and the Youth Parliament in Scotland were highlighted as good practice, but these forums for children's participation must receive additional support. There should also be opportunities for children to engage and participate elsewhere in a meaningful way, in the media, for example.

The committee recognized one area that severely impedes children's opportunities to engage in society, namely, their lack of freedom to assemble peacefully. It affirmed the rights of children to freedom of movement as well as peaceful assembly and the importance of these rights in children's development. The UK's use of "mosquito devices" and "dispersed zones" to stop children from assembling was seen as undesirable. Additionally, the committee was "concerned that, with the sole exception of Wales, the right to play and leisure is not fully enjoyed by all children in the State party."[11] The committee drew attention to poor infrastructures for play, particularly for children with disabilities. The loss of public spaces designed specifically for play and the ever-increasing Anti-Social Behaviour Orders (ASBOs) have led to a reduction in opportunities for children to meet and play. Children's right to rest, play, and leisure, together with their right to participate freely in cultural life and the arts, is seen as needing attention, especially in the case of children with disabilities.

Children with disabilities were seen by the committee to require special protection through legislation. A national strategy is required to enhance inclusion opportunities. A further recommendation was that the UK consider ratifying the International Convention on the Rights of Persons with Disabilities and its Optional Protocol. These initiatives would raise awareness of issues associated with disability and the rights of those children who have disabilities, therefore tackling problems of discrimination and the institutionalization of such children. Training for those working with children with disabilities should be provided. Scotland already has the Standards in Scotland's Schools Act (2000) and the Education (Additional Support for Learning) Act (2004). These presume provision of mainstream schooling for all children, making local authorities provide the additional support needed by all children, including those with disabilities.

Regarding health services, a lack of coordination between health policy, practice, and the people these services serve was reported to result in significant inequality in access and provision. As to mental health services, the committee was concerned that approximately only 25% of children in need have access to the services and treatment they require, and that some children are still treated in adult psychiatric wards. The situation in Northern Ireland was reported as "delicate" due to the conflict there. The committee advocated that additional resources need to be dedicated to health services. As for infant and adolescent health services, the committee recommended implementation of the International Code of Marketing of Breastmilk Substitutes. Breastfeeding should be encouraged in nursery training. The first legislation on breastfeeding was passed by the Scottish government in 2005: the Breastfeeding (Scotland) Act. Concern was expressed over the high rate of teenage pregnancies, with a recommendation that the UK provide adolescents with appropriate and accessible reproductive health education. Efficient education and related services should also be available to adolescents regarding alcohol, drug, and other toxic substances with a view to tackling the root causes of these problems. Mental health and counseling services should be available, providing accurate and objective information for those working to stop their use or dependency. This support should take the form of informal as well as formal education.

The committee noted that "significant inequalities persist with regard to school achievement of children living with their parents in economic hardship,"[12] as with children with disabilities, asylum-seeking children, Traveler and Roma children, teenage mothers, and nonattendees for health reasons, among other groups. Northern Ireland has already made efforts to end the unequal two-tier education system criticized by the committee. On top of the inequalities noted in the different education systems in the UK were the unacceptably high number of children permanently and temporarily excluded from school. The committee also reported that attendance is likely to be diminished for some children due to the widespread problem of bullying. Children's opportunities to have their voices heard on school issues as well as in complaints procedures tend to be restricted, and often it is parents whose views are heard. The committee noted that Looked After and Accommodated Children are further marginalized because of lack of parental support. There was a strong recommendation in favor of "truly inclusive education which ensures the full enjoyment to children from all disadvantaged, marginalized and school-distant groups."[13] This should be addressed by increased resources to support and represent those with difficulty in accessing the appropriate services and systems, while also addressing the issue of school exclusion. The Every Child Matters reform in England was welcomed by the committee; though it will not specifically address education, it will still impact educational experiences. Scotland has developed several early intervention strategies to capture children in the preschool sector, and the Scottish government has now stipulated that those responsible for young children, for example, in nurseries, must possess a degree-level qualification, for example, a bachelor's in Childhood Practice. Such professional education will raise awareness of children's rights, something the committee found generally lacking in those working professionally with children and young people.

This need for greater awareness was brought into focus in the UK in late 2008 and early 2009 with the distressing case of "Baby P," a two-year-old child who died due to persistent abuse but who did not receive the intervention desperately needed, despite the child being on the local authority's social work department's child protection register. This has been the latest in a series of high profile news stories of the failures of the public social services. Media and public pressure in this case are likely to push the UK government to further heed the committee's recommendation, so that given "any unexpected death or serious injury involving children,"[14] an independent and public review will be automatically be instated. Related recommendations call for monitoring violence, sexual abuse, maltreatment, neglect, and exploitation (article 19). This monitoring should take account of what happens in families, schools, and other institutions responsible for care. Professionals working with children—for example, teachers, social workers, police, health care employees, and the judiciary—should be trained to ensure maximum protection of children from violence, abuse, and neglect. For those suffering from these abuses the state should provide support and ensure that, when legal proceedings occur, the child or young person does not further become a victim during the legal process. Services, such as counseling, should be available to aid recovery.

The state was encouraged to ensure that all corporal punishment is prohibited in all schools and in any other institution caring for children. Nonviolent approaches to discipline are to be fostered in such institutions, but also at home with the notion of "reasonable chastisement" being questioned. The committee further recommended in society at large that taser guns and attenuating energy projectiles used by the police in England, Wales and Northern Ireland should not be used on children. In addition, a review of Antisocial Behaviour Orders is encouraged with a view to abolishing their application to children. This illustrates the committee's concern over the number of children under the various nations' judicial systems who are treated as adults. Until early 2009 Scotland had the lowest age of criminal responsibility in Europe: children at eight years old were considered to be capable of being criminally responsible. In Northern Ireland, Wales, and England the age was ten. While the Scottish government has claimed that children were in the majority of cases dealt with through the children's hearings system, some children are still tried in adult courts. However, on March 2, 2009, the Scottish Commissioner for Children and Young People (SCCYP) announced on its website that within days, plans for raising the age of criminal responsibility from eight to twelve would be revealed. The committee holds that children should never be tried in adult courts, "irrespective of the gravity of the crime they are charged with,"[15] that they be held in detention only "as a matter of last resort and for the shortest period of time,"[16] and that alternatives to detention should be sought.

Child detention and the judicial process further entered the committee's recommendations on asylum-seeking and migrant children. The UK's Asylum and Immigration Act (2004) was criticized for subjecting children over the age of ten as liable to prosecution should they arrive in the UK without valid documentation. The committee counseled that the UK government consider amending the act "to allow for a guaranteed defence for unaccompanied children"[17] who lack valid documentation. The UK was encouraged to provide guardians for unaccompanied asylum seeker and migrant children, and for children whose age is under question, with the benefit of the doubt afforded to the child, and with experts' guidance sought on how best to determine age.

A further aspect of UK asylum and immigration legislation that concerned the committee was the detention of asylum-seeker and migrant children. Again, this measure should be used as a last resort for the briefest time possible. The Scottish government, in their draft response to the UN committee's report, repeats its opposition to the detention of children in Dungavel Detention Centre in Scotland, and states that "it has made its position clear to UK Government Ministers on a number of occasions."[18] In fact, the Scottish government and NGOs speak with one voice on the matter, and more specifically on "dawn raids" on the homes of asylum seekers and migrant families, with their ill effect on children.

The care of children, either within or outside the family context, also received the committee's attention. The standing of children living in foster care or with either one or both parents in prison must be upheld and opportunities for maintaining parental contact, where possible, should be facilitated. Parents and those providing care for children should be assisted. Further, children should not find themselves in care due to low parental income. This raises a central issue.

POVERTY IN THE UK

Despite the UK's relatively high per capita income, throughout the committee's report the question of poverty, inequality, and disadvantage looms large. While the UK government has increased spending on children in recent years, it in no way satisfies the great need experienced by ever-increasing numbers of children. The committee was "concerned that poverty is a very serious problem affecting all parts of the United Kingdom, including the Overseas Territories, and that it is a particular concern in Northern Ireland, where over twenty per cent of children reportedly live in persistent poverty."[19] This picture is echoed in Scotland. Nutrition, clothing, and housing are key areas where support should be provided for children and families in need. Indeed, the committee recalled the promise made by Prime Minister Tony Blair on March 18, 1999, to halve child poverty from 2.7 million children in 2006-07 to 1.7 million children by 2010 on the government's path to eradicating child poverty by 2020. He stated: "Our historic aim will be for ours to be the first generation to end child poverty forever, and it will take a generation. It is a twenty-year mission, but I believe it can be done." The UK government, in the first half of 2009, announced that it will not be able to meet its promise for 2010. The Child Poverty Action Group (CPAG) in Scotland, the leading charity campaigning for the abolition of child poverty in the UK, reports that "despite Scotland's undoubted wealth a staggering one in four of our children still lives in poverty. What's more the latest official statistics suggest recent progress in reducing child poverty has stalled."[20] Given the new government's declared intention in May 2010 to address the deficit in public finances by proposing a 20% cut in public spending, the poverty gap can only grow and children will be further disadvantaged.

If we consider the persistent poverty of "children in households with incomes below different income thresholds in at least three out of the last four years,"[21] the UK Department for Work and Pensions' 2008 statistics show that "around one in ten children experience persistently low income before housing costs are accounted for, and nearly one in five after housing costs are accounted for."[22] These factors impact implementation of the CRC. Further, many children in poverty are unable to engage fully with educational opportunities. Children with disabilities have insufficient support or resources. The UK government simply has not done enough to pull children out of the poverty in which they find themselves.

PARTICIPATION RIGHTS

Beyond protection and provision as determined by the CRC, the other area of the children's rights agenda that remains stunted, largely through the inequality children experience in their everyday living, is that of participation. The idea of participation is closely associated with that of children's voice and the realization of article 12, where children have the right to express their views in matters concerning them. Where failures in realizing protection and provision rights are often traceable to inadequate funding, in the case of participation rights the failure is due more to a lack of political will.

Children's voice and the opportunities to have their views heard was commented upon repeatedly in the committee's report. In matters of health care, complaints systems relating to family and alternative care, children and young people's parliaments, and education, children need to have the opportunity and a forum established to make their views known. In education and schooling some provision for children to air their views is most likely to be found. Increasingly, schools have Pupil Councils where pupils elect representatives to sit in the council to discuss key aspects relating to the life of the school. In Scotland it is expected that every school will have a Pupil Council chaired by a pupil, with the minutes being taken by a pupil. However, the tokenistic nature of consultation at Pupil Councils and the lack of power actually available for the children in determining how their schools should run have been often noted.[23] Despite the model in Scotland, resulting from section 6 of the Standards in Scotland's Schools, etc., Act 2000, which requires head teachers to show in their school development plans how they will consult with pupils regarding decisions about the daily running of the school, the all too common picture across Scotland and the rest of the UK is that Pupil Councils are often left to discuss only three main features of school life: school uniform, food available to buy at break times, and toilet facilities. Indeed, Pupil Councils are often the first thing to go when time constraints become tight during the course of a school week. This is illustrative of the value placed on children's participation and voice in the context where they will undoubtedly spend a large proportion of their time. Since the percentage of children educated privately is very small and since there is no particular homeschooling movement to speak of in the UK, state schools, as the responsibility of local public authorities, have the responsibility and the power to promote participation by children in educational matters.

Laura Lundy presents a new framework under which article 12 of the CRC might be considered.[24] Her proposition is that voice is not enough. She offers four key elements that should be in place to implement article 12: space, voice, audience, and influence. Without consideration of these four factors,

Lundy argues, children's participation is seriously compromised. It is not adequate for children to be given a voice and for this voice to have space and an audience. The audience itself should not be passive but should engage, while ensuring opportunities for real influence as a consequence. If children, with their different voices, are consulted and included in debate and dialogue with no further purpose, the exercise has limited value. Indeed, this lack of meaningful opportunities for participation points to the key problem of the role and status of children in society.

A number of commentators call attention to this participation deficit. Adrian James makes clear that the issue of status is reinforced by legislation, or the lack of it. In discussing family law in England and Wales, he suggests that "because children have no legal right to be consulted, this allows adult decision makers to set aside a child's wishes and feelings if the decision maker feels that these are contrary to the child's long-term interests."[25] While it is, of course, important that the child's best interests be central to decision making, James further comments that the "ambivalent attitudes of the state and of adults towards children"[26] are emphasized due to the established construction of the concept of children and the consequent treatment of children and childhood by the law.

Michael Freeman sees a denial of children's entitlement to be active in society, with their interests too often ignored and their participation not requested in the first place.[27] He further highlights the problem of child status when he notes that "nothing is a clearer statement of the position that children occupy in society, a clearer badge of childhood and what we associate with it, than the fact that children alone of all people in society can be hit with impunity."[28] It is clear from the UN committee's report that this is still a cause for concern.

Rudi Roose and Maria Bouverne-de Bie recognize that status and participation rights are linked to citizenship.[29] They hold that relational citizenship is based upon the relations individuals have with others. They suggest this is closely associated with achieving a desirable society in which participation is encouraged and promoted among all. Dympna Devine also recognizes that active agency and participation by children helps form a social identity.[30] Jens Qvortrup, too, recognizes the key role of citizenship status, and holds that the visibility of children and who they are and what they do is central to their status within society.[31] Children should be listened to, acknowledged, respected, and recognized "as persons in their own right."[32] This is the crux of the matter.

Elsewhere I have offered a Kantian concept of what it means for a child to be a person, and have argued that children are not currently considered by society to be persons.[33] Recalling the Kantian claim that we should treat a person as an end in himself or herself and never simply as a means, children very often continue to be treated as a mere means to an end, that end being adult-hood with full powers for participation.

In this volume, Butler appears to allow the dialogical participation of children, but he sees this simply as a preparation for adulthood, holding that children are not equal to adults regarding their ability to participate in dialogue. He considers that a redistribution of power in society that shifts to a more "child-centred society" should be avoided, that children should not be allocated decisive influence. He does not hold that children should be treated merely as a means, but that the best way to treat them as a means to equality in dialogue with adults is to treat them as an end in themselves as childhood dialogue partners. The suggestion here is not that all power should be handed over to children, but that children should be able to participate, that they should be given opportunities to join in deliberations and learn how to participate and make decisions effectively. Children should, in short, not be powerless individuals who have to wait their turn before they are allowed to *be* in society.[34] The negative notion of the child as a *becoming* has gathered momentum in the last ten years,[35] and unless it is addressed, there is not likely to be a change in the status of the child as we currently know it in the UK and the wider global context.

At present, the child's status is often subsumed under that of the family. James cautions that, in placing the child in the context of the family, "children's agency and their capacity for autonomous decision making, and their rights"[36] may diminish as a result of children, parents, and family becoming synonymous with one another. What is more disturbing for children than their status being overridden by parents' or family views is that, for a large part of their day-to-day existence, the views and consent of children's parents are not required for the state to interfere with children's privacy. The UN committee expressed concern in its report that children's privacy was not protected. It raised issues surrounding children and the media, citing both "negative media representation and public 'naming and shaming'"[37] and the insufficient protection of children in reality television programs. What is most pointed, however, is the need for stronger regulations governing data protection, particularly in keeping records of children's DNA when they have been charged with a crime, irrespective of guilt. In the UK, Scotland does not have a national DNA database, but Terri Dowty highlights the dangers recognized by the UN committee and goes on to explore the ways in which children are under surveillance for, potentially, twenty-four hours a day in the UK.[38] Examples such as CCTV cameras, scanned tickets used for school meals, and even tracking devices in clothing illustrate just how simple it is for children to be observed by a range of mechanisms throughout their childhood. It remains unclear why such surveillance is necessary, but "privacy is about far more than secrecy or furtive activities: it is about our autonomy."[39] Again, by denying autonomy and thus assigning to children diminished status, we fail to treat children as persons in their own right with a full and participative role in society.

Morwenna Griffiths outlines three phases under which children's empowerment, including agency and participation, could be arranged and discussed.[40] First, empowerment is ascribed to certain groups or individuals. Second, the power held by an individual or group must allow them a capacity to effect change, to act and alter an existing situation for themselves by virtue of "a theoretical possibility of agency."[41] Third, individuals or groups must be able to pass power on from one to another. She holds that this transfer of power might allow new actions to occur beyond what was previously possible, resulting in a shift in power. It may be an idealized notion to think that the power balance might be redressed to allow children sufficient power to meet Griffiths' criterion of the "possibility of agency." Without this, however, it seems unlikely that children can reach her third phase. Indeed, even to get to the first and second phase, it would appear that adults have to engage authentically with the third phase and relinquish some of the power at their disposal if there is to be any meaningful engagement of children in society.

There is limited evidence of ways or structures under which children could become full, active, participative, and political individuals who are able to engage and act within their society. Often the scope for children's engagement is very limited. There needs to be a conscious and deliberate inclusion of children, so their participation is not an add-on, as some kind of hoop-jumping exercise to show compliance with children's rights. What is required is a way of equipping children with the tools to engage as persons in the full sense.[42]

Community of Philosophical Inquiry (CoPI)[43] is a practical philosophy that grew out of the Philosophy for Children (P4C) movement.[44] While P4C was designed specifically for children, CoPI is a practice used with adults and children in the same manner.[45] In encouraging children to reason and reflect about the world around them through CoPI they are more likely to become active, participative, and political citizens. CoPI demonstrates that children are able and willing to comment on matters of concern to their daily life. They have opinions about what goes on in their environment, and not simply their immediate local environment. In CoPI, children from as young as three are able to reason and reflect.[46] CoPI is blind to status and is egalitarian in theory and practice. It can be used as a tool for children's empowerment, promoting engagement, and fostering a desire to effect change. In allowing children voices that are listened to, children's status is raised as they move toward realizing their participation rights and personhood.

Greg Mannion and John l'Anson conclude that notions of child and childhood are based firmly in adults' memories of what it was to be a child, and that "child and adult agency are interconnected."[47] However, if notions of childhood and child status depend on adults' memories of their own childhoods, given the current poor level of opportunities for child engagement and participation, it will be a long time before those with memories of full and active participation in society as children will be in a position to enact all of the CRC to allow children the right not only to protection and provision, but also to participation. By teaching children how to engage in dialogue and in facilitating that dialogue, an approach such as CoPI or P4C can increase the opportunity for children's voices to be heard.[48] The UN committee's report on the UK's provision for children's rights recognized aspects of initiatives for children such as the various youth parliaments, but these parliaments are far from engaging all children and are unlikely to include children from already disadvantaged groups.

It is easy to grant that children living in poverty should not have to do so, and that poverty threatens protection and provision rights. If the UK government has a will to end child poverty it can do so. It is harder, however, to address participation rights. It is all too easy to pay lip service to children's participation and voice, to allow tokenistic approaches, often for those already in positions of advantage socially, and to allow the voices to speak out without, as Lundy suggests,[49] either an audience or, more importantly, influence. There is no organized opposition to children's rights in the UK. However, the popular, or populist, press occasionally depict children's rights as nothing more than political correctness with the implication that things are going too far, that parents are losing their rights to parent as they see fit.

This attitude resonates with Farris's notion, in this volume, that according children greater rights by ratifying the convention would lead to a uniform model of parenting in all situations. Yet there is no suggestion in the convention that all children are the same, that they exist in the same social context, that they share common life experiences and life chances, and that the environments they inhabit are all identical. Certainly parents generally will not lose authority, but their authority ought sometimes to be questioned—by others as well as themselves. Attention should be directed to the power relations between parents and their children. Parents should be there to protect and provide for their children, materially and emotionally, in order that their children might engage more fully with their world.

In conclusion, we may ask whether the children's rights movement has advanced further in countries where the CRC has been ratified. In Scotland, the

Standards in Scottish Schools, etc., Act 2000 would not have happened without the CRC. Equally, the Children (Scotland) Act 1995 is fully informed by the convention, particularly in relation to family break-up. Previously, the adults' views rather than those of the children within the family were paramount. Now, with the presence of article 12, children's views are central when decisions are taken in relation to the family. As Katherine Covell and R. Brian Howe assert,[50] rights-respecting societies are likely to result only from rights-based approaches to law and policy making affecting children. In rights-respecting societies there would be no need to make special reference to rights-based approaches, since this would be the overall approach in the first place.

What is essential is that the convention has highlighted the role those in power, adults, have in fulfilling their responsibilities for children. The convention provides a clear framework for the provision of quality services for children and young people. Ratification of the convention facilitates public awareness raising and professional development. Without consciousness raising, without a framework with which to consider children's rights, disadvantaged and disempowered children will have lower status. Article 12 holds that children's views should be given "due weight," but only "according to the age and maturity of the child." This leaves unanswered questions surrounding competency and just what matters might affect the child, thus firmly maintaining power in the adult domain. Without status, children and young people have no voice, there is no one to hear them, indeed, no one need hear them, and their participation is not encouraged or even promoted. It is crucial that children and young people are seen as ends in themselves; that they are beings and not simply becomings.[51] Mark Drakeford, Jonathan Scourfield, Sally Holland, and Andrew Davies conclude that "children identify interaction as at the heart of their sense of their own place in the scheme of things, so their accounts of civic space are . . . dominated by images of debate, exchange and dialogue."[52] Without the CRC, children are socialized into a society that behaves towards them for their potential as future adults. In ratifying the convention, the United Kingdom has taken a step toward engaging children as participants in society while offering them the protection and provision that they are unable to offer themselves. Ratification, however, serves as an embarrassment to a society that lacks the political will both to adequately fund implementation of the convention and to support fuller participation by children in decision making affecting their lives.

Notes

1.   J. Williams, "Incorporating Children's Rights: The Divergence in Law and Policy." *Legal Studies* 27, no. 2 (2002): 261-87.

2.   I. Maclagan, "Making Rights Stick: Children's Rights Commissioner Work in Oxfordshire," *Support for Learning* 17, no. 2 (2002): 133-37.

3.   United Nations Committee on the Rights of the Child, *Concluding Observations: United Kingdom of Great Britain and Northern Ireland, Considerations of Reports Submitted by States Parties Under Article 44 of the Convention* (Geneva: Office of the United Nations High Commissioner for Human Rights, 2008). (Hereafter cited as CRC.)

4.   Ibid.

5.   Ibid.

6.   Ibid.

7.   Ibid.

8.   Ibid., 5.

9.   K. Covell and R. B. Howe, "Human Rights Education: Developmental Considerations," in this volume.

10.   The Curriculum Review Group, "A Curriculum for Excellence," *The Scottish Government Publications*, December 16, 2011 (Edinburgh: Scottish Executive, 2004), accessed March 16, 2009, http://www.scotland.gov.uk/Publications/2004/11/20178/45862.

11.   CRC, 16.

12.   Ibid., 15.

13.   Ibid., 16.

14.   Ibid., 7.

15.   Ibid., 19.

16.   Ibid., 19.

17.   Ibid., 17.

18.   "Improving the Lives of Children in Scotland—Are We There Yet?" in *The Scottish Government's Response to the 2008 Concluding Observations from the UN Committee on the Rights of the Child* (Edinburgh: Scottish Government, 2008), 44.

19.   CRC, 14.

20.   "Child Poverty: The Statistical Analysis of the Latest Poverty Statistics," *The Scotland Child Poverty Action Group (CPAG)* (2008), 11, accessed March 13, 2009, http://www.cpag.org.uk.

21.   Ibid.

22.   Ibid.

23. W. Stainton Rogers, "Promoting Better Childhoods: Constructions of Child Concern," in *An Introduction to Childhood Studies*, ed. M. J. Kehily (Maidenhead: Open University Press: 2004); A. B. Smith, "Children and Young People's Participation Rights in Education," *International Journal of Children's Rights* 15 (2007): 147-64.

24. L. Lundy, "'Voice' Is Not Enough: Conceptualising Article 12 of the United Nations Convention on the Rights of the Child," *British Educational Research Journal* 33, no. 6 (2007): 927–42.

25. A. L. James, "Children, the CRC, and Family Law in England and Wales," *Family Court Review* 46, no. 1 (2008): 54.

26. Ibid., 56.

27. M. Freeman, "The Future of Children's Rights," *Children and Society* 14 (2000): 277-93.

28. Ibid., 287.

29. R. Roose and M. Bouverne-de Bie, "Do Children Have Rights or Do Their Rights Have to Be Realised? The CRC as a Frame of Reference for Pedagogical Action," *Journal of Philosophy of Education* 41, no. 3 (2007): 431-43.

30. D. Devine, "Children's Citizenship and the Structuring of Adult-Child Relations in the Primary School," *Childhood* 9, no. 3 (2002): 303-20.

31. J. Qvortrup, "Are Children Subjects or a Liability?" *Childhood* 13, no. 4 (2006): 435-39.

32. Ibid. 435.

33. C. Cassidy, *Thinking Children* (London: Continuum, 2007).

34. C. Cassidy and S. Jessop, "Public Action, Public Voice, Public Children: Reconceptualising Children's Public Action," paper presented at the British Educational Research Association Conference, Edinburgh, September 2008.

35. C. Jenks, *Childhood* (London: Routledge, 1996); A. James, and A. Prout, eds., *Constructing and Reconstructing Childhood: Contemporary Issues in the Sociological Study of Childhood* (London: Falmer Press, 1997); A. James, C. Jenks C. and A. Prout, *Theorizing Childhood.* (Cambridge: Polity Press, 1998); Allison James and Adrian James, *Constructing Childhood: Theory, Policy and Social Practice* (New York: Palgrave Macmillan, 2004); C. Hallett, and A. Prout, eds., *Hearing the Voices of Children* (London: Falmer Press, 2003); Cassidy, *Thinking Children*.

36. A. L. James, Children, "The CRC, and Family Law in England and Wales," *Family Court Review* 46, no. 1 (2008): 56.

37. CRC, 8.

38. T. Dowty, "Pixie-Dust and Privacy: What's Happened to Children's Rights in England?" *Children and Society* 22, no. 5 (2008): 393-99.

39. Ibid., 397.

40. M. Griffiths, "Research for Social Justice: Empowerment and Voice," paper presented at Joint Glasgow/Strathclyde Research Group on Teacher Education and Teachers' Work Seminar, University of Glasgow, May 13, 2008.

41. Ibid. 7.

42. Cassidy, *Thinking Children*

43. C. McCall, *Stevenson Lectures on Citizenship* (Glasgow: Glasgow University Press, 1991); C. McCall, *Transforming Thinking* (London: Routledge, 2009); C. Cassidy "Child and Community of Philosophical Inquiry," *Childhood and Philosophy: Journal of the International Council of Philosophical Inquiry with Children* 2, no. 4 (2006), accessed May 28, 2010, www.filoeduc.org/childphilo/n4/ClaireCassidy.htm; Cassidy *Thinking Children*; C. Cassidy, "Philosophical Citizens—A Contradiction In Terms?" *Critical and Creative Thinking* 16, no. 2 (2008): 5-21.

44. M. Lipman, *Philosophy Goes to School* (Philadelphia: Temple University Press, 1988); M. Lipman, *Thinking in Education*, 2nd ed. (Cambridge: Cambridge University Press, 2003); M. J. Pardales and M. Girod, "Community of Inquiry: Its Past and Present Future" *Educational Philosophy and Theory* 38, no. 3 (2006): 299-309; M.-F. Daniel, "Learning to Philosophise: Positive Impacts and Conditions for Implementation. A Synthesis of 10 Years of Research (1995-2005)," *Thinking* 18, no. 4 (2008): 36-48.

45. Cassidy, *Thinking Children*.

46. McCall, *Stevenson Lectures on Citizenship*.

47. G. Mannion and J. I'Anson, "Beyond the Disneyesque: Children's Participation, Spatiality and Adult-Child Relations" *Childhood* 11, no. 3 (2004): 303-18.

48. Cassidy, "Child and Community."

49. Lundy, "'Voice' Is Not Enough."

50. Covell and Howe, "Human Rights Education."

51. Cassidy, *Thinking Children*.

52. M. Drakeford, J. Scourfield, S. Holland, and A. Davies, "Welsh Children's Views on Government and Participation," *Childhood* 16, no. 2 (2009): 247-64.

PART 3

CHILDREN'S RIGHTS IN THE DEVELOPING WORLD

Nine

Motivating Political Responsibility for Children in Poor Countries

☞ STEPHEN L. ESQUITH ☜

Article 12.1. States Parties shall assure to the child who is capable of forming his or her own views the right to express those views freely in all matters affecting the child, the views of the child being given due weight in accordance with the age and maturity of the child.

Article 29.1.d. States Parties agree that the education of the child shall be directed to the preparation of the child for responsible life in a free society, in the spirit of understanding, peace, tolerance, equality of sexes, and friendship among all peoples, ethnic, national and religious groups and persons of indigenous origin.

—United Nations Convention on the Rights of the Child

INTRODUCTION

More so than any of the other rights in the United Nations Convention on the Rights of the Child (CRC), the rights of participation, especially the right to form and freely express one's own views "in all matters affecting the child," depend upon a right to an education appropriate to "the preparation of the child for responsible life in a free society." When read together, articles 12 and 29 underline the importance of a democratic political education for all children.[1]

Who is responsible for providing democratic political education? The CRC assumes that "State Parties" have the primary responsibility for the realization of the rights of children under this treaty between nations. International and multilateral organizations have been involved from the very beginning in discussions of the rights of children, but the burden of the CRC has fallen most heavily on states to prepare their own children to participate in their own society and advance their own legitimate interests through a democratic political process.

In this essay I argue that there are other parties responsible for the democratic political education of children besides the state, nongovernmental organizations such as Save the Children, and multilaterial organizations such as UNICEF. These other parties are the individuals and institutions who benefit through their relationships with children in need in poor countries. Some are domestic and some are foreign. As sponsors of orphanages, agents of international adoption, and employers of household labor, individuals, and institutions, primarily but not exclusively from rich countries, incur a responsibility for the democratic political education of children in poor countries.

My argument for this responsibility is in two parts. First, I introduce two concepts of responsibility for the violation of children's rights: cause responsibility and benefit responsibility. Cause responsibility is the responsibility that perpetrators and collaborators have for the violation or unfulfillment of children's rights, particularly the use of child soldiers, the use of child labor, and the exploitation of children in sexual trafficking. Cause responsibility for these violations of children's rights has a moral and legal dimension, depending upon the severity of the harm and the particular causal connections between the antecedent acts or omissions and the harm done. It is sometimes national and sometimes cosmopolitan. Benefit responsibility is typically the responsibility of parties who do not occupy a place within the extended chain of cause and effect that defines moral guilt and legal liability.[2]

Benefit responsibility is political, and it belongs to parties who may unintentionally and sometimes unwittingly inherit or otherwise enjoy the subsequent benefits that accumulate from the violation or unfulfillment of the rights of others, including children. Benefit responsible parties may be the adoptive parents of adopted children, the institutions that facilitate these adoptions, or the employers of household workers and their children. The political responsibilities of these benefit responsible parties are not to renounce their adopted children or discharge child workers and their families, but rather to educate these children so that the children (and their children) are more able to exercise their rights under the CRC to participate in determining the course of their own lives.

The second part of the essay addresses the problem of how to motivate parties who are benefit responsible for the violation or unfulfillment of children's rights to recognize and act on these political responsibilities. The solution

I offer is neither Humean nor Kantian. That is, it is not a matter of cultivating a sympathy for children in need, nor is it a matter of sharpening one's rational understanding of cause responsibility. This type of political motivation is more effectively prompted by reenacting the violation or unfulfillment of children's rights so that benefit responsible parties can 1. see themselves within the frame of reference of a longer political story than an emergency rescue story such as those told by Peter Singer and Jeffrey D. Sachs,[3] and 2. imagine themselves playing a constructive role in the democratic political education of the children whose rights have been violated or left unfulfilled.

I will present two examples of this idea of deepening narrative reenactment, one that offers more promise than the other, as a way to motivate political responsibilities for the protection and fulfillment of children's political rights. There is nothing inherently democratic about reenactment, any more than simulations are inherently depoliticizing. However, the evolution of NGO pitches, using quick simulations of child suffering in eliciting donations, or other quick action relieving the conscience of comfortable viewers, does make their use as tools for democratic political education quite limited. Reenactments drawing viewers into the more dramatic situations in which children in the developiong world fall avoid some of the pitfalls of such simulations, although they can have problems of their own, as one of the examples I introduce illustrates.

Two Concepts of Responsibility

According to *New York Times* correspondent Jeffrey Gettleman, it is well known that Somalia's radical Islamist insurgents are plucking children off soccer fields and turning them into fighters.[4] But Awil is not a rebel. He is working for Somalia's transitional federal government, a critical piece of the American counterterrorism strategy in the Horn of Africa. According to Somali human rights groups and UN officials, the Somali government, which relies on assistance from the West to survive, is fielding hundreds of children or more on the front lines, some as young as nine.

Somali government officials concede that they have not done the proper vetting. Officials also revealed that the United States government was helping pay their soldiers, an arrangement American officials confirmed, raising the possibility that the wages for some of these child combatants may have come from American taxpayers. Like many other children here, the war has left Awil hard beyond his years. He loves cigarettes and is addicted to qat, a bitter leaf that, for the few hours he chews it each day, makes grim reality fade away. He was abandoned by parents who fled to Yemen, he said, and joined a militia when he was about seven. He now lives with other government soldiers in a dive of a house littered with cigarette boxes and smelly clothes. Awil does not know exactly how old he is. His commander says he is around twelve, but birth certificates are rare.

The United States and Somalia are the only two countries that have not ratified the CRC since its passage in 1989, although the United States has ratified the subsequent optional protocol prohibiting the use of children in armed conflict. In what sense, if any, are the American taxpayers Gettleman refers to responsible for this violation of children's rights? Similar questions could be raised about US government contributions to economic policies in many other poor countries that indirectly perpetuate the use of child labor and the denial of children's rights to equal educational opportunities. In what sense, if any, are American taxpayers, or American citizens more generally, responsible? For example, consider the possible effects of US government crop subsidies to American cotton farmers. These subsidies allow US growers to reduce the price they charge on the world market and thereby make it more difficult for cotton farmers in poor countries to compete with them unless the farmers in poor countries reduce their own labor costs (or introduce other cost-reduction measures). One way to reduce their labor costs is to use their own children as workers rather than allow them to continue in school. Are American taxpayers indirectly contributing to practices that violate the principles of child welfare that their own government affirms in their name?

One response to this question, articulated in detail by David Miller, is that indirect international contributions do not establish strong causal connections, and therefore cannot be the grounds for this kind of responsibility. These international contributions lack the requisite intentionality and proximity. Indirect contributions, especially international ones, are more complex and tenuous than domestic contributing factors.[5]

This argument for the priority of national responsibility holds that states like Somalia and their own citizens have primary responsibility for the violation of their own children's rights. For example, in some cases of forced labor, families respond to desperate domestic situations and sell their children to traders who put them to work elsewhere. Take the case of six-year-old Mark Kwadwo, a Ghanaian child sold into forced labor by his family, also profiled in the New York Times article.[6] Some West African families see child labor as a survival strategy. In a region where nearly two-thirds of the population lives on less than a dollar a day, the compensation for the temporary loss of a child keeps the rest of the family from going hungry. Some parents argue that their children are better off learning a trade than starving at home.[7]

As heartbreaking as the stories and images of Awil and Mark may be, according to the argument from national responsibility, domestic factors are more likely to contribute to the grim living conditions of these children than international factors. Furthermore, in a world in which national sovereignty is valued above cosmopolitan citizenship, appeals to national responsibility are more likely to have a remedial effect on problems such as these than attempts at international and regional coercion or persuasion.

I have stressed only one side of this debate. The case for global responsibility made by Thomas Pogge and Richard W. Miller, for example, can be equally persuasive when the issues involve trade in other commodities more directly linked to government corruption and worker exploitation.[8] (I will return later in this essay to Pogge's view in the context of the motivational problem.) However, whichever side one takes, the debate over cause responsibility until recently has overlooked a very different concept of responsibility for the violation of children's rights and human rights in general in poor countries. This is the concept of responsibility based upon benefits. Cause responsibility focuses our attention on the guilt or liability of perpetrators and collaborators. It has both a moral and a legal dimension. At one extreme are unrepentant perpetrators who are both morally and legally responsible for violating children's rights. These are typified by kidnappers who traffic in child soldiers and child labor. At another extreme are desperate parents who reluctantly entrust their children to seemingly responsible friends and relatives in hopes that the child at least will have adequate food and lodging. They may have failed morally as parents out of negligence, but it would be difficult to hold them legally liable for abuse. Like the American taxpayer who has contributed indirectly to the violation of children's rights, these desperate parents are morally implicated but not legally culpable.

In contrast to national and cosmopolitan cause responsibility, some forms of benefit responsibility are neither primarily a matter of moral guilt or legal liability. They occur after-the-fact of displacement and disenfranchisement, and they create a political responsibility that cannot be discharged the way that moral and legal cause responsibilities can. Compensation may mitigate some of the harm done, but making apologies or amends is not enough.

I say "some forms of benefit responsibility," because there are other forms of benefit responsibility that do entail moral and legal responsibilities, often very severe ones. The patrons of child prostitution, for example, benefit from this practice in a perverse sense and also create a market for its continuing practice. Some patrons are predators; others are lonely, confused, and convince themselves that they are rescuing children.[9] Both types of patron sometimes, but not always, are simultaneously cause responsible and benefit responsible for child prostitution. Like the drug user's demand for drugs, the patron's demand for child sex contributes to the violation of children's rights on the supply and the demand sides. However, neither the drug user nor the purchaser of child sex is benefit responsible in the political sense that I want to stress. In other words, the exploiters of Awil and Mark are morally and legally responsible in a causal sense. The patrons of child prostitution are morally and legally responsible in both an antecedent causal sense (contributing to the harm of a minor) and one particular benefit sense (creating a market demand for future harm to minors). The beneficiaries of the violation of children's rights I am particularly interested in are benefit responsible in a political sense.

What does this political benefit responsibility look like? I have alluded to displacement and disenfranchisement. What exactly do these terms mean in the context of children's participatory human rights? They do not own property or vote, so how can individuals and institutions benefit from their displacement the way dam companies benefit from the displacement of villagers and ruling elites benefit from the disenfranchisement of immigrant workers?

Let me begin with an analogy to a different kind of forced labor, the use of "leased convicts" in the United States. In a July 2001 article in the *Wall Street Journal* reporting on the entanglement of major US corporations with slave labor, Douglas A. Blackmon described the following case. On March 30, 1908, Green Cottenham was arrested by the Shelby County, Alabama sheriff and charged with vagrancy. After three days in the county jail, the 22-year-old African American was sentenced to an unspecified term of hard labor. The next day, he was handed over to a unit of US Steel Corporation and put to work with hundreds of other convicts in the notorious Pratt Mines complex on the outskirts of Birmingham. Four months later, he was still at the coal mines when tuberculosis killed him. Born two decades after the end of slavery in America, Green Cottenham died a slave in all but name.[10]

When Blackmon asked US Steel officials about such practices, they denied that they had occurred and then suggested that there is no reason to revisit these matters. For corporations that believe they are being responsible citizens now, historical injustices are not an issue. Nonetheless, corporations such as this (including many of their employees and stockholders) continue to enjoy benefits from these past unjust practices. They share institutional responsibilities to bring these benefits to light and create appropriate political methods for addressing them fairly.

This web of political responsibility can extend in surprising directions. In his subsequent book-length study of "industrial slavery" beginning in the mid-nineteenth century until 1945, Blackmon locates the Cottenham case alongside other similar stories, including his own family's use of forced labor. "I had no hand in the horrors perpetrated by John Pace or any of the other twentieth-century slave masters who terrorized American blacks for four generations. But it is nonetheless true that hundreds of millions of us spring from or benefit as a result of the lines of descent that abided those crimes and benefited from them."[11] While the beneficiaries of severe violence are often large corporations and other institutions, sometimes small business owners like Blackmon's family and even other immigrants, refugees, and displaced persons can be the reluctant beneficiaries of the unjust actions of others.

Is there a similar responsibility for the violation of children's rights for those who benefit from the trafficking of child soldiers? Gettleman challenges the American taxpayer: if you knew your money was going to support the use of child soldiers in Somalia, would you consent to it? The question is similar to the one posed by fair trade activists. If you knew that child labor was being used to produce the commodity you have purchased, would you still buy that commodity? This is not the question one should pose to the owners of stock in US Steel today. Divesting themselves of this stock or not buying products that use US Steel does not address the harm done to Green Cottenham and his descendants. It might be argued that some compensation or reparations is owed to these descendants, but the economics and mathematics of such a task have proved insurmountable when the time elapsed is so great.

If purchasing fair trade commodities does not point us in the right direction, are there other violations of children's rights that are analogous to the disenfranchisement of leased convicts? One is the case of support for orphans in poor countries. Another is the case of hiring children to do household labor in poor countries. A third is international adoption from poor countries to richer ones. The children in these cases do not literally lose their homes or their voting rights, but they are denied their right to a democratic political education as it is expressed in articles 12 and 29 of the CRC.

DONATING TO ORPHANAGES IN POOR COUNTRIES

Orphanages and the young, innocent children who live there are an obvious object of affection for tourists and other visitors to poor countries. In situations where street children seem to be at the mercy of unscrupulous adults who are all too ready to exploit them, orphanages present an apparently safe way for citizens of richer countries to provide aid and make a difference. Children who have been rescued from the street or their village to become orphans seem to feel the same way. Andrea Freidus relays the following images and comments from one such orphan in Malawi at an orphanage by the name of Miracles.

> Mphatso is a sixteen-year-old who has resided in Miracles for three years. In the first panel of her storyboard drawing about life in her village she in-

cluded a house without electricity or running water, and with a dirt floor. The drawing is a self-portrait. She explained that in that picture she is sad, her clothes are worn-out and she lacks food. Mphatso said she was abused by her stepmother and forced to work more than others in the house. The second panel is of Mphatso at the orphanage, appearing happy and well-dressed. She is smiling and stresses the importance of school—"I am go[ing] to school, very happy" is written under her picture. She explained, "[n] othing is missing at Miracles." Her drawing is similar to those made by her peers reflecting common vulnerabilities faced by children living in poverty.[12]

The benefits of aid to orphanages flow both ways. Recipients like Mphatso receive more regular schooling, more frequent meals, and adult supervision. Benefactors receive the satisfaction of knowing that even a small contribution will have an impact. The benefits to donors, while primarily psychological, are not negligible. In countries that struggle to make use of the foreign aid they do receive, private aid to orphanages stands out as a relative success story. What's not to like about it?

Freidus does not shy away from the costs of this kind of orphan rescue. Even in orphanages like Miracles that do not swoop down on unsuspecting families who think they are only boarding their children temporarily, there are costs to the orphans in terms of their relationship to their village, to their extended family, and to their culture in general. In the orphanage they may become more individualistic and possessive about the material goods that they have received through the orphanage. As satisfied as donors may be that they have rescued children from difficult circumstances, they also should recognize that the orphans themselves may pay a more long-term price for becoming orphans.

Donors who benefit psychologically from their contributions to orphanages like this tend to be more inclined to give to a program with a tangible institutional presence than support a more diffuse village kinship network. However, institutionalized care for orphans may create the very problem that it is designed to solve. Children who have lost one or both parents, but still have a kinship support system available to them, may be labeled orphans in order to provide new young residents for an orphanage in search of donors. Helen Meintjes and Sonja Giese have argued that with "orphanhood" in the case of South African children orphaned by the AIDS/HIV epidemic there has been this kind of ambiguity.

In some instances, children without biological parents adopt an identity as an orphan or get labeled that way by others. They replicate and recirculate a global notion because it has economic valence, while having to take on the derisive connotations that derive from local linguistic histories. This is a choice that provides them with one of very few opportunities to access material support. It is also a choice that enables characteristically underresourced children's support organizations to garner funding. In the process, orphanhood becomes a condition embedded with contradiction. It is a globally circulated commodity at the same time that it becomes an identity lived in struggle. It is a state that is both positive in its potential access to resources for children and their social networks and negative in its associations with failure of and rejection by social village networks.[13]

Benefit responsibility in this case, then, is the responsibility that donors have to recognize that the psychological benefits they enjoy from supporting orphanages may impose a cost on the very children they have tried to help. They are not exactly stockholders in US Steel, but they are stakeholders in an institution whose continuing effects may be more equivocal than the sense of satisfaction they receive from knowing they have rescued a few needy children. It is true that there is an element of cause responsibility in this case. As donors they may encourage unscrupulous people looking to sweep up needy children and label them orphans in order to make a profit. But, even in cases like Miracles, where donor demand for orphans is not creating orphanhood, the psychological benefits enjoyed by donors carries with it a separate benefit responsibility to mitigate the negative effects of institutionalization. Benefiting donors who have a stake in maintaining these legitimate orphanages have a responsibility to raise appropriate questions about the stigmatization and possessive individualism of orphans. Eroding the supportive kinship system that orphans appear to be inclined to renounce may unintentionally make it more difficult for needy children who are not institutionalized to make a life for themselves.

ADOPTING CHILDREN FROM POOR COUNTRIES

Consider a second case of benefit responsibility, international adoption. Like the case of orphanage donors, this is also a mixed case with an element of cause responsibility as well as benefit responsibility. Adoption has become the object of serious philosophical reflection in recent years, in part as a result of feminist and race theories of personal identity. Mixed race adoptions and adoptions by single-sex couples have cast some traditional metaphysical and epistemological questions in a new light. Adoption also has raised anew the moral status of children and their rights vis-á-vis parents and the state.[14] Much less has been said about international adoptions beyond some general concerns about its imperialist overtones and the unwillingness of adoptive parents to take the culture of their international adopted child very seriously.

I begin with the strong assumption that international adoptive parents enter the adoption relationship conceiving of themselves, not their adopted child, as the primary beneficiary of the adoption. Some adoptive parents certainly may be responding to a natural disaster or emergency when they adopt an abandoned or orphaned child from a poor country. But they will also view international adoption as a way of having (more) children of their own, expanding their own cultural horizons, and teaching tolerance to themselves and other members of their family. The combination of generosity toward a child in a poorer country, the desire to enrich culturally their own family, and in some cases the chance to have a child that they have not been able to have through the available means of reproduction makes it difficult to rule out benefit responsibility. In international adoptions, the adoptive parents do have a cause responsibility to the adopted child: they have taken them from their native culture and have a cause responsibility to make sure that this is a soft landing with opportunities to remain in contact with that native culture. Beyond that, what benefit responsibilities do the adoptive parents in rich countries have to their adopted children from poorer countries?

Again, the answer depends upon viewing these benefit responsibilities from a political rather than a moral or legal point of view. International adoption, like all adoptions, does not end with childhood or adolescence. There is a continuing long-term relationship between adoptive parents and their adopted children in which the benefit responsibility of the parent becomes increasingly important and takes on a more concrete political character as the child matures into an adult. It becomes, in short, a responsibility for democratic political education that extends beyond the formal education of the adopted child.

Pursuant to articles 12 and 29 of the CRC, there is a responsibility to teach the international adopted child how to express her own views about international adoption and familial responsibilities. This means introducing the child to other cultures, including her native culture, in an appropriately developmental manner. It means conversing with her in a respectful way about the dangers of discrimination and stigmatization that adopted children may face, and the particular biases and assumptions that people may have in her adopted country but also from her native country toward adopted children and adoptive parents. In some cultures, for example, there is an assumption that families will only adopt children who have been conceived through the husband's extramarital affair. In some cultures, international adoptions are viewed by the poorer native culture, especially its political elite, as a sign of failure to provide for its own children. Just as orphanhood carries a stigma in some native cultures, so too does international adoption. The inability of the international adopted child to speak her native language fluently and the fact that adoptive family may not practice her native customs (even if she herself has studied them) will create barriers between her and other children from her native country whom she may encounter.

As the beneficiaries of a tolerant multicultural family life that international adoption may afford, adoptive parents have a strong positive responsibility to teach themselves, other biological children, and their international adopted children about these obstacles to toleration and participation which international adopted children, immigrants, naturalized citizens, and refugees often face throughout their lives. These obstacles will arise in school, in social life, and in civil society in general.

EMPLOYING CHILDREN TO DO HOUSEHOLD LABOR IN POOR COUNTRIES

Children are often employed in poor countries to do menial housework, and it is the primary form of child labor for many young girls. Most child advocacy groups like Save the Children and Anti-Slavery International consider this a form of child slavery or indentured servitude. Child domestic workers are on call around the clock throughout the year. They are susceptible to arbitrary termination without pay and at risk of brutal corporal punishment.[15] Another interpretation, however, is that these relationships are more ambiguous and provide the children and their family a form of contact with middle-class families that serves as a social safety net of sorts. In this interpretation, the child laborer may be part of a rural family that is employed by a middle-class native family in the city to do the cooking, cleaning, and other routine chores. Sometimes these children attend school and receive special gifts from their employer that "mystify" the contractual agreement. In some cases, by the time they have reached adolescence, they are working full-time for their employer, but the relationship is not purely one of exploitation.[16]

I am interested in a variation on this phenomenon of child household work, the employment of young adults and adolescents by, for example, Western expatriates working temporarily in poor countries. What are the benefit responsibilities of these expatriates to the families of their household workers, especially the young and future children of these workers? This is not a topic on which I am aware much research has been done, although there are intervention programs in place that address the legal and educational needs of young girls working in these situations.[17] My remarks are based on my own limited experience. The benefits I list below are not surprising or extraordinary. The responsibilities that I believe are entailed by them are not moral supererogatory duties. They are part of the political geography that household workers and expatriate employers inhabit together.

One dilemma that the expatriate employer faces in the household labor market is how much salary to offer. Middle-class neighbors who also employ housekeepers and watchmen will resent expatriates who pay their household workers more than the going market rate. On the other hand, the household workers themselves realize that their chances of working for wealthier expatriates are limited, and they do not see their higher salary as affecting the overall wage rate for household workers. The labor market, from their perspective, is segmented. The result is often something in the middle: the expatriate pays more than the going rate but less than the expatriate can actually afford. This is the first benefit expatriates receive: low-cost household service that is typically much more than they can afford in their home country.

A related benefit is the reduced price for perishable goods and other household items that the household worker is able to bargain for in the market as the agent for the expatriate. Even though the household worker quickly is identified as an agent for an expatriate and therefore is charged somewhat higher prices in the market than other native consumers, these inflated prices are still lower than the prices the expatriate would get alone, assuming he or she had the time to go to the market.

A related benefit is information. Household workers provide important information about social networks, handymen, cooks for special occasions, and the like which the expatriate will need if he or she is living and working in the poor country for more than just a short visit. Door locks break regularly, plumbing must be repaired, bills may have to be paid by standing in long lines in the heat or rain, and all these things require the ability to negotiate in the native language about technical details. An experienced expatriate with near fluency in the native language can do this alone, assuming he or she has the time. But for most expatriates, the time and energy required to attend to these quotidian chores and fix these problems are prohibitive. Household workers either can do these chores themselves, and or find someone who can do them.

Finally, the expatriate benefits from the sheer stamina and physical strength that household workers have who are more accustomed to the climate and living conditions of their native country. Negotiating impassable streets by foot in the rainy season and enduring the direct rays of the sun for just short periods of time, let alone driving through heavy traffic, can be exhausting for the expatriate unfamiliar with the rules and contours of the road.

Now, what should be recognized is that this mutually beneficial relationship between household workers and expatriates is temporary and intermittent. There are more housekeepers, cooks, chauffeurs, and watchmen than there are positions for them with expatriate households. When the expatriate leaves, the household worker will return to the potentially more exploitative household labor described above, and this may involve their female children as well as themselves. In order to cushion this return to the lower segment of the household labor market with all its dangers and ambiguities, the household worker will try to establish a continuing relationship with the expatriate employer. The expatriate, on the other hand, may want to do more than temporarily raise the household worker's salary by helping the household worker invest and save for the future. This may involve setting some salary aside for future professional training or creating a small savings account to cover the school fees of the household worker's children once employment with the expatriate is over.

These small savings and investments are simple enough to imagine, but much more difficult to negotiate with the worker and implement. The household worker will have immediate family expenses for health care, funerals, transportation, and so on. To forego these things in order to take advantage of the expatriate's seeming largesse (for example, setting aside funds for secretarial training or funds for the school fees of the children of the household worker) requires that the household worker have a support system that she or he may not have. If the worker has left his or her village to seek employment in an urban area, it is often in order to send money home, not to save it. The worker may be the support system for others.

The benefit responsibility of these employer expatriates is to the family of their household worker, particularly future generations, not just the worker herself. The extended family and its future generations are the ones who will benefit from these modest savings and investment arrangements. But to meet this benefit responsibility, expatriates and the current household worker must engage in a difficult conversation about the sacrifices that may have to be made in current consumption in order follow through on savings and investment plans. In conversations like these both the expatriate and the household worker will have to confront some deeply held assumptions and an obvious power inequality. The expatriate will have to realize that savings and investment for education in poor countries are much more difficult and riskier than they are in richer countries. There are fewer assurances that the investments will pay off and immediate consumption can be foregone. The household worker will have to realize that despite the goodwill of the expatriate, future support for her savings and investment plans may decline. Once the expatriate has returned to home, he or she may not have the same level of disposable income to support these plans, or over time may lose the sense of closeness and responsibility for former household workers.

The inference that I draw from this is that to make support for savings and investment plans such as this sustainable, some kind of institutional structure has to be created beyond the charity of individual expatriate employers. Relying on a gift relationship between expatriate and household worker is not enough to provide greater educational and employment opportunities for future generations when there is so much uncertainty. In this far from perfect political conversation, the expatriate and the household worker must focus on the participation rights of future generations and the kind of education they will need to escape the poverty that forces them back into indentured housework, orphaning their children, or placing their children up for international adoption.

Two Ways to Motivate Benefit Responsibility

Thus far I have described three cases where benefit responsibility arises, and I have argued that this responsibility is political in a particular sense. It is a responsibility for democratic political education owed to children. Donors to orphanages in poor countries, parents adopting children from poor countries, and expatriates employing household workers in poor countries all may have some form of cause responsibility of a moral or legal nature. They should not contribute to orphanages that lift children out of kinship support systems and thereby create a need for more donations to more orphanages. That would be immoral. They should not adopt children from poor countries who have been taken from their biological families in haste or under false pretenses. That too would be immoral and possibly criminal. They should not use their power as employers to make coercive wage and benefit offers to household workers of any age contrary to the CRC and other international laws. However, these moral and legal prohibitions do not address the more ambitious provisions of the CRC dealing with the rights of children to participate in the formulation of their own successful life plans. Participatory rights are political rights; they depend upon compromise, deliberation, and fairness. Most of all they depend upon a democratic political education so that, as children mature, they are prepared to participate in this fashion. The three cases discussed above illustrate how as beneficiaries of their relationships with children and their parents in poor countries, citizens in and from rich countries incur a benefit responsibility for this kind of democratic political education.

However, arguments like this can only take us so far. Motivating political responsibility is more complicated than just making good arguments. In the second part of this essay I introduce the distinction between two ways of motivating political responsibility: *simulation* and *reenactment*. These two methods for motivating donors, parents, and employers to recognize and act on their responsibility for democratic political education have some things in common, but there is also an important difference. Reenactment has the potential to prompt a more democratic conception of political responsibility than simulation.

Hugh LaFollette and Larry May, following the eighteenth-century philosopher David Hume, have argued that bystanders have a shared moral responsibility to help chronically malnourished children, whether we are responsible for their suffering or not. Their argument is built upon an individual natural sentiment of sympathy for suffering children, which they extend in the following way. If you have sympathy for one child who is suffering because she is denied basic educational opportunities, they argue, then you should feel an analogous sympathetic responsibility to contribute to educational institutions that offer the best strategy for educating as many needy children as possible without making undue sacrifices of your own.[18]

Onora O'Neill believes arguments like this are not enough. As complicated as causal arguments about responsibility for suffering may be, they can and should be made (only) where injustices such as violence, coercion, and deception have occurred.[19] According to O'Neill, a cultivated Humean sympathy like the one LaFollette and May describe is not likely to be enough to motivate and guide institutional solutions to the chronic problems of adults who have been harmed in these ways. Two more rational duties exist: a strong duty (what Kant called a "perfect duty") not to condone, not to participate in, or otherwise support an unjust offer or policy complemented by the additional responsibility (what he called an "imperfect duty") of beneficence. This responsibility of beneficence is not merely the option to give charity, O'Neill stresses, even though it is also not a matter of legal obligation. Like "perfect duties" of justice, it rests upon a well-reasoned respect for individual autonomy and an analysis of the institutional causes of suffering.[20]

Thomas Pogge also favors this kind of argument for motivating cause responsibility over direct appeals to sympathy, charity, and beneficence. He rejects the idea that citizens in rich countries are bystanders to global poverty. On the contrary, he argues that they often are deeply implicated in global poverty through their participation in and through the benefits they derive from harmful global economic institutions and practices. The more they participate in and benefit from the current global economy, the more they perpetuate and aggravate global economic inequality.[21] But mere knowledge of the causal roles played by the international trading and borrowing privileges accorded by rich countries to authoritarian regimes will not be enough to make everyday bystanders take their political responsibilities more seriously. There are too many uncertainties about the relative weight of national and cosmopolitan cause responsibilities for this rational argument to motivate those who think of themselves as innocent bystanders.

Regardless of whether one prefers a Humean, Lockean, or Kantian explanation for the sentiments of justice and beneficence, LaFollette and May are correct that one purpose of all these philosophical theories is to motivate those who do have responsibilities for suffering and violence to recognize these responsibilities and begin to act upon them. Arguments for why cause responsibility has this motivational force have thus far proved insufficient.

SIMULATION

Consider a totally virtual refugee camp like one that has been sponsored by Médecins Sans Frontières. It consists in a series of images of a tour of a refugee camp in the place of an actual tour. In this virtual tour, watched from the comfort of your home, "you," led to adopt the standpoint of the refugees themselves, are asked questions like "Where will I live?" "Where will I find water?" "Where will I find food?"[22] Faced with wide-eyed and hungry children—but not so alien from us as to be covered with flies or bellies swollen—puzzled and sad, we immediately sympathize with them, and are ready to learn more.

Bystanders thousands of miles away can tour the camp and simulate what it is like to witness the hardships of internally displaced persons, exiles, and other refugees who are fleeing severe violence. Like other simulations, this one offers bystanders a way to better understand the plight of refugees and imaginatively test various strategies for helping them before the work of actually begins. As we click deeper into the hypertext, eventually we can "learn more about food aid," including how to get it and how much to get. The needs for nutritional balance can be quantified. Shipments can be estimated. Arrangements can be made. We are cautioned that we must not forget the refugees: "above all listen to their opinions and allow them to describe their needs."

Something very important has happened on this virtual tour. The simulation begins by addressing us abstractly as potential refugees ("Where will I live?" "What if I get sick?"). We are at that point encouraged to identify with parents desperate to find food for their hungry children. However, as we search for more detailed information, we discover that this is after all not about us, but about "them." We gradually come to be cast as representatives of agencies responsible for providing medicine, food, and clean water. We are there to help the refugees. We have identified and sympathized, and now we are asked to step back and help fix this problem.

A more interactive video game that also simulates life in a refugee camp is the MTV game *Darfur is Dying*. There is an attempt to lead the player toward greater activism and engagement, specifically with regard to the genocide in Darfur.[23] The first move is to choose a victim and then try to outrun the Janjaweed.

If "you" are a young girl, then you are quickly caught and probably raped. If you want, you can try again, only to be caught and raped again. When you do resign yourself to life in the refugee camp, it proves to be not much better. After glimpsing the fear and frustration that defines life in Darfur, you can watch an interview with a Darfurian who breaks down in tears. Finally, if you are finished impersonating the virtual characters in the game, you can take real action by sending a message to the president or your congressional representative. There are instructions for starting a divestment campaign on your own college campus or submitting a new game of your own to MTV. You also can play the games that were awarded runner-up prizes.

Darfur is Dying has received considerable publicity; however, as a video game it is not technically sophisticated. It is not so much a game as it is an interactive virtual experience of genocide. No matter which character you choose, you always end up suffering ignominiously. Consequently, *Darfur is Dying* is not likely to persuade those who do not already feel that they have an obligation to take action. It is more likely to offend by trivializing the suffering victims are facing in Sudan and nearby refugee camps. The Médecins Sans Frontières web site and others like it appeal more directly to sympathy, particularly sympathy for the individual child. Simulations trade on the apparent fact that the face of one suffering child is more likely to motivate a response by donors than the face of many,[24] even if the face makes them viscerally uncomfortable as the face of a child with cleft lip or palate does for many of the viewers of the media advertisements of Operation Smile.[25]

This is both the strength and weakness of simulations. They may evoke a powerful sympathetic response, but they also objectify the suffering children and situate the viewer on the outside looking in. Without more common ground between them, the only relationship available to the donor and the child is the apolitical relationship of emergency rescue.

REENACTMENT

Simulations like the ones I have described above are sophisticated training films. They are designed to prepare the viewer to respond efficiently and effectively to difficult situations, sometimes without warning.[26] The flight simulator remains the archetypical form of a simulation. The danger, of course, is that the algorithms built into the simulation condition a narrow-minded, arguably single-minded response that is not open to revision, let alone democratic deliberation. They are uncritically and sometimes unwittingly taken on faith, thereby creating what Sherry Turkle has called a depoliticizing "culture of simulation"[27]

The purpose of a dramatic reenactment is to create a political space for critical self-reflection and political dialogue. The emphasis in reenactment is not on speed, sympathy, and conditioned response, but rather is designed to slow things down so that assumptions (like the algorithms of the simulation) can be questioned. Reenactments can certainly shock their viewers with larger-than life-faces of suffering children. This is one way to free them from the assumptions they may be holding uncritically, at least initially. But if a reenactment is to prompt greater self-reflection on the political responsibilities which expatriate employers of household workers, international adoptive parents, and donors to orphanages in poor countries have for the democratic political education of children in these situations, it has to be more open textured than a training film whose goal is fiercely defined in advance, and it cannot rest content with the evocation of sympathy. A deeper connection or bond must be built.

To illustrate, let me compare two film reenactments of children caught in difficult situations not unlike the ones I have described more generally above. The first is the film *Holly* (2007),[28] about a young adolescent Cambodian girl, Holly, sold into prostitution by her economically desperate parents. Holly is befriended by an aimless American expatriate who takes it as his mission to rescue her from the clutches of a series of violent abusers and exploiters. The second film is *Cautiva* (2005),[29] the story of a fifteen-year-old Argentinean teenage girl, Cristina, who in 1994 is suddenly forced by the state to leave her adoptive parents on the grounds that they had illegally obtained her during the "Dirty War" in the mid-1970s when her parents were executed by the military junta. Neither film presents itself as a documentary, but the practices they dramatize are historically well documented. While *Cautiva* evokes a powerful feeling of sympathy for its main character, it is not as effective as *Holly* in building a more lasting bond between children like Holly and its viewers.

In *Cautiva*, Cristina gradually learns, through the help of a politically enlightened fellow student and the kindness of her surviving biological grandmother and aunt, that her adoptive parents were well aware of the fate of her biological parents and intentionally hid from her all of the facts of her adoption. When she confronts them with this, her adoptive father reacts violently and berates her for her political naiveté. She has no idea, he shouts, of the threat the country was under from communists like her biological parents. He and his wife not only rescued her from a personal life of ruin, but as a police officer he helped to rescue the country from the likes of her parents.

The judicial system surreptitiously removes Cristina from her middle-class adoptive parents and initially appears authoritarian, but it is her adoptive parents who gradually become the villains of the story as Cristina learns the truth. Is it fair, director Gaston Biraben asks, to force an adolescent to confront her true personal identity in order to correct the larger political record? The answer seems to be that you can have it both ways. Cristina learns to live with her true historical identity and Argentina can settle accounts with one of the more unsavory parts of its "Dirty War," the state-sanctioned kidnapping of the orphans of the disappeared.

In fact, the historical record is more complex. As efforts have been made to reunite surviving members of the biological families of the disappeared with orphaned children like Cristina, some children have chosen to remain with their adoptive parents and some adoptive parents have sought compromise arrangements with the surviving biological families.[30] *Cautiva* portrays this legacy of violence against children in a Manichean way and Cristina's political agency falls out of the picture. Instead of asking, pursuant to article 12.1 of the CRC, what role these orphaned adolescents—who are coming of age in a postauthoritarian democracy—should play in the creation of their society's collective political identity, *Cautiva* continues to treat them as wards of the state. The difference is that the state is now benevolent. There is no sense of responsibility to educate Cristina and her cohort so that they can play an active role in Argentine public life. The assumption of *Cautiva* is that if the children of the *desaparecidos* ("disappeared") are told the truth in a compassionate way, eventually they will return to their extended biological families and the nation will be whole.

What makes *Cautiva* unnerving initially is the shock that someone could grow up not realizing that the adults she thought were her biological parents actually had collaborated with the government that killed her parents. However, once this initial shock wears off, the story of rescue rings hollow. There is nothing left to talk about for viewers who might otherwise suspect that their own collective political identity has been built on fear—whether it is the fear of communism or more recently the fear of a worldwide terrorist network.

Holly, on the other hand, turns a story of rescue into a story of political coming of age. Where Cristina learns the political history of her family but does not become a more active political agent in her own life, director Guy Moshé takes Holly's story in a very different direction. Throughout the film, Holly's would-be rescuer, Patrick, repeatedly gets physically and emotionally too close to Holly for the viewer's comfort. Whether it is lifting her up from behind by the waist to pick fruit from a tree, resisting her explicit overtures to be his wife so he can take her with him back to the United States, or rinsing himself off in the shower after almost succumbing to his own carnal desire for her prepubescent body, the director does not shy away from pressing the viewer to confront Patrick's confusion and emotional immaturity. Patrick fails, somewhat melodramatically, and Holly is left to fend for herself, but the story is not only one of Holly's tragic fate. It is primarily a story about the misguided altruism of rescuers like Patrick and their complex mixed motives that they only dimly understand themselves. Saving Holly by "taking her back to the US" is a metonymic device for representing a variety of other seemingly less drastic forms of foreign adoption. The viewer, who initially wants Patrick to succeed, is gradually encouraged to question what other alternatives there should be for children like Holly in her native country. By indulging his own desire to "have" Holly, Patrick has only satisfied a transient and self-destructive desire of his own. He attacks one of Holly's attackers and is quickly taken into custody. By reenacting the rescue narrative rather than simulating a successful rescue mission, *Holly* prompts the viewer to go a little slower next time. The nongovernmental organization Red Light Children, which the film is affiliated with, provides opportunities for viewers to donate to educational and residential programs in-country for children like Holly.[31]

CONCLUSION

The moral and legal status of children's rights are no longer seriously in doubt. This does not mean that everyone agrees on exactly what they are. For example, the acceptance of the most recent optional protocols for the CRC that explicitly prohibit the use of child soldiers and the abuse of children through organized prostitution and pornography are heavily qualified country by country. However, whatever the reservations and qualifications about these protocols may be, they are still qualified acceptances. Similarly, whether children's rights are justified on the basis of human needs, interests, or liberties, their moral status in general is not in question. Childhood, as distinguished from adulthood, has its own moral imperatives and ends. In UNICEF's 20th anniversary edition of *The State of the World's Children*, the authors claim that "to fulfill the rights of children, it is imperative to protect childhood as a period that is separate from adulthood, to define a time in which children can grow, learn, play and develop."[32]

This same report, however, does not shy away from the gap between aspirations and achievement. The actual state of the world's children is still a matter of grave concern. Despite the progress that has been made since the United Nations Convention on the Rights of the Child, there isn't an area of the health, education, and welfare of the world's children that does not still require attention. In this context, it may seem misguided to emphasize the participatory rights of children when there are so many other grave unmet needs. The underlying assumption of this essay on the rights of children to a democratic political education is that without this participatory right for children and the motivation to realize it, the abuses and violence children like Holly and Cristina suffer will continue to afflict them and their children.

Notes

1. By political education, I mean an education in power and participation, not what modern political science calls political socialization or what liberal political theory describes in terms of an education for autonomy and tolerance. See S. L. Esquith, *Intimacy and Spectacle: Liberal Theory as Political Education* (Ithaca, NY: Cornell University Press, 1994). A democratic political education is an education in the dynamics of power and violence that prepares citizens to generate, hold, and distribute political power fairly and limit the effects of violence.

2. Benefit responsible parties are sometimes described as bystanders, but this is a complex term which I avoid using here despite its importance for the general notion of political responsibility. See S. L. Esquith, *The Political Responsibilities of Everyday Bystanders* (University Park, PA: Penn State University Press, 2010).

3. P. Singer, *The Life You Can Save: Acting Now to End World Poverty* (New York: Random House, 2009); and J. D. Sachs, *The End of Poverty: Economic Possibilities for Our Time* (New York: Penguin, 2005). Also see J. Rubenstein, "Distribution and Emergency," *Journal of Political Philosophy* 15 (2007): 296-320.

4. J. Gettleman, "Children Carry Guns for US Ally, Somalia," *New York Times*, June 13, 2010.

5. See D. Miller, *National Responsibility and Global Justice* (New York: Oxford University Press, 2008).

6. S. LaFraniere, "Africa's World of Forced Labor, in a Six-Year-Old's Eyes," *New York Times*, October 29, 2006.

7. T. Pogge, *World Poverty and Human Rights* (Malden, MA: Polity Press, 2002); and R. W. Miller, *Globalizing Justice: The Ethics of Poverty and Power* (Oxford: Oxford University Press, 2010).

8. D. Butt, "On Benefiting from Injustice," *Canadian Journal of Philosophy* 37, no. 1 (March 2007): 129-52.

9. For an interesting critical contrast of these two types of patrons see the film *Holly* (2007) produced by the K11 Project as part of its Redlight Children's Campaign, http://www.redlightchildren.org/films.php.

10. D. A. Blackmon, "From Alabama's Past, Capitalism and Racism in a Cruel Partnership," *Wall Street Journal*, July 16, 2001, A1. Also, see M. J. Mancini, *One Dies, Get Another: Convict Leasing in the American South, 1866-1928* (Columbia: University of South Carolina Press, 1996).

11. D. A. Blackmon, *Slavery by Another Name: The Re-Enslavement of Black Americans from the Civil War to World War II* (New York: Doubleday, 2008), 396.

12. A. Freidus, "Raising Malawi's Children: Unanticipated Outcomes Associated with Institutionalised Care," *Children & Society* 24, no. 4 (2010): 293-303.

13. H. Meintjes and S. Giese, "Spinning the Epidemic: The Making of Mythologies of Orphanhood in the Context of AIDS. *Childhood* 13 (2006): 407-30.

14. For example, S. Haslanger and C. Witt, eds., *Adoption Matters: Philosophical and Feminist Essays* (Ithaca, NY: Cornell University Press, 2005).

15. J. Blagbrough and E. Glynn, "Child Domestic Workers: Characteristics of the Modern Slave and Approaches to Ending Such Exploitation," *Childhood* 6 (1999): 51-56.

16. S. Wasiuzzaman and K. Wells, "Assembling Webs of Support: Child Domestic Workers in India," *Children & Society* 24, no. 4 (2010): 282-92.

17. For example, see the story of J. Dembelé ("Madame Urbaine"), who has developed an education program for young domestic workers, in T. Cappello, dir., *A Powerful Noise*, Unify Films in association with Crazy Legs Productions (2011), accessed December 20, 2011, http://apowerfulnoise.com.

18. H. LaFollette and L. May, "Suffer the Little Children," in *World Hunger and Morality*, ed. W. Aiken and H. LaFollette, 70-84 (New York: Prentice-Hall, 1996). On Hume's original conception of sympathy, see P. Mercer, *Sympathy and Ethics: A Study of the Relationship between Sympathy and Morality with Special Reference to Hume's Treatise* (Oxford: Clarendon Press, 1972).

19. O. O'Neill, "Ending World Hunger," in *Matters of Life and Death,* ed. T. Regan, 264 (New York: McGraw Hill, 1993).

20. O'Neill, "Ending World Hunger", 269. For O'Neill's discussion of imperfect obligations to children in particular, see her "Children's Rights and Children's Lives," *Ethics* 98, no. 3 (1988): 445-63.

21. Consistent with his emphasis on institutionally mediated causal responsibility, Pogge also has written that "with a better understanding of the role global institutional factors play in the persistence of severe poverty, many would take this problem much more seriously." "'Assisting' the global poor," in *The Ethics of Assistance: Morality and the Distant Needy*, ed. D. K. Chatterjee, 280 (New York: Cambridge University Press, 2004).

22. *A Refugee Camp in the Heart of the City*, Médecins Sans Frontières (MSF) Canada, accessed August 29, 2010, http://www.refugeecamp.org.

23. "In partnership with the Reebok Human Rights Foundation and the International Crisis Group, mtvU launched the Darfur Digital Activist Context, an unprecedented competition bringing together student technology and activism to help stop the genocide in Darfur . . . *Darfur is Dying* is a narrative-based simulation where the user from the perspective of a displaced Darfurian, nego-

tiates forces that threaten the survival of his or her refugee camp. It offers a faint glimpse of what it is like for the more than 2.5 million who have been internally displaced by the crisis in Sudan." *Darfur is Dying*, The Human Rights Foundation, The International Crisis Group, and mtvU, 2009, accessed December 20, 2011, http://www.darfurisdyiing.com/aboutgame.html

24. P. Slovic, "'If I look at the mass I will never act': Psychic Numbing and Genocide," *Judgment and Decision Making* 2 (2007): 3.

25. *Operation Smile*, access date December 20, 2011, http://www.operationsmile.org.

26. The distinction between simulations and reenactments is developed in more detail in Esquith, *The Political Responsibilities of Everyday Bystanders*, ch. 4.

27. S. Turkle, "Virtuality and Its Discontents: Searching for Community in Cyberspace," *The American Prospect* 7, no. 24 (1996): 50-57.

28. G. Moshe, dir., *Holly*, Priority Films, 2007.

29. G. Biraben, dir., *Cautiva*, Laemmle/Zeller Films, 2006.

30. L. Oren, "Righting Child Custody Wrongs: The Children of the 'Disappeared' in Argentina," *Harvard Human Rights Journal* 14 (Spring 2001).

31. A documentary film, *Red Light*, by G. Jacobson and A. Ezroni, Priority Films, 2010, provides the background for *Holly* and information for those interested in political lobbying on this issue. *Red Light the Movie*, accessed December 20, 2011, http://redlightthemovie.com/index.html

32. UNICEF, *The State of the World's Children Special Edition: Celebrating 20 Years of the Convention on the Rights of the Child* (New York: UNICEF, 2009), 2.

Ten

"The Right Child": Challenges and Opportunities of Child Rights Legislation in Theory and Practice

⌐ KRISJON OLSON ⌐

The United Nations Convention on the Rights of the Child (CRC) has been used by international aid agencies and the Guatemalan government to bolster community reconstruction following the armed conflict (1960-1996). Child rights discourse, with its particular logic of protection, is in tension with a postwar context where children are both the survivors and perpetrators of violence. An anthropological study, based on a decade of ethnographic fieldwork, demonstrates that, as young people have become a focal point for reconciliation and social reintegration, conflicting ideas of the "right child" emerge in contemporary Guatemala.

INTRODUCTION

The view that human beings have rights, simply because they are human, is one of the most common moral ideals in the world today. The idea of human rights creates an intricate web of people and places that seems to characterize late capitalism.[1] By closely examining the implementation of children's rights norms by humanitarian organizations and the embodiment of those ideals in a Guatemalan youth movement for peace I consider several questions.[2] What are rights, and on what basis do people claim or argue for them? What reasons have been offered for doubting or rejecting these claims? How are humanitarian interventions and human rights activism changing ideas about young people? These are questions I have asked ordinary people, children, donors, and activists in Guatemala.[3]

The armed conflict in Guatemala (1960-1996) is familiar to outside observers as a site of multiple conflicts. It is sometimes known as a conflagration of Cold War politics, a dirty war against a rebellious populous.[4] The violence has also been variously categorized as "ethnic warfare" with shifting claims on Mayanist liberation.[5] What most scholars agree upon is that the course of the war inflicted massive violence upon the Guatemalan people, with as many as a quarter of the nation's population displaced and hundreds of thousands killed.[6] In a conflict that spanned thirty-six years, war enveloped the lives of nearly all those who remained. Following the signing of the Peace Accords in 1996, the vulnerability of life itself came to the forefront of this protracted conflict as local people failed to reap the benefits of social reform. Citizens, young people, and activists raised questions about how to end enduring violence, transform a buckling social and economic infrastructure, and rein in political corruption.

Today, according to the most recent United Nations report, Guatemala has one of the highest infant mortality rates and the lowest life expectancies at birth of any country of the Americas. In spite of its being the largest economy in Central America, deep inequality and social stratification are often singled out as most significant to understanding Guatemala's ongoing poverty and entrenched racism. At the same time there is continuing impunity for those who engaged in genocide, torture, forced disappearances, and extrajudicial executions during the war. It is the issue of ongoing violence that saturates everyday conversations. Local newspapers chronicle the bodies that have piled up on the streets and crime that touches every corner of the country as the homicide rate has doubled since the signing of the Peace Accords in 1996. Most observers agree that such violence is not attributable to any single factor.[7] But many peace workers argue that a lack of educational and professional opportunities make young people prone to violence and children have become a focal point of local, national, and international humanitarian interventions.

Since the decades of war in Guatemala have officially come to a close, a proliferation of international and local nongovernmental organizations has engaged in humanitarian work to secure children's rights and create a movement for social reform for and by young people. Reconstruction and reintegration take place through an intricate network of education, medical care, and community participation. The involvement of young people, who were both innocent and under fire during the conflict, is seen as key to securing human rights and postwar reconciliation. While the armed conflict has formally ceased, the fear of war is a way of life in Guatemala.[8]

I shall describe how the CRC is employed by international aid agencies and the Guatemalan government to reconstruct communities in crisis. The youth movement carries a range of political and material meanings that continually alter the Guatemalan landscape. International child rights instruments recast power and everyday practices as young people and peace workers use these new legal instruments and humanitarian interventions for their own purposes. This anthropological study, based on a decade of ethnographic fieldwork in the western highlands of Guatemala, demonstrates how conflicting ideas of the "right child" emerge in contemporary Guatemala. Here I trace the establishment of one nongovernmental association, called Apoyo, for the protection, education, and social welfare of children and examine its impact on the Ixil area of Nebaj. This influential association is part of a major philanthropic venture in The Hague to improve the well being of young people in adverse circumstances, a prevailing strategy to redress the impact of genocide. While the "right child" is inflected with global legal orthodoxy, it also surfaces through the practices of local organizations, donors, peace workers, and children themselves.

A FOREIGN ELEMENT: TRANSNATIONAL CONFIGURATIONS OF CHILDREN'S RIGHTS

In 1991, interested in reinvesting in Guatemala as the first refugees returned from Mexico, Marcel Mastenbroek[9] of the de Jong Foundation contracted a local medical doctor to study organizations working with children and identify new partners in the region. The first visit, by the foundation director, was to the country office of the United Nations Children's Emergency Fund (UNICEF) that was financing supplementary feeding stations, malaria reduction initiatives, and a large urban services program, all directed at increasing child survival[10] in the midst of the armed conflict. A Dutch expatriate working in the UNICEF office pointed Marcel to a program for the comprehensive care of children in the mountainous northwest of the country which was implemented by the French organization, Children Refugees of the World (CRW). She offered to provide Marcel with a UN vehicle to visit the area, which at that time was nearly sixteen hours by road from the capital city. He was escorted by a French woman named Dianne, who had worked in the Ixil area since 1986.

Dianne is a chain smoker, talkative, and introduced Marcel to young people caught between present and future violence in their own hometown. At least sixty percent of the returned refugees in Guatemala were children, some 20,000 are believed to have participated in army civil patrol units, and children represent one in three of the bodies exhumed from mass graves.[11] At that time the Ixil area had already endured more than 100 massacres, and was in the midst of resurgent violence.[12] Children Refugees aimed to address this war on childhood with the guiding principle that "a child who does not play dies." In her seminal volume, *Children and the Politics of Culture*, Sharon Stephens notes that the domain of play, the absence or presence of it, is central to most notions of childhood. She writes, "We might see play as active exploration of imagined environments, built up in spaces of existing social life. In this light, play is the ground of a notion of culture as living resource, rather than objectified project."[13] The French organization attempted to recover a space of play, exercised with some degree of safety and adult guidance, as a protective mechanism, by pairing groups of children under the age of seven with outgoing young Ixiles "to preserve and recapture the Mayan Ixil culture, and to validate it," explained Dianne. Mr. Claudio, who became the team coordinator in 1995, describes a preservation of values based on suffering over a lifetime: "The region in which the Ixil people live suffered most from the armed conflict that continued in Guatemala for so many years. Here it generated great violence and uncounted deaths. . . . [D]espite so much suffering, the Ixil people have jealously preserved their culture and its values. We wanted to develop innovative approaches to early childhood education, and ways for children to play, drawn from this culture."

The suggestion that "a child who does not play dies" is tied up in contemporary concerns about the loss of cooperation and imagination in late capitalism. Advocacy on behalf of endangered young Ixiles, the centrality of their play to peace, rests on the presumption that childhood must be attended to as a space of sanctuary.

Reflecting on that first trip more than a decade later Marcel recounted to me:

> Frankly there was not much of a plan for Guatemala, there was no country study. It was anybody's best guess what was happening to children in remote parts of the country, where the violence was overcoming life. I found it a very interesting project [in the Ixil area], and because of my information from UNICEF about the difficult situation at the time I realized that it didn't make much sense to work through the government. I realized that it wouldn't be bad to work with an international NGO. At that time, it was too dangerous for local, Guatemalan agencies to be active in the region as they could become targets either for the military or the guerrilla groups. It was what we could handle, without a real survey of the country. We have always said we should work now with the international agency, but move to a direct relationship with a local counterpart. It was more or less a coincidence though, coming into contact with Children Refugees of the World. It was fortuitous that it lined up with some of the priorities we have on indigenous children, marginalized and all of that. Ever since then

it comprises a large part of the portfolio. I've never visited their programs outside of Guatemala, but I do know that it spans the globe.

In 1993 Children Refugees submitted a substantial request for support from the foundation, titled *Indigenous Displaced Children,* for a period of three years, which was approved the following year.

The 75-page project proposal details how in the mid-1980s there was pressure on the international community to intervene on behalf of the communities most affected by the internecine conflict.[14] In 1986 Children Refugees constituted the first large-scale intervention in the Ixil area, designed to develop an integral approach to the problems faced by children in the midst of a war against the civilian population. At its inception the project was a large emergency operation with expatriate and local staff. European professionals and Ixil peace workers occupied several houses in the town of Nebaj, extending the terrain of their work each year. Initially there were three components: medical care, education, and community mental health. Within these broad categories five pilot projects were initiated that involved traditional midwives, rural health workers, preschool education, child centered health, and community youth centers. The application submitted to the foundation describes fourteen teams including French doctors, Spanish educators, community animators, and Ixil staff. These groups would implement short-, medium-, and long-term projects "developing a vocation for humanitarian attention to the comprehensive needs of the child not only through reflection, but by direct action" toward the well-being of between 600,000 and one million orphaned youth and displaced children.[15] A diagram annexed to the proposal describes a complex distribution of responsibilities between an "expatriate team" and "local promoters" that organized matters of solidarity and collective interests for the office in Guatemala. What can be drawn from this account of humanitarianism in the Ixil area relates, beyond moral intentions, the ways in which humanitarian work itself is transformative in unexpected ways.

The typewritten observations of one expatriate staff member, written after the completion of the first year of the pilot project, are worth noting: "It would have been desirable, seen from here [in Nebaj], to have had the opportunity to start the project after this first year. We could have dedicated ourselves more to observation, would have had direct contact with the problems and been able to know the community in more depth." His 17-page report recounts military control in the communities, financial difficulties, and his own ideological struggles.

> I have never been clear about what our countries would be capable of doing in favor of development. It is easy, more comfortable really, to have a leftist ideology in a society of capitalist robes, when vital individual compromises

are given to the demand of the circumstances. To struggle against the tendency of the majority is complicated; it presupposes that we renounce our
customary equilibrium. It would seem easier in a communist country, but
quite to the contrary it takes work to deny the privileges that keep us on
the other side of the line. To think, on the global level, that our countries
can escape this contradiction through international help and cooperation
seems to me an illusion.

Something unusual emerges from the state of destruction from which
the man finds himself reporting: "If we had understood well the military control of the community, it would have hardly made us more judicious from the
start." His notions of voluntarism are wounded by the immediacy of war. The
infinite scope of his responsibility for others is all consuming because concern
alone cannot eliminate suffering. The work of Emmanuel Levinas locates the
ethical primacy of this altruism and responsibility in our encounter with the
suffering of others. This "face-to-face" relation is a fact of consciousness that
commands responsibility toward the other. In *Entre Nous*, Levinas writes: "To
envisage suffering, as I have just attempted to do, in the inter-human perspective–that is, as meaningful in me, useless in the Other—does not consist
in adopting a relative point of view, but in restoring it to the dimensions of
meaning outside of which the immanent and savage concreteness of evil in a
consciousness is but an abstraction."[16] Drawing on the work of Levinas, Nancy
Scheper-Hughes writes, in *Death without Weeping*, "Accountability, answerabil-
ity to 'the other'—the ethical as I am defining it here—is 'precultural' in that
human existence always presupposes the presence of another. That I have been
'thrown' into human existence at all presupposes a given, moral relationship."
The backdrop to suffering in this case is one of disastrous dependency where
poverty provides the competitive advantage in the economies of international
aid.[17] The work of reaching children subjugated by violence involves an appeal
to ethical universalism. Such sentiments can be traced over Children Refugees'
first decade of work in Guatemala.

Many of the expatriate staff, like Dianne, are "sentimental about rights."
They take pride in their proximity to suffering; it is nearly elegant, and they
venerate it. Even a woman like Dianne, who is ready to lay bare human despair,
often speaks with emotion about it:

> Our intention here is that we, strangers in Ixil country, have tried to recover
> the wave of the memory, the best, the wisest, and most profound of what
> still remains for children. Such is the memory of the Mayan peoples [*pueblo
> maya*]; it has never been extinguished. It is for this reason that we, strangers
> in the Ixil country, have permitted ourselves the task of recopying, joining,
> and distilling the wise memory of the ancestors to soothe the suffering of the

young. So that today, the hearts and minds of children know how to play, sing, and dramatize this memory left for generations that will never die.

This is what Dianne told me the first time we met. It was during the rainy season in 1998, during a meeting between Marcel and Dianne. The foundation had just approved a three-year renewal for the Indigenous Displaced Children Project in the Ixil area. This brought the total investment by the foundation, over six years, to nearly one million dollars. In an area where the municipal budget for the entire region was less than $300,000 per year, and the daily wage for an agricultural worker falls under one dollar, this represented both a hefty sum and more than 100 lucrative jobs. Children Refugees had extended its work to twenty-two different communities in the region with financing from the European Union, the UN, and the de Jong Foundation. At their Ixil headquarters was a large map painted over wood, marking out their domain of intervention in school buildings, community health centers, six libraries, textile cooperatives, and a veterinary clinic. It hung next to a white board that detailed the schedule of the "expatriate team" and the "local team" for each day of the week. The three of us sat in the courtyard that spans the width of Children Refugees office as I learned about the relationships of patronage and collaboration that were quick drawn in the program. Our discussion went late into the night, with both Marcel and Dianne taking puffs of cigarettes and short gulps of instant coffee. In the dark she explained the two-fold ethic of humanitarianism, at once collectivist and hierarchical, marked by claim and obligation.

CONTESTED EXPERTISE: RIGHTS CLAIMS AND OBLIGATIONS

"You have to understand a man like Mr. Claudio if you want to understand the problem of rights here," said Dianne to me one day. Mr. Claudio is a middle-aged Cakchiquel man who had come to work on the "local" team of Children Refugees five years earlier. He is from Patzún, a town distant from the Ixil area. Dianne continued:

> What he recognizes is that Children Refugees is the roof that covers everything here. Those are his words. It is under our roof that he has become an expert. He has become an expert on the psychology of Ixil children with knowledge about culture and cultural repair. Working here he began to understand that this is not a simple task of poverty alleviation. And yet he is convinced that Ixil people alone must promote and defend their own culture, decide what they want in this world. The reality is that we do not know how the Ixil people can think about rights in the midst of violence. I have nothing against Claudio, he is a good person. It is the men of his background, people who hold his isolationist values, that will be the beginning and end of rights in this place. But even he cannot deny that we give them a roof.

Among the staff of Children Refugees Mr. Claudio had become a touch-stone for controversy. When he first arrived, as a professional educator, he acted as a moral compass for many of the peace workers on the team. Central components of traditional development work and child rights instruments, such as participation and empowerment, seemed strange until Mr. Claudio proffered them up as lessons on Ixil character and marked them with idioms of familiar expression. He would often say in meetings that Ixiles had to "live their name." The word Ixil is thought to come from the phrase "carrier of pots," from the time when clay vessels made in the area were used cooking and carrying water. The fabrication and sale of clay pottery were the origins of commerce in the region. In Ixil, *Ij* means to carry or carrier. *Xhiil* is translated as pot or pots. Thus *Ij-Xhiil* referred to people who carried pots to and from the market.[18] Mr. Claudio suggested that Ixil people should now "carry development as a marker of who you are." His became a language of humanitarian ethics, a new code for conducting oneself in relationship to the prevailing moral discourse of peace. He provided a way to grapple with the presence of the past and the uncertain promise of peace. The idea that it was their obligation to carry the development of their community seemed sensible to most members of the team. The notion that their work with children, on the other hand, held any kind of redemption was somewhat suspicious. What claim could children make on progress? Development was understood as an achievement, not something protected by law. It was difficult to imagine that children could make claims on the future of the Ixil area.

The distinction between claim and obligation became clear as Mr. Claudio began to advocate for two young people from Nebaj to take over jobs occupied by French and Italian expatriates. Although both had been previously employed as Ixil peace workers, Santos was a sober young fellow who left his job teaching in a rural village to join the office for the Displaced Indigenous Children Project. In his work he focused primarily on community mobilization, marshalling the interest and support of parents to build school properties and cook snacks for their children. By contrast, Maco had spent his years in the same program focused on children's rights to identity, recreation, and freedom. When the two men put forward their candidacy to lead a new Ixil organization within Children Refugees their fellow peace workers responded favorably to Santos but shunned Maco, who was said to "want nothing but the emancipation of children." From that time forward Santos was known in town as "the little dictator" powerful enough to overcome foreign influence "and impose a new kind of thinking on the French."

Dianne, who eventually left the Guatemalan office to head up Children Refugees in Paris, describes an ethics based on proximate relations with others that is an umbrella for a sort of universal humanity. For her, a foreign element was essential antidote to the "problem of rights." Our conversation was no coincidence. Marcel had conditioned the renewal of the Indigenous Displaced Children Project by the foundation on the phased withdrawal of all French staff from the Children Refugees offices in Guatemala and the creation of a local association within the program "to build up local capacity of young indigenous Guatemalans that can, in a scheduled way, assume full responsibility for the activities in their community." For Dianne this meant the loss of both a significant source of revenue and a program that she had built over the course of her career. Children Refugees is a French nonprofit and 75 percent of its funding comes from the public sector of the French Ministry for Exterior Relations and the European Union. The condition of this financial arrangement is that Children Refugees must cover 25 percent of its budget with through other financial streams, like grants from the de Jong Foundation. Her quandary highlights the immediate and distant consequences of the humanitarian enterprise, detachment with intimate effects on work for social change. For Marcel this designation would occupy him for more than a decade of his career, as Ixil people began to reinvent childhood. Years later in an interview with me at the foundation, Marcel reflected on the decision to condition his support of Children Refugees in this way.

> What I have experienced through the years with Children Refugees—they always have this foreign element when you go to Guatemala. There is always someone who is foreign. I find the presence very dominant, not only in terms of being representative of a French organization but also in terms of their thinking for the program. The way things are presented can be a form of lecturing, consciousness raising, which is negative. I don't think they do it intentionally, but it has something to do with the French culture and the French way of doing things. It is very outspoken way of understanding people and things. It is as if their doctrine is the best, and the only one that really serves a purpose. That is why I have always insisted on creating an organization in Guatemala. I wonder if there is too much bias to understand what is really going on—it is very much a focus on the individual child. What kind of process is taking place here? Children Refugees is both a funder and implements projects. So it is different from us—there is a different relationship of being involved directly in day-to-day activities that are carried out by people in the community.

Foreignness for Children Refugees constituted a social tactic, a mode of operation. And now, in Nebaj, it has become routine practice. One local government official, who continues to work in close coordination with the Indigenous Displaced Children Project, explained, "They [the expatriate staff] arrived and were strange in some way. We hardly knew what it was they intended to do. But they worked, and went on in conversation, when we were accustomed to silence. And now, there are so many organizations in our town, who knows what they do. They ask for letters, support, and participation. They demand it, and we hardly know what it is they do. Who knows if it is good or bad?" What can be familiar, and what is marked as foreign, surfaced across the town as an early childhood education program initiated by French relief workers became a social movement.

A MODEL CHILD: THE UN CONVENTION IN PRACTICE

At the time of my first meeting with Dianne and Marcel I was working on a national campaign to change the laws protecting Guatemalan children. It was my task, and no easy one, to raise awareness around the obligations inscribed in the CRC, which had been approved by the Guatemalan Congress in 1990. The Children Refugees programs had been repeatedly recognized[19] as a paradigm for "successful and culturally appropriate interventions with young people" because the organization encouraged children to live and develop their full potential. The passage of the CRC in the late eighties drew attention to the impact of armed conflict on children,[20] and initiatives such as the Indigenous Displaced Children Project became multilateral funding priorities for international agencies. New monies became available to mitigate the effects of warfare on children. As one staff member explained:

> We began a psychosocial support program because there was money available. The resources were available, you know, because we are victims of the war. And people were concerned about the mental state of the children. We hardly knew what it meant, but we went ahead. It was like there was a model for what it meant to be a child. Our program was supposed to reform the minds of children, to repair them in the image of themselves. It hardly matters, so long as the interim report has the right jargon.

Over the years the Indigenous Displaced Children's Project was involved in a number of efforts to promote the rights of children in the Ixil area. At the time Children Refugees was best known for its implementation of an early childhood education program for children three to six years of age. Young Ixil men and women were trained by French and Spanish *animateurs* to teach children about hygiene, self-expression, and Ixil and Spanish language and to foster play in preschool centers. The organization justified this intervention on the basis of the CRC, citing article 2 (nondiscrimination), article 24 (health care), article 28 (education), article 29 (aims of education), article 30 (children of minorities or indigenous populations), and article 31 (leisure, recreation, and cultural activities)—a convention to which the Guatemalan government was the sixth signatory. It found further legal backing for its work in a policy put forth by the Guatemalan Ministry of Education as a part of the peace agreement which obliges the state to "attend to groups that have traditionally been marginalized or excluded from educational services . . . especially monolingual populations, women and children with learning problems, street children, migrants, refugees and the displaced."[21] As a part of its ongoing work, Children Refugees sought to identify and draw attention to violations of these rights and generate public awareness about the issues of indigenous children living in poor rural areas of Guatemala that comprise well over half of the country's population. During a push to gain local support for the 1996 Code for Children, which would have done away with the 1979 Code for Minors that criminalized "irregular conduct" and did not differentiate between juvenile delinquents and children who are endangered, impoverished, or abandoned, Children Refugees held a number of workshops in the rectory of the Catholic church. Dianne invited me to attend.

In the meeting hall rows of chairs had been set up around the model of an early childhood education center. There were books lining one wall, with a row of cups and toothbrushes on another, and a reading area with grass mats covered the floor. In one corner a group of children was using finger paints to make pictures of animals that a teacher named first in Ixil, then in Spanish. Another corner was filled with a group of boys playing the marimba. A girl carried small pieces of wood toward a makeshift fire where a woman stirred a pot. When I arrived Santos explained to me, pointing toward the girl, "This is a model child, it is our idea of education for our people." Above the reproduction of the preschool area hanged a banner which said, "A New Vision of Rights, Childhood with our Values." The gathering started in the same way in which most in the town of Nebaj do, with formal introductions and expressions of gratitude on the part of participants. During this time a young woman, named Juana, sat next to me. She had been sent as a representative of The Organization of Displaced Peoples in North Quiche, who paid for her transportation, meals, and attendance at the meeting. As the meeting began she whispered to me, "You know it well, in this town human rights are an office. Nothing more than that. It is a simple building with a placard. There are no values there. Rights, we are tired of hearing about them and never having any. The real value we have as humans is what we can create for ourselves." The children's rights workshop reinvented quotidian activities as rights. Over the course of the day it became clear that through their participation in the Displaced Indigenous Children's Project, Ixil people began a complex exploration of the rights, responsibilities, and limitations of childhood in Guatemala.

A man named Miguel, who had worked for the project since its inception, described his experience building the Displaced Indigenous Children's Project as a way to live in tumultuous times. He spoke to the audience with a hat tipped forward on his head. He looked at his knees, occasionally looking up at the room filled with onlookers.

> I am Miguel Ramírez Gomez, and I was born in the village of Xeucalvitz, Nebaj in 1964. I am Ixil. I began to study at the age of twelve, but after the third grade I left to work as an agriculturalist. I continued studying by correspondence until the conflict gained strength, and I left my studies once again. They said that those of us who lived in rural areas were organized by the guerrilla, so the army came and burned all of the houses, the crops. They killed children, old people, women. My mother, they killed her for just walking on the hillside. On the 27 May 1985 the army came and killed twenty-six people of all ages: men, women, children, young and old. We opened up the earth and buried them together. In 1988 the violence was worse, they destroyed our bridges and said that we were part of something called the Communities of Populations in Resistance. We couldn't take it any more and we decided to come back here to town. There were thirty families. Since we couldn't all remain together, they separated us. We were seven, together with my wife and five children, living under a roof made of plastic in Las Violetas. There was no firewood, no land, there was nothing. That is when I realized that Children Refugees was building a preschool, and I asked to do the wood work. Then the organization sent me to teach women to plant tubers, a women's project. We had been living in Las Violetas for one year and we wanted to return to our village, but the army would not give us permission. Instead they took us to practice shooting blanks, and when we learned they gave us a rifle. Finally they authorized us to return to the community and form civil patrol units. When we returned to Xeucalvitz we worked the land. But we realized that our children were not cultivated. Together with my brother we decided that we should cultivate our children in the same way that we cared for our land. We asked for help from Children Refugees because they had the model. With the community we built a school with a roof of plastic and began to take care of the children. Later we went to ask for help in the Catholic church, but later they got rid of us because they said that the children sung songs that weren't Christian. Eventually teachers from the Ministry of Education returned to the village but they would only accept children that spoke Spanish.
>
> From 1992 to 1996 the violence had lessened, but we still patrolled the community. We had thirty rifles and we took turns. But the war was sad, the people of the village divided between the guerrilla and the Army. I didn't take sides, but I had to take part in the civil patrols. For me this was a very bitter experience, to know that the conflict existed because of injustice and inequality. These qualities were within us, and had become the values of our children too. This is how it went until the peace was signed in 1996. It was at that time we resolved to find a resolution to our problems and change our children. We carried the bricks for the school on our shoulders, bricks

we found any way we could. It was when Children Refugees and the Fund for Peace began to help us that we began to see that we could make things right, for our children and community.

Here the education of children is directly linked to experiences of war and displacement and the possibility for social change in the postwar period. The provision of emergency relief in the form of education and medical and food supplies is one of the most prominent justifications for children's rights in the Ixil. In the first instance humanitarian intervention provides for the possibility of employment. As part of the peace process community members are persuaded to transform their children into different kind of people. Community members in attendance at the workshop were told that it was the right of their children to play, to have freedom and liberty of expression. Any sort of activity, in the hands of a professional, can overcome violence: washing hands, brushing teeth, parades, weaving, and gardening all have life-affirming properties that advance peace. The process of promoting and defending children's rights takes place through physical, affective, and sociocultural change that ultimately allows "the true child to emerge," workshop facilitators explained.

Dianne interjects:

> The possibility for play that you see here today comes to us from the distant past. It is universal, existing in every part of the world, always. In the *Popul Vuh* they tell how children managed to escape persecution by the men from Xibalbá thanks to their music, their masks, and their ability to play. In this way we think that for children caught up in every war, all kinds of expressive play is the surest way to oppose the most desperate situations. It is from this premise that we have started to work with the children.

In postwar Guatemala, a bevy of vigilant nongovernmental organizations have led parents to measure their children with a global yard stick. The rhetoric of the "right child" in Miguel's story betrays both a desire for change and its impossibility. In the Ixil area rights are often understood only in their violation, as matters of violence. The right child, a new promise in the community, is a source of character to be cultivated like the corn fields once the peace comes.

Children were constituted in legal terms as targets, and not mere contingent casualties, of armed conflict.[22] The publication of the 1996 study by Graça Machel on the *Impact of Armed Conflict on Children*,[23] in the same year that the Guatemalan Peace Accords were signed, drew further attention to the Children Refugees program, which was one of the few organizations formally addressing the needs of children during the war. The Machel report was the first human rights assessment of war-affected children which used the CRC as a guiding framework of analysis. A new consensus was emerging across the world on the matter of rights,[24] and children's rights were taking new salience in the peace process.[25] The UN Security Council emphasized the need for children to be actively involved in the peace process,[26] spearheading a movement to dignify child victims of the war in Guatemala. The notion of the "right child" in the Guatemalan peace process was based on a certain understanding of age and socioeconomic conditions, especially changing notions of positive rights and justice, which have precipitated new forms of organizing and identity around young people.

A widely distributed illustrated book, *Let's Debate the Rights of the Child*, features a dove with an olive branch on its title page. It showcases each of the 54 articles of the CRC with a comic strip. This illustrated version of the first article of the convention states, for example, that "a child means every human being below the age of eighteen years."

The work of *sensibilización*, or consciousness raising, regarding various aspects of children's rights and the CRC in Guatemala, was carried out largely by nongovernmental organizations like Children Refugees and UNICEF. Peace workers often explained that the special role of children in community reconstruction was due to their age or "unique period of development." The CRC, unlike its 1959 predecessor the Declaration of the Rights of the Child, emphasizes the capacity of children to act independently from adults.[27] Four principles in the convention are notable—nondiscrimination (article 2), best interests of the child (article 3), the right to life, survival and development (article 6), and the right for children to have their views heard and considered in decisions affecting them (article 12). Pamphlets titled *New Vision*, *New Organization*, and *New Legal Path*, which outlined these articles of the CRC in relationship to Guatemalan law, were particularly popular in meetings organized to educate community leaders. One prominent Ixil politician noted: "We were informed that our children—the registration of their names, birth certificates, and education–are the only thing that can secure peace. Imagine that—before their heads are fully formed they are responsible for our people." Guatemalan legislation,[28] from 1996, reads as follows: "There is a need to educate children in the spirit of peace, dignity, tolerance, freedom, equality, and solidarity, while conceiving of childhood and youth as singular subjects of social, economic, and cultural rights which would allow them to become protagonists in their own development with a framework of solidarity, for the strengthening of the state of law, social justice, peace, and democracy."

In the years following the war in Guatemala children were increasingly designated as bearers of a peace process that periodically gave way to extreme violence. In 1999 constitutional reforms, which were meant to solidify the peace accords, included changes to national legislation surrounding the rights of children. But they failed to pass popular referendum. Under the circumstances,[29] I concluded that the Code for Children was generally perceived as a ploy by international organizations that granted special treatment to delinquents. Many donors and development professionals began to question the viability of a rights-based approach to childhood in Guatemala.

In 2002 a report of the UN Human Rights Commission concluded: "Unfortunately, the measures adopted by the Guatemalan government, including ratification of international human rights instruments and acknowledgement of state responsibility in cases submitted to the Inter-American Human Rights System, have not improved the situation of human rights or children's rights in Guatemala."[30]

Children's rights are premised on a new politics of equal treatment. A universal ethic is identified with the old utilitarian principle of minimization of pain and maximization of happiness in human experience. How successful is this sort of utilitarian argument? In this case, one respects the rights of others because they understand that to do so will make everyone better off. No matter how utility is defined—as pleasure, desire fulfillment, or as a numerical representation of human choice—there would seem to be some need to go beyond this simple valuation of ethical practices. Especially because the ratification of international children's rights instruments does not necessarily change state practices, though it does set important precedents for making rights claims. A substantial body of literature from anthropology criticizes the CRC[31] for normalizing a Western understanding of childhood in which children are active participants.[32] It is remarkable that the particularistic understanding of value in the CRC is underwritten by a host of universalistic, prescriptive claims about children. Accounting for this expansion of neoliberal discourse, I would like instead to examine the idea of rights, particularly children's rights and childhood, as generative concepts that create new attitudes and behaviors.

While the rhetoric of rights can be politically powerful in the world today, I suggest that it is also important to examine the practices of peace workers that promote those rights as they relate to children. The very notion that the humanity of children is, in part, defined by its violation calls into question our capacity to respond. Children become exemplars of the universal, singular humanity of each survivor in Guatemala. The consequence of making children into rights bearers is that it effectively constructs them as a demographic and cultural imaginary entity both outside of violence and responsible for it. This practice humanizes children in a particular, minimal way. Hannah Arendt writes convincingly: "The concept of the Rights of man, based on the supposed existence of a human being as such, collapsed in ruins as soon as those who professed it found themselves for the first time before men who had truly lost every other specific quality and connection except for the mere fact of being human."[33]

Following Arendt and Michel Foucault, philosopher Giorgio Agamben argues that the primordial political element of sovereign power is "the life of *homo sacer*... situated at the intersection of a capacity to be killed and yet not sacrificed, outside the human and divine law."[34] Children are imbued with life when they are exposed to death. Are these acts of horror which could, literally, set a young person apart from childhood? How does one come to accept, or to commit, such acts of cruelty? It may be, as Miguel suggests, the desire to nurture a different sort of son or daughter.

At the same time, for people from the Ixil area, the reputation of a child is predetermined. A child's character and conduct is inherited from his or her namesake, or *che'x*. The child is always known, from the day of his or her birth, and over time the moral fiber of that child is confirmed by experience. While the concept of rights is used to defend Ixil children from genocidal military tactics, it also legitimates an understanding of children as immature figures that are born without a namesake. The question of rights, then, becomes a matter of how children can reform themselves according to the universal terms of humanity. In the Ixil this entails a complex movement of reversals by men like Miguel who, having been displaced, calls for intervention on behalf of his children, and also seeks to manipulate the interveners to support his (sometimes violent) agenda in a divided village. By way of response, nongovernmental organizations working in the Ixil area have developed their own technical rationale for children's rights which is uncoupled from the everyday responsibilities of Ixil children. At the children's rights workshop the mayor of Nebaj spoke to young people in the room about their rights and obligations:

> We are very concerned about the attitude of some young people today. I have always thought that it is difficult to understand why we do not have respect any longer. And I don't know the reason. But we are all human beings that have a heart, a way of thinking, a soul. And we know that God governs our life. We should allow God to govern our life, but we also have to do our part as human beings—as young people and children. We have to think over the situations in our life. All situations have solutions. And the solution is that each young person has the responsibility to take care of him- or herself, and find love for him- or herself. The first solution is to kneel before God and beg him for life. The second solution is to respect our parents. You must respect them, first before anything else. If you cannot show respect here on Earth, there is no doubt that you will suffer badly. Today you must learn values and take them to your friends and neighbors.

A foundation official in attendance at the workshop responded with a reflection on the obligation of peace workers toward children. We must understand that one part of childhood is the movement toward maturity: "Whether one is young or old in age, it is our wish that every person become aware of the consequences of their conduct. Even from a young age children ideally should feel such responsibility in their heart. In this way child's rights and the 'right child' are not separate, but one. This is the calling of those who set out to do good for young children today."

Even when the lives of children are protected by rights, that same protection exists in reference to the possibility of a world without rights. In Nebaj, people complain, children have embraced their rights but not their responsibilities, leading to what is called *xovisa aama*, or threats to the soul.[35] It is precisely these unexpected effects of children's rights discourse that become the motivation for a close study of the relationships between humanitarian organizations and young people. In the Ixil children's rights work becomes a question of political legitimacy. There is a tension created by the force of a young person's participation[36] and the recognition of that participation as a legitimate one. In 2001, I conducted a study of the participation of children in decisions related to family life in Nebaj.[37] When neither parent was educated, and when both parents were educated, children's reported participation in decisions was 23 percent higher. It was significantly lower when only one of the parents had formal schooling. Cross-tabulation of the data for schooling of parents shows that for 74 percent of the 123 couples in this group it was the father who had some education. In families where children had significant participation in decisions it was described as *tx'olo'm*, or learning to better oneself. The ethical obligation of responsibility to participate in family decisions differentiates some children from others. It also marks the beginning of a different sort of community. And in the Ixil, community begins with particular kinds of obligations (toward family and family relations) and values (to suffer well in the face of adversity). The embedding and disembedding of childhood—new forms of play, hygiene, and law—have come to dominate the town of Nebaj in the postwar period.

The work of children's rights is fundamentally about a particular way of making oneself human, transforming oneself in the pursuit of peace. Children are marked by the dyadic relation of claim and obligation. It is a relation between parents and children, linking donors and peace workers, invested with logic of protection.

CONCLUSION

In 1999 a group of young farmers, educators, and demobilized soldiers invited me to join them on a piece of land just outside of the town of Nebaj to gather cement blocks and build a community center. All of them had worked as *promotores*, at one time or another, with Children Refugees of the World. As David Stoll notes, in *Between Two Armies in the Ixil Towns of Guatemala*, these Ixil professionals have long played an important role in political and social change in the region. Vincente Ixcotoyac, who was twenty at the time, talked to me as he carried materials to the construction site about how he became involved:

> What I can tell you about this organization is that it is time to have something that is ours, with our name and vision. What I can tell you about myself is what I can tell you about the example of my mother. She has always been one of the people who has struggled to overcome her circumstances, our suffering. She has a vision and involves herself with whatever group. Not my father, he is never inspired. She has always been organizing women, and projects, with different organizations. Sometimes they don't work out, or the funds disappear. Often it is the very same group of people who create something, is the same one that will dismantle it. Remember that. Today we are carrying bricks. But before you know it we could be taking them apart. In one way or another there is always *divisionismo*. That is our problem. Sometimes, as sons, we don't look well on it because in one way or another it creates problems. In the end you have people with one criticism or another. And sometimes, because of all of the involvement with groups, a mother forgets to take care of her family. But she has a desire to see the community overcome its problems, the obstacles. I carry that with me, and it is how I end up here today. We have always been self-sufficient. We are people originating from our communities and we offer services in those children in our communities. We speak Ixil and Spanish and are able to help our children integrate into the world that surrounds them.

Apoyo y Autosuficiencia Ixil is a local association oriented towards the protection, education, and social welfare of children. Several large international organizations working in the Ixil area, and town officials, helped Apoyo gain legal status and access remote areas of the region. In 2001 the executive committee of the association wrote a preliminary request to the de Jong Foundation and received an initial donation of $300. The letter, penned by a Flemish volunteer, acknowledging the donation reads: "After a long work with Mr. Marcel we are very pleased. Mostly because the foundation also has as its primordial interest children, just like us. Evidence of this is the donation received from Marcel, that will be used for needy children in our communities." The association also submitted a request for $8000, which was approved by the foundation with the following justification by Marcel Mastenbroek. He wrote:

> To obtain sustainability, this phase will be used to transfer increasingly responsibilities for operational activities from Children Refugees to the local associations, in particular to Apoyo in Nebaj. In order to prepare for this transfer, Apoyo is to receive financial support from the foundation to set up its operational structure. A clear plan will be defined as how to further

transfer responsibilities for the whole program so that Children Refugees can withdraw, or at least reduce to a minimum its involvement in Guatemala. . . This development, however, is not without consequences and risks. First, we will have to accept that the Apoyo staff will have to learn *en concreto* how to run their own organization and supervise the program. The potential is there, and Children Refugees staff is obviously present and available but it may not always go without friction. Second the creation of this new organization, or to be more precise, the decision to support the development of Apoyo from an association of local youth into a local NGO does require our ongoing financial commitment.

When the grant was approved Santos Bernal left his job in Children Refugees to become head up Apoyo. Santos was still known in town as "the little dictator" by many folks. "But one has to admit that it is impressive, the way he [Santos] has managed to corral international bosses," said the owner of the cafeteria around the corner from the community center that houses Apoyo. Together with a staff of ten people, and an association of sixty educators, Santos began to develop a strategic plan for the organization. In the intervening years he met foundation officials, including visits with several board members, who came to assess the "exemplary work" of the Indigenous Displaced Children's Project. Santos and Marcel both welcomed my participation over the years. I was a strange sort of interloper, translating for foundation board members, scribbling notes on Apoyo project proposals, and visiting with children I had come to know over the years. Why, I asked Santos, do you want to create a new organization focused on children?

As with most descriptions of Apoyo, his response first mapped its origins within the humanitarian intervention of Children Refugees in the Ixil area. Then he turned to the "nature" of Apoyo. He leaned back, pushing his glasses up on his nose.

> As Ixil people we must be protagonists in our own development. Our approach is based in our community, centered on children, and sustained by the peace agreement which calls for educational reform in our nation. It is true that the local team was created with support from foreigners, their finances. Now we do not have a need for assistance, and now it has become a question of their confidence in our abilities. For many years we followed a foreign element here on our own land. Then we began to create a curriculum made by ourselves for our children. With Children Refugees we labored under the idea that "a child who does not play, dies." Now we have another thought which is that "to educate with love is a shared commitment."

The workers, Santos explained, would not be technicians that taught games and rhymes to small children. There would be no foreign element of distance, "we no longer need to be protected by strangers." Ixil educators would be "trained to care, to love children." The plans to "train educators to care" through capacity building and follow-up on the "professionalization process" were laid out in a 50-page proposal submitted to the de Jong Foundation under the name, *U tzelem unq'a talintxa,* which translates roughly as "the smile within children."

In 2004 in Guatemala City the staff and supporters of both Children Refugees and Apoyo gathered for a meeting on the sustainability of a youth movement in the Ixil area. This was designated as *transferencia* "to officially transfer responsibilities from Children Refugees to Apoyo" by the foundation. The process took several weeks, opening and closing with a divination by a daykeeper. The daykeeper prayed for energy, resources, strength, and respect and for a road to open that would allow Apoyo to help its own people. He explained that this was a day when everyone would feel fear akin to the fear a parent feels when he releases his child's hand for the first time. The meeting was initiated with a phrase that became a topic of hot debate: "Social processes are built and they are built by human beings." Who, and what, creates the possibility for social change involves money, political conditions, and children themselves. When Dianne stated that the sole purpose of her participation in the meeting was to "protect children and the program," Nila, who had worked with the program since the start, responded by explaining: "People cannot be protected because of their age alone." As the meetings progressed, candles placed at the center of the room burned black, a bad omen. Amilcar proposed: "At the end of the day what we want is a child who becomes socially different, not someone who only wants to play."

Santos explained what he learned during the armed conflict was that "the enemy of my enemy is my friend." How, he asked, does one measure or quantify willingness to change your own peoples beliefs? "As an Ixil person I added my ingredient, but it is added to a French and Dutch recipe that is decades old. What we really are as peace workers is finders and vendors of knowledge, because that is what we can sell to a government who only governs for thirty percent of our country. Without vigilance the government would dedicate themselves either to drug dealing or making piñatas. It is real love for our people that we bring to our work with children." The "expatriate" and "local" teams proved impossible to reconcile. Accusations of racism, financial mismanagement, and corruption flew around the room. At the heart of the discussion was the ability of Apoyo to *convencer,* or to convince, and make people of the town believe in the centrality of children to community life. During the fractious encounter between the two organizations Apoyo introduced its new icon, a red butterfly with a child's handprint in the corner. It replaced the symbol of a refugee child with his arms and legs intertwined, which had dominated signs, buildings, and forums in the Ixil region for nearly twenty years. When Nila presented the new symbol she explained that, like Apoyo, the butterfly starts out in a cocoon but grows to travel wherever it needs to be. Likewise, a child leaves her first handprint, grabbing on to whatever is close by, before she goes making her way in the world. It is the teacher that extends his hand to reach the child and show him a new world. She says: "We are all committed, we have sacrificed to these ends, to change the way that young people in our communities live. Conflict is important in life, perhaps we cannot understand or give appropriate weight to what the other has accomplished. If there have always been good intentions, perhaps we do not know how to manage them."

It was then that Vincente Ixcotoyac raised himself up for the first, and last, time during the meeting. He said:

> When I was in the mountains, before I had returned to town I was offered a job with UNICEF. Many times they say [he raises a book] here are our experiences in the world. And this has been the experience of our people that someone comes with a book raised up and waves it before our people. Here is what I am going to speak in front of you here today and tell you that I don't bring anything written down. If you do not believe in our capacity to change this world then come with me, accompany me [applause]. It isn't so much what one can defend in writing [he raises a book again]. It is what we practice. And today I am here in the great capital city, with mud on my boots, to explain what we can do. That is our value. It is a sad fate of our people to have divided and divided again over the difficulties of ideology when we should be united and work together so that we do not continue to make pieces of what should be whole.

Here the idea of what is right for a child does not emanate from ardent love for humanity as a whole, but in a commitment to a particular place that is in excess of any sort of universal humanity. Codes and laws may exist to protect the rights of a child but the exercise of commitment occurs from person to person and in practice. No matter how intolerable inaction might be, Vincente claims that action can no longer come from a distance.

In the time that followed, UNICEF, the European Union, Children Refugees, and Save the Children "transferred responsibility" for twenty-two rural early childhood education centers, youth centers, and infant stimulation programs to Apoyo.

This was part of the exit strategy for international organizations from a country where postwar reconstruction was, by this time, perceived as a failing proposition. Apoyo and similar projects were incorporated into the national government's tenuous initiative for accessible, equal education that was a veiled attempt to comply with the Peace Accords. The question of how to deal with a growing young population had fallen from the domain of state and familial responsibility into the hands of nongovernmental organizations in the Ixil area. By taking care of the youngest Ixiles, Apoyo and the young people that run it moderate limited, discriminatory, public services that had long been entirely absent from the region. Apoyo also provides a space where young people can access new political and social opportunities. Their practice of educating children has transformed over the years into complex forms of self-care that align with the life-affirming demands of the peace process. In my work at Apoyo I could see how practicing certain forms of care (bodily reform by hygiene, citizenship through education, and increasing individualism) reinforced, through a lack of resources we take for granted, a sense of suffering in the postwar period. These kinds of interventions, in the Ixil moral milieu, demonstrate how understandings of what are good, right, exemplary, and correct are under revision. Against an expanding discourse on children's rights, we are confronted with the limits of organizational forms and infrastructures where these rights are realized in a new political economy of peace.

In my view these rights are not simply rhetorical devices of late capitalism inexorably embedded in contemporary peace processes. Instead, my ethnographic study reveals that the theory and practice of children's rights is generative of new knowledge, space, and ideology. The implementation of the CRC by international aid agencies and the Guatemalan government has created new forms of everyday experience for and by young people in the postwar period. And while child's rights discourse, with its particular logic of protection, may be a paradigm for political action by humanitarian organizations, it has also become a source of self-expression, organization, and controversy in Guatemala. In short, rights are not only what has been codified in law but what children make of them in everyday life. The act of carrying out children's rights as part of community reconstruction in postwar Guatemala has created a youth movement for peace that both incorporates and exceeds the CRC. While the "right child" is inflected with global legal orthodoxy, it also emerges through the practices of local organizations, donors, peace workers, and children themselves.

NOTES

1.   J. Comaroff and J. Comaroff, eds., *Millennial Capitalism and the Culture of Neoliberalism* (Durham: Duke University Press, 2001).

2.   As an anthropologist I have explored how the peace process incorporates human rights instruments such as the CRC as refugees returned from refuge. My fieldwork for this chapter straddled the Ixil highlands of the Department of Quiché in Guatemala and the offices of humanitarian organizations in

Europe. Here I describe how international donors, activists, and youth are engaged in a social movement that promotes postwar reconciliation.

3. For excellent studies of this phenomenon outside of Guatemala, see P. Reynolds, "Children of Tribulation: The Need to Heal and the Means to Heal War Trauma," *Africa* 60, no. 1 (1990) on South Africa; K. Felsman, "Children and War Project: Maputo Mozambique" in *Refugee Children in Malawi*, ed. D. Tolfree, Save Alliance, 195-220 (Boulder: Westview Press, 1991) on Mozambique; also see K. Cheney, *Pillars of a Nation: Child Citizens and Ugandan National Development* (Chicago: The University of Chicago Press, 2007) on Uganda; and S. Shepler, "Shifting Priorities in Child Protection in Sierra Leone since Lomé" in *Sierra Leone Beyond Lomé, Challenges and Possibilities for a Post-War Nation*, ed. M. Mustapha and J. Bangura, 35-48 (New York: Palgrave MacMillan, 2011).

4. G. Grandin, *The Last Colonial Massacre* (Chicago: University of Chicago Press, 2004).

5. K. Warren, *Indigenous Movements and Their Critics: Pan-Maya Activism in Guatemala*, (Princeton: Princeton University Press, 1998); J. Wantanabe "Culturing Identities, the State, and National Consciousness in Late Nineteenth-Century Western Guatemala," *Bulletin of Latin American Research* 19, no. 3 (2000): 321-40.

6. There is a wealth of literature which explores the violence in Guatemala that constituted three decades of armed struggle which included acts of genocide. See, for example, J. Zur, *Violent Memories: Mayan War Widows in Guatemala* (Boulder: Westview Press, 1998); L. Green, *Fear as a Way of Life* (New York: Columbia University Press, 1998); J. Perlin, "The Guatemalan Historical Clarification Commission finds Genocide," *ILSA Journal of International and Comparative Law* 6, no. 2 (2000): 389-414; V. Sanford, *Buried Secrets: Truth and Human Rights in Guatemala* (New York: Palgrave Macmillan, 2003); B. Manz, *Paradise in Ashes. A Guatemalan Journey of Courage, Terror and Hope* (Berkeley: University of California Press, 2004).

7. See "The Comision para el Esclarecimiento Historico (CEH)," *Guatemala, memoria del silencio* (Guatemala: CEH 2000).

8. L. Green, *Fear as a Way of Life* (New York: Columbia University Press, 1998).

9. All identifying information of individuals and organizations has been changed, unless otherwise specified.

10. In the introduction to her edited volume on the subject of child survival, Nancy Scheper-Hughes notes, "the social construction of child survival as a ... problem about which something can and should be done is fairly recent. ... It would take political conflict and economic emergencies ... to provoke state

interest in the regulation and control of population, including a concern with child survival, which has recently achieved the status of a 'master' social and political problem in the "modern' world." Also see N. Scheper-Hughes and C. Sargent, *Small Wars: The Cultural Politics of Childhood*. (Berkeley: University of California Press 1998).

11. See Witness for Peace, *A People Damned* (Washington, DC: Witness for Peace, 1996).

12. Of the 420 army massacres documented by the Recuperation of Historic Memory project, 111 occurred in the Ixil area, where Nebaj is a municipality. See the "Oficina de Derechos Humanos del Arzobispado de Guatemala (ODHAG)," in *"Guatemala: Nunca Más*, vol. 3 (Guatemala: ODHAG 1998).

13. S. Stephens, ed. *Children and the Politics of Culture* (New Jersey: Princeton University Press, 1995), 34.

14. Since 1981, the French organization Refugees of the World has led sixty-one projects in sixteen countries affected by violence, including projects that I visited in Rwanda and Honduras. It is relevant to note, however, that the rapid influx of international aid and organizations in the Ixil area took place over a short period between 1994-1998, after the work of Children Refugees of the World was already well underway.

15. This is the number cited in the Children Refugees proposal which can be found in the foundation archive.

16. E. Levinas, *Entre Nous: On Thinking of the Other* (New York: Columbia University Press 1991), 100.

17. J. C. Cambranes, *Coffee and Peasants: The Origins of the Modern Plantation Economy in Guatemala, 1853-1897* (Antigua: Centro de Investigaciones Regionales de Mesoamérica, 1985); R. Feinberg and B. Bagley. *Development Postponed: The Political Economy of Central America in the 1980s* (Boulder: Westview Press, 1986).

18. Today the spelling is most commonly hispanicized as Ixil, while the Academy of Mayan Languages determines its spelling to be Ixhil.

19. "Education: UNICEF 50th Anniversary 1946-1996," in *Fact Sheet of Achievements* (New York: UNICEF,1996).

20. Articles 38 and 39 of the treaty state that should children fall victim to armed conflict they have rights to protection, care, physical and psychological recovery, and social reintegration. While CRC is the central instrument of international law protecting children, the measures of the Geneva Conventions are also relevant.

21. *La Política Educativa*, no. 9 (Guatemala City: Ministerio de Educación, 1998). My translation.

22. On May 25, 2000, the UN General Assembly proposed a new protocol to the CRC, the Children in Armed Conflict Protocol, with provisions meant to promote international cooperation and assistance in the rehabilitation and social reintegration of children who have been "victimized" by armed conflict.

23. G. Machel, *Impact of Armed Conflict on Children*, United Nations Report A/51/306 (1996). The report, which makes recommendations related to the participation of children in armed conflict, also explores the protective standards needed to promote the well-being of such young people. Education, as reported in the study, is crucial at the outset of an emergency because educational opportunities provide structure, constancy and routine within community life.

24. See, for example, G. Mohan. and J. Holland, "Human Rights and Development in Africa: Moral Intrusion or Empowering Opportunity," *Review of African Political Economy* 88 (2001): 177-96.

25. Prior to the release of the Machel report there had been no Security Council Resolutions that dealt with children in the midst of armed conflict. More recently the Security Council has adopted a number of important resolutions on the topic: S/RES/1261 (1999), S/RES/1314 (2000), S/RES/1460 (2003).

26. A/55/163-S/2000/712 and S/RES/1261 (1999), paragraph 7.

27. Stephens, ed., *Children and the Politics of Culture.*

28. Decreto Número 78-1996, *Codigo de la niñez y la juventud*, El Congreso de la República de Guatemala, September 27, 1996. My translation.

29. As the leader of the Guatemalan Congress Efrain Ríos Montt refused to recognize the peace process and upon taking office he effectively derailed the *Code for Children*. When young people were denied their ancestral rights to land as they returned from refuge, they became violent actors in rural communities. They claimed public parks through thievery, defaced municipal buildings, and terrorized local markets in a language of refusal, creating a place for themselves even where one was not available. Children of poor displaced peasants emerged in the local news as a residual category of the war. In May 2000, President Alfonso Portillo resorted to military intervention, calling thousands of troops into rural communities to combat the anarchy and disorder. Opinion polls in the national papers registered strong support for the military intervention from within the communities themselves. Children that I interviewed during this period often defended the violent attacks as an acceptable form of social control.

30. Misión de Verificación de las Naciones Unidas en Guatemala, "Los Linchamientos: un flagelo que persiste," *Informe de Verificación* (Guatemala City: Misión de Verificación de las Naciones Unidas en Guatemala, 2002).

31. See J. Comaroff, "Conscientious Subjects: Moral Beings in the Modern World," *Suomen Antropologi: Journal of the Finnish Anthropological Society*

2 (1994): 1-29; J. Boyden, "Children's Experience of Conflict-Related Emergencies: Some Implications for Relief Policy and Practice," *Disasters* 18, no. 3 (1994): 254-67; N. Scheper-Hughes and C. Sargen, eds., *Small Wars: The Cultural Politics of Childhood* (Berkeley: University of California Press, 1998); O. Nieuwenhuys, *Children's Lifeworlds* (London: Routledge, 1995).

32. N. Ndebele, "Recovering Childhood: Children in South African National Reconstruction," in *Children and the Politics of Culture*, ed. S. Stephens, 321-23 (Princeton: Princeton University Press 1995); P. Reynolds, *The Ground of All Making: State Violence, The Family and Political Activists* (Pretoria: Human Sciences Research Council, 1995).

33. H. Arendt, *The Jew as Pariah* (New York: Grove Press, 1978), 55-57.

34. G. Agamben, *Homo Sacer: Sovereignty and Bare Life* (Stanford: Stanford University Press, 1999), 71.

35. For an extended discussion of *xovisa aama*, see K. Olson, *Youth without Sanctuary: The New Ethics of Humanitarianism in Post-War Guatemala* (Berkeley: University of California Berkeley, 2007), 235-45.

36. For an excellent study of politics in the lives of children, see R. Coles, *The Political Life of Children* (Boston: Houghton Mifflin, 1986).

37. The survey team asked questions related to common decisions in family life that were administered in the Ixil language. The survey inquired as to the role of all household members as to: 1) Whether or not to buy household items like a cellular phone, gas stove, or a cow?, 2) What to do if a child of the family becomes ill?, 3) Whether or not to buy medicine for a person in the family is ill?, and 4) Whether or not to send a child to school?

Eleven

Pragmatism, Capabilities, and Children's Rights in Development Ethics

JENNIFER CASELDINE-BRACHT

The United Nations Convention on the Rights of the Child (CRC), adopted by the General Assembly in 1989, went into effect on September 2, 1990. Internationally, public opinion tended to be overwhelmingly in favor of this convention, the most ratified international convention on record. As of November 2008, 193 countries have ratified it; the only members of the United Nations that have not ratified it are the United States and Somalia. In this paper, I will examine the philosophical underpinnings of such approval and argue that the capabilities approach, coupled with a pragmatic methodology, is the most promising path towards actualizing more children's rights. I will address the issue of the universalizability of children's rights. The current notion of rights , I believe, can often be understood as inflexible and hence may inadvertently stifle further thoughts on the matter. Regarding human rights and gender, Martha Nussbaum argues that at least a tentative list of universalizable capabilities is necessary if we are to actually treat each person as an end.[1] I will examine her argument within the context of children's rights and demonstrate how it can complement the Deweyian distinction between aims and ends. Finally, I will examine the appropriate roles that developing, in contrast to developed, countries might assume to ensure the positive development of children in those countries. The CRC can of course be amended, or additional protocols can be ratified, although amendment may be protracted or difficult because of the canonical nature of such a nearly universal legal text. For this reason children's rights advocates should not confuse the "is" of the letter of existing international law with the "ought" in the ethics of children's rights. The ethics of children's rights may evolve over time, which should lead us to view the CRC as a living instrument even without formal amendment.

In order to examine some of the philosophical justifications for the CRC, it may be enlightening to examine some of the arguments made against it. For example, Onora O'Neill has argued that securing children's rights in conventions and declarations is not necessarily in the best interest of children. She writes, "The crucial difference between [early] childhood dependence and the dependence of oppressed social groups is that childhood is a stage of life, from which children normally emerge and are helped to emerge by those who have most power over them. Those with power over children's lives usually have an interest in ending childish dependence. Oppressors usually have an interest in maintaining the oppression of social groups."[2] She argues that for those people interested in the welfare of children, it is much more useful to think in terms of adult obligations instead of children's rights. Each child is at a different stage of development, but the language of rights tends to talk as if they were all members of one easy-to-distinguish group. This unqualified language of "child rights" is not helpful at all when one is actually dealing with children. What is right for a three-year-old will be much different than what is right for a twelve-year-old. Thus, article 12.1 of the CRC states: "States Parties shall assure to the child who is capable of forming his or her own views the right to express those views freely in all matters affecting the child, the views of the child being given due weight in accordance with the age and maturity of the child."

However, O'Neill's point is that it is not that the convention does not recognize that these differences exist, but rather that it is not up for the children— regardless of their age—to decide how capable they are of forming their views or determining how much weight their views should receive. This is up to the adults to decide on behalf of the children. Hence, due to this uncertainty as to the age and extent to which children claim article 12 rights, why not simply talk about the obligations adults have to children? She argues that rights talk is not the most practical route to ensuring the protection of children. After all, children are not generally in a position to demand their rights in the way that other oppressed groups are able to do. Furthermore, the rights are ultimately written to caution people from acting (or not acting) in a way that is detrimental to children. These rights are actually more of a second-hand approach to addressing adult obligations to children, so it is more direct and practical to simply cut to the chase and talk about obligations to children rather than rights which children can supposedly claim.[3] Child rights are more certainly inferred from adult obligations rather than the other way around.

While I agree with O'Neill that rights of children and other oppressed groups are in some ways disanalogous, there are other ways in which the analogy is very strong. We can examine how the capabilities approach intersects with both child rights and children's education and look at ways in which the capabilities approach helps children which are analogous to other oppressed groups. I will show later in this paper that a focus on children's rights can increase the well-being of children around the world in significant ways. The capabilities approach measures the progress of human beings in a way that includes but also goes beyond mere economic definitions of well-being. Amartya Sen and Martha Nussbaum both endorse a capabilities approach to empowering children, but their ideas regarding how this should be done sometimes differ. Sen's idea of justice takes a comparative view towards capabilities, whereas Nussbaum's view links up more directly with the current human rights approach. Sen rejects traditional transcendental theories of justice as proposed by respected philosophers such as Rawls. A transcendental theory of justice tries to develop a theory of a perfectly just society. Sen is not interested in developing this type of theory. Rather, he prefers to focus on comparative judgments regarding what is more or less just in the operation of existing societies—judgments which develop and emerge from the comparative advantage of certain current institutions. He writes,

> Indeed, the theory of justice, as formulated under the currently dominant transcendental institutionalism, reduces many of the most relevant issues of justice into empty—even if "well-meaning"—rhetoric. When people across the world agitate to get *more* global justice—and I emphasize here the comparative word "more"—they are not clamoring for some kind of "minimal humanitarianism." Nor are they agitating for a "perfectly just" world society, but merely for the elimination of some outrageously unjust arrangements to enhance global justice.[4]

He does not want a list of capabilities introduced before public discussion of what these capabilities should be. However, Nussbaum provides such a tentative list and encourages the UN to develop policies and goals which will help people achieve all of the capabilities on the list. The UN has taken on her challenge. Since 1990, the *Human Development Report* has incorporated the capabilities approach along lines Nussbaum suggests into its analysis of human rights progress. This linkage can be used to focus on children's well being in a way that has the potential to be beneficial to them. Nussbaum argues that all humans need things other than money, such as proper self-esteem and the ability to think and reason in a way that has been developed through a proper education, in order to flourish. She makes the case that, in order to create a more robust account of development, we need to look at the interconnected web of conditions that are required to create a valuable life. Nussbaum claims that at least a tentative list of universalizable capabilities is necessary if we are ever to live in a world of flourishing human beings.[5]

Having an approach such as the one Nussbaum endorses encourages respect for universal human rights. This is especially important for children because they are often the first ones to suffer when the discussion starts to drift away from rights. Onora O'Neill has pointed out that normative human rights talk is often logically incoherent. For instance, it is deeply problematic if there is no symmetry between the obligations which the declarations and conventions specifically assign to states and the universal human rights which are promised to individuals. With so many rights being respected, and so few people being actually punished or forced to do their part to actualize the legal rights enshrined in the CRC, the rhetoric of rights does not make logical sense to her. She argues that a normative right entails specific obligations, or else rights talk is "at best aspirational."[6] However, the rights of children are normative claims that are legally supported by most of the international community, even though the corresponding obligations are not always clear cut.

Yet by insisting children have certain rights, we push along the discussion in an important way. Nussbaum's tentative list of universal capabilities are interconnected and a loss of any one of the capabilities is a tragedy. There is a use in acknowledging the tragedy of the situation which O'Neill does not fully address. What is the case is not necessarily what ought to be the case. If this distinction is not carefully observed, a group of people may deem, for instance, that military expenditures for security are more important than child health care, and then conclude based on the mere fact of so deeming, that it ought to be more important than child health care. It may then be easier for governments to come up with weak reasons for not doing everything they can to provide a framework wherein people can flourish by inadvertently giving them an easy excuse to drop some of requirements which are truly necessary for human flourishing.

For example, the leaders of a country might say that it is too bad there is child labor in their country, but families need the money so children need to get to work. This argument can lend it self to being set up as a simple disjunctive syllogism:

Premise 1: Today either we have child labor or families starve.
Premise 2: We want families not to starve more than we want to avoid child labor.
Conclusion: Therefore, we will allow child labor.

This is a valid argument, but is it sound? This would require empirical verification. If it is a sound argument, it should also lead to questions such as, why is the situation such that there is such an awful choice between children working or families starving? Is there anything the international community can do in order to help avoid such a tragic choice? If it is not a sound argument, namely, because the disjunction in the first premise is falsely understood to exclude a third alternative of neither child labor nor starvation, then what has the government, or the international community, done wrong to allow for such a tragic situation? By insisting it is a tragic situation that should be avoided if at all possible, then we can put necessary pressure on the government, or international community, or the most powerful within the group, to do more in order to end an unjust state of affairs? The capabilities approach coupled with the UN Convention on the Rights of the Child is important for two reasons: 1. Child rights claims are normative claims with the potential, because of the crying need of countless children, for generating consensus among a wide range of people with differing metaphysical commitments and ethical perspectives; and 2. The pressure of such normative claims can be genuinely helpful when dealing with recalcitrant governments, or with a sometimes apathetic international community.

In some of Nussbaum's earlier work, her capabilities list was sometimes criticized for being too dogmatic. There is a definite tension between insisting on a list of basic capabilities and also being open minded and willing to change the list of capabilities she has in mind. Of course, nobody can exercise all of their capabilities. There are moral constraints bounding the capabilities we may exercise. Even using Nussbaum's list, conflicts regarding where those boundaries ought to be drawn will arise from time to time. Her position allows for some flexibility of boundaries. In *Women and Human Development*, she writes: "Since the intuitive conception of human functioning and capability demands continued reflection and testing against our intuitions, we should view any given version of the list as a proposal put forward in Socratic fashion, to be tested against the most secure of our intuitions as we attempt to arrive at a type of reflective equilibrium for political purposes."[7] This is something to keep in mind when thinking about children's rights. For example, we may remain steadfast regarding our commitment to provide a framework by which the flourishing of children is possible no matter where a person is born or what gender she happens to be, while recognizing that there may be different ways to achieve this goal. For instance, article 29 of the CRC upholds "the development of respect for the child's parents, his or her own cultural identity, language and values, for the national values of the country in which the child is living, the country from which he or she may originate, and for civilizations different from his or her own." If we do not view such values dogmatically, but only as a point of departure, then perhaps they could eventually yield to a right to an education that is not necessarily derived from these particular sources. An example could be values in a world not comprised of nation-states, or perhaps a development of respect for values in a more communitarian spirit rather than "respect for the child's parents," as illustrated by a Kibbutz. While this may not be a perfect example, it points in a direction of an approach that, while opening the door to a vast array of possibilities, is neither a relativist view nor one that rejects the importance of the CRC. On the contrary, it is vital to recognize the importance of children's rights while realizing that how we understand them may evolve over time. In *Democracy and Education*, John Dewey writes about the aims of education. He does not believe that aims can be completely developed in advance of trying to realize them:

> The aim as it first emerges is a mere tentative sketch. The act of striving to realize it tests its worth. If it suffices to direct activity successfully, nothing more is required, since its whole function is to set a mark in advance; and at times a mere hint may suffice. But usually—at least in complicated situations—acting upon it brings to light conditions which had been overlooked. This calls for revision of the original aim; it has to be added to and subtracted from. An aim must, then, be *flexible*; it must be capable of alteration to meet circumstances. An end established externally to the process of action is always rigid.[8]

Dewey notes that when our ends are already fixed, then our activity to achieve these ends may tend to march forward mindlessly, without any account of how experience may alter our original ends. If we are simply achieving ends that we have been told we should achieve, our activity may feel like nothing more than drudgery.[9] But through developing our aims and realizing they are not absolutely and permanently fixed ends, we become freer to consider other possibilities and other types of aims. Instead of our activity being reduced to work that must be completed in order to achieve some predetermined ends, it becomes an adventure in which our aims change through what we learn while engaged in our various endeavors in trying to realize them. To be stuck on some fixed ends set up externally from the beginning is to miss out on developing notions of rights that might result from reflecting on all the experiences we gain throughout our activity and the input we receive from children who will eventually be adding to the discourse of rights. Hence, flexibility may be an essential feature to include in our ongoing strategy for developing children's rights.

Different approaches are obviously called for in different regions of the world. Often families need children to work in order for the family to survive, and education can seem like an unaffordable luxury. Even if education is tuition-free, there are often other costs to the family to consider when children go to school rather than work. Child labor is still an enormous impediment to reaching the goal of universal primary education. Article 32 of the CRC declares that states parties recognize the right of the child to be protected from economic exploitation and from performing any work that is likely to be hazardous or to interfere with the child's education, or to be harmful to the child's health or physical, mental, spiritual, moral, or social development. Yet the International Labor Organization (ILO) is correct that not all child labor should be eliminated. Activities such as doing some chores around the family home, working part-time at the family business, working part-time after school to earn some money, and so forth can aid in the development of a child. However, there are other times when child labor is detrimental to the child. Regarding types of child labor that should be eliminated, the ILO offers the following guidelines: "[Detrimental labor] is mentally, physically, socially or morally dangerous and harmful to children; and interferes with their schooling by: depriving them of the opportunity to attend school; obliging them to leave school prematurely; or requiring them to attempt to combine school attendance with excessively long and heavy work."[10] Several developing countries profess they want to abolish the type of child labor that the ILO argues should be eliminated. Yet they often interpret these words, what Dewey calls "a tentative sketch," in ways that allow the pursuit of conflicting ends which, human rights groups argue, exploit children. Without examining the sketch within the perimeters of the concrete experience, and using it as merely a starting point, one will have a severely limited approach to child rights development. According to *Human Rights Watch*, there is some very vague language included in some of the work study programs regulated by the Ministry of Education in China.[11] They argue that this language can be read in a way that encourages types of child labor that the CRC would disallow. For instance, Chinese law prohibits the use of child of labor under age sixteen but allows exceptions under some circumstances. For children on nonacademic tracks who pursue athletics or the arts, or who are receiving some sort of vocational education, exceptions can be made. The work study programs stipulate that children in middle and junior high schools cannot engage in hazardous work and that their work must not interfere with their education. However, there are no specific limits regarding the number of hours that may be worked or the kind of work that may be done. With aims that are stated in such a way, many businesses and schools exploit the exceptions to find creative ways to use these loopholes. Schools make creative use of the recommendations to develop programs that will bring much needed money into the schools. When schools can make money from this scheme, the temptation to interpret the CRC's and the ILO's provisions loosely is obvious. When the government lacks money it is often the education budget that gets slashed. When the education budget gets slashed, vulnerable schools cannot continue to be operational without collecting money from some source, which is how the problem develops on a slippery slope.

Our general aim may be to educate children nonvocationally as well as vocationally, but the way this aim is achieved in China or India will be different from the way it is achieved in the United States. Of course, there can be clear ways of implementing the right to an education, which need to be distinguished from equally clear ways of violating it. Nussbaum shares some observations she made from a trip to rural Bihar. There were people helping a group of girls who happened to herd sheep all day. These people provided the girls with a basic education, helped them save money to buy their own goats, and instructed these girls on how women in other regions managed to avoid the dowry system. Nussbaum points out that this sort of help was more useful than truant officers rounding up girls that are not in school. Additionally, it is a more realistic approach than simply hoping for secondary education for all at this point in time. There are lamentable economic realities that must be dealt with in a more substantial way than "waving a wand and saying even 'universal compulsory primary education.'"[12] By honestly pursuing the aim, in this concrete situation, we may at least understand what needs to be considered in order to then accomplish the next step. It may be a type of tightrope act to do what we can with what we have, while still holding it is a tragedy that there is not universal compulsory primary education.

The capabilities approach still leaves a great number of unanswered questions. For instance, when is child labor acceptable? Is it alright for a child to engage in some vocational work? How does one go about determining such things when using the capabilities approach as a template? These are all important questions that need to be seriously considered. The capabilities approach at least provides an outline for thinking about some of these issues. It takes us beyond thinking about mere economics as development. For instance, it provides an argument against traditional beliefs that girls are not as valuable as boys, making the case that there should be universal compulsory primary education for both girls and boys. The capabilities approach has been a valuable tool for providing philosophical justification for human rights development. As our understanding of important capabilities may evolve, so may our understanding and implementation of children's rights. This is valuable because girls are still often pulled out of school more frequently than boys. Enculturation and tradition are powerful forces which are not easily broken. Many people around the world do state that they do not think girls should be treated unequally and that universal compulsory primary education is important for both girls and boys. This split between the way things are and the way many people claim they ought to be is powerful. Pushing at the pressure point on this split is potentially a tool for chiseling away at discriminatory ideas which persist through tradition and enculturation. Having a quasi-universal list of capabilities enshrined in declarations, conventions, and constitutions which holds equality as a universal value puts pressure on those that hold contrary ideas based on enculturation, resulting in a challenge to their belief system. If a person wants to deny a portion of the tentative universal list of capabilities, then that person is more likely to try to think of reasons why equality is bad, for instance. When a person starts thinking of reasons for their beliefs, then it allows for a crack to develop in the armor of enculturation.

I have argued that part of the reason that children's rights are not implemented may go back to lethargy and discouragement in the face of the prevailing absolute and universal language surrounding the rights of the child proclaimed in the convention when the obligations are unfairly defined or distributed. It may be important to read more works by Thomas Pogge, Elizabeth Anderson, Amartya Sen, and others in order to develop a better understanding of what these obligations ought to be. A developing country faced with a seemingly uncompromising but impossible millennium development goal of universal primary education by 2015 may verbally agree but not bother to make a useless effort. For instance, schools that do not get funding, so that their only source of funding is through employing child labor, find themselves in a real dilemma. Either the schools close or children engage in child labor. Which is the lesser of two bad choices? Sometimes human rights groups condemn the child labor practices and point to abstract words in conventions and show how certain provisions within the convention have been violated without always fully considering the very real difficulty of implementation, such as the problem of child labor violations in China. Once again, this will involve empirical investigation to determine if there are enough resources to obtain all of these important moral ideals.

Pragmatic intelligence coupled with the capabilities approach to children's rights, when used, is often quite helpful to finding creative solutions to real life problems. It is not only businesses, schools and governments that are responsible for child labor violations. Families often feel that their children should work in order to help support the family. In order to address this issue, some countries have tried to find ways to help the families to help their children. According to the Center for Global Development, tying compensation for families with school attendance has worked in countries as diverse as Brazil and Bangladesh. Research shows that from 1994 to 2005, Brazil's federal government paid mothers a stipend of approximately eighteen dollars per month for sending their children to school. Incomes of participating Brazilian families rose between 20 and 30 percent, while drop-out rates declined.[13] This program has successfully built in a mechanism for parents who wanted to send their children to school and sincerely desired to end the cycle of poverty but who felt like they could not afford to think of future benefits when their present needs were so overwhelming. By linking education to a current increase in the standard of living for poor families, this program has developed a potentially sustainable pragmatic approach, adapted to the situation of these countries, towards realizing the millennium goal of a primary education for all of their children.

Bangladesh's program, which offered incentives for families that sent their children to school, showed significant success, too. The Bangladesh Food for Education (FFE) program started in 1993 and has grown throughout the years. It is a program that offers rice and wheat to families that have at least one primary school-age child attending school. There are random checks incorporated into the plan to ensure that children participating in the program attend school at least 60 percent of the time for the family to be eligible to receive the grain. The current cost of the program is about ten cents (US) per day per student. Xin Meng and Jim Ryan analyzed the data from household survey data submitted in 2000: "Eligible children on average have 15 to 27 percent higher school participation rates, relative to their counterfactuals that were not but would have been eligible for the program. Conditional on school participation, participants also stay at school 0.7 to 1.05 years longer than their counterfactuals."[14] This program is an example of how relatively little financial investment can benefit the lives of many children in developing countries, as well as potentially having benefits for future generations to come.

Different programs directed at eliminating poverty need to be implemented in different countries. The amount of money or food that would provide adequate incentive for parents to send their children to school will differ from one country to another. For instance, in 1997, Mexico initiated an incentive program to alleviate extreme poverty. The program, initially known as Progresa, and now as Oportunidades, has taken a three-pronged approach to addressing issues of poverty. The program addresses education, nutrition, and health. Originally the program's goal was to increase the number of children who would successfully complete their primary education. However, the program has now evolved to raise the amount of money families receive for children as they go on to complete a secondary education, which historically has had a very high drop-out rate. The rate of girls who dropped out was exceptionally high, so there are now extra incentives for families who send their female children to school.[15] The Oportunidades program also offers scholarships and school supplies, and links these incentives to regular school attendance. There are strong controls to ensure that children are going to school. These incentives, coupled with a robust mechanism for keeping track of children's attendance, have led to a significant improvement in the number of children that attend high school. According to the *New York Times*, "Oportunidades has also cut child labor and led to more schooling. In rural areas, the number of children starting high school increased by 85 percent.[16]

It is worth noting that this is a highly adaptive program. Since 1997 there have been many changes and improvements to ensure that the program is doing what it was designed to do. When it is not working properly, changes are implemented. Sunset provisions apply. In 2008, when it became apparent that there was a global food crisis, the program added a food aid for better living supplement to families involved in this program. The Oportunidades program is an example of a flexible approach to solving the problem of poverty. The program administrator reads the external data reports, learns from them, and maintains a willingness to change portions of the program if there are unintended consequences. The results have been so impressive that cities around the world, including New York City, have used it as a template to develop their own strategic plan to reduce poverty.[17]

It is beyond the scope of this paper to go into any great detail regarding the problem of poverty and how it relates to institutions and structural reforms. The reform of International Financial Institutions (IFI) is currently on the world's agenda, and is needed to realize the worthwhile aim of universal primary education in Burkina Faso and similar countries. However, it is clear that the United States and Western Europe often exasperate poverty in developing countries through unfair trade agreements such as agricultural subsidies. These arrangements can directly and negatively impact the rights of children in developing countries without specifically intending to do so.

According to the United Nations, part of the reason for poverty in some developing countries is unprofitable state-controlled corporations.[18] Both developed countries and developing countries have agreements and structures unique to them that can be improved upon, which may also eventually improve the educational quality of lives for the children. While the capabilities approach advocates moving beyond solely economic measurements, the issue of poverty is obviously not trivial. It must maintain a prominent part of any capabilities effort to improve the lives of children. To really get at the root of some of these problems, it is important to consider how these institutions operate in both developing and developed countries, and what can be done to make them work for all people. It is vital to realize the fundamental children's right to an education which is not merely vocational may be best realized by not merely making that aim the goal or end, but by also intelligently pursuing additional ends such as economic development both domestically and globally, and by the reform of IFI institutions.

Notes

1. M. Nussbaum, *Women and Human Development: The Human Capabilities Approach* (New York: Cambridge University Press, 2001),106.

2. P. Alston, S. Parker, and J. Seymour, eds., *Children, Rights and the Law* (New York: Oxford University Press, 1992), 38-39.

3. Ibid., 39-40.

4. A. Sen, *The Idea of Justice* (Cambridge: Harvard University Press, 2009), 26.

5. This list can be found in Nussbaum, *Women and Human Development,* 78-80 . The list is also available online, e.g., see "Capability approach," *Wikipedia,* accessed June 30, 2010, http://en.wikipedia.org/wiki/Capability_approach.

6. O. O'Neill, "The Dark Side of Human Rights," *International Affairs* 81, no. 2 (2005): 427-39.

7. Nussbaum, *Women and Human Development,* 77.

8. J. Dewey, *Ethics, Logic, Psychology,* in *The Essential Dewey,* ed. L. Hickman and T. Alexander, 2:252 (Bloomington: Indiana University Press, 1998).

9. Ibid., 253.

10. "International Programme on the Elimination of Child Labor," *International Labor Organization,* December 2, 2007, 1, accessed December 15, 2008, http://www.ilo.org/ipec/facts/lang--en/index.htm.

11. "China: End Child Labor in State Schools 'Work and Study' Programs Put Hundreds of Thousands of Children at Risk," *Human Rights Watch,* December 7, 2007, accessed July 29th, 2009, http://www.hrw.org/en/news/2007/12/02/china-end-child-labor-state-schools.

12. Nussbaum. *Women and Human Development,* 77.

13. "Making it Pay to Stay in School?" *Center for Global Development,* March 2005, accessed October 17, 2006, www.cgdev.org/files/3222_file_Making_it_Pay_CGD_Note.pdf.

14. X. Meng and J. Ryan, "Does a Food for Education Program Affect School Outcomes? The Bangladesh Case," *Institute for the Study of Labor,* accessed August 24, 2009, ftp://repeAc.iza.org/RePEc/Discussionpaper/dp2557.pdf.

15. "Paying for Better Parenting," *New York Times.* October 17, 2006.

16. Ibid., 1.

17. Ibid.

18. "Landlocked Developing Countries and Small Island Developing States," *UN Office of the High Representative for the Least Developed Countries, Burkina Faso.* April 2009, Accessed August 24, 2009, http://www.un.org/special-rep/ohrlls/ldc/LDCs-List/profiles/burkina.htm?id=854.

Annotated Bibliography

The endnotes of this book already offer many avenues for further reading. This annotated bibliography directs readers to reading beyond what is referenced in the chapters. These readings are wide ranging, both historically and geographically. The study of children's rights, just like that of human rights, if undertaken concretely rather than merely abstractly, becomes at once a study of comparative world cultures. I have chosen publications that address the general educated public and that include international human rights law without presupposing special expertise in the field.

Anderson, Gail, and Marcia Hill, eds. *Children's Rights, Therapists' Responsibilities.* Binghamton, NY: Haworth Press, 1997.
> A collection of essays offering feminist approaches to treating mental health issues among children.

Archard, David William. *Children: Rights and Childhood.* New York: Routledge, 1993.
> A volume written by one of the best respected philosophers on children's rights issues.

Burguière, Andrè, ed. *A History of the Family.* Cambridge, MA: Harvard University Press, 1996.
> In two volumes. The first demonstrates the variety as well as universality of the family throughout the ages, and of children within the family. The second examines the family in response to the shock of modernity, beginning with the industrial revolution.

Butler, Clark. "Jack Donnelly on Human Rights," *CLIO* 33, no. 1 (2003): 107-13.
An article providing a brief statement of themes in the book *Human Rights Ethics*, which states the normative ethical theory developed with regard to children in chapter 1.

Conde, H. Victor. *An Encyclopedia of Human Rights in the United States.* Amenia, NY: Grey House Publishing, 2011.
In two volumes. A reference work accessible to the general educated public.

Conde, H. Victor. *A Handbook of International Human Rights Terminology.* Lincoln, NE: University of Nebraska Press, 2004.
A reference work accessible to the general educated public.

DeMause, Lloyd, ed. *The History of Childhood.* Lanham, MD: Jason Aronson Publishers, 1991.
A collection of essays documenting the systematic abuse of children from the Middle Ages through the nineteenth century and examining changing parental attitudes toward their children.

Dwyer, James. *The Relationship Rights of Children.* Cambridge, UK: Cambridge University Press, 2006.
A volume concluding that the law should ascribe to children rights equivalent (though not identical) to those which adults enjoy, and that this would require substantial changes in the way the legal system treats children, including a reformation of the rules for establishing legal parent-child relationships at birth and of the rules for deciding whether to end a parent-child relationship.

Farrell, Courtney. *Children's Rights.* Edina, MN: ABDO Publishing, 2010.
A book examining the historical background of child rights abuses around the world and corrective efforts leading up to the UN Convention on the Rights of the Child.

Finnis, John. *Human Rights and Common Good.* Oxford: Oxford University Press, 2011.
A noted natural law ethicist in the Catholic tradition addressing child rights among other human rights issues as timeless natural rights, rather than as valid historical constructs since the eighteenth century.

Freeman, Michael and Philip E. Veerman, eds. *The Ideologies of Children's Rights.* The Hague: Martinus Nijhoff, 1992.
A collection of essays examining different cultural perspectives on children.

Gaither, Milton. *Homeschool: An American History.* London: Palgrave Macmillan, 2008.
An objective study investigating the largely Christian homeschooling movement in the United States.

Gooneskere, Savitri, Shaheen Sadar Ali, Emilio Garcia Mendez, and Rebeca Rios-Kohn. *Protecting the World's Children.* Cambridge, UK: Cambridge University Press, 2007.
A volume documenting the impact the Convention on the Rights of the Child has had in different regions of the World Relief Fund (UNICEF). Published with the sponsorship of UNICEF, the United Nations Fund for Children.

Guggenheim, Martin. *What's Wrong with Children's Rights.* Cambridge, MA: Harvard University Press, 2005.
A book offering a contrarian view in the face of the child movement's use of the convention, especially when it opposes the rights and best interests of the child to the rights and interests of parents and adult society, and suggesting that adult child rights activists may benefit more than the children.

Haeussler, Chara and Glanzer, Perry, eds. *American Educational Thought: Essays from 1640-1940.* Charlotte, NC: Information Age Publishing, 2009.
A work seeking to provide teachers, contemporary scholars of education, and policymakers with the most significant arguments made on the subject of American education during this time period.

Halasz, G.. "The Rights of the Child in Therapy," *American Journal Psychotherapy* 50, no. 3 (1996): 285-97.
An article discussing the evolution of psychotherapy for children under the influence of the child rights movement reflected in the UN convention.

Hawes, Joseph. *The Children's Rights Movement: A History of Advocacy and Protection.* Boston: Twayne Publishers, 1991.
A book providing a historical perspective on the children's rights movement, tracing its evolution from colonial times in America to the present.

John, Mary. *Children's Rights and Power: Charging up for a New Century.* London: Jessica Kingsley, 2003.
A volume documenting the historical powerlessness of children and contemporary possibilities of empowerment.

Lawrence, Frederick, ed. *Home Schooling: Status and Bibliography*. New York: Nova Publishers, 2007.
A collection surveying the literature surrounding the homeschooling controversies from different points of view.

Liljeström, Rita. *Young Children in China*. Clevedon, Avon, UK: Multilingual Matters, 1982.
A multi-authored study examining Chinese children in different socio-economic strata, with special attention to education, both traditional and under the Chinese People's Republic.

Marrou, Henri Irénée Marrou. *A History of Education in Antiquity*. Lanham, MD: Sheed and Ward, 1956.
A study surveying the evolution of education in Greco-Roman antiquity, including education at the primary and secondary school level.

O'Neill, Thomas, and Dawn Zinga, eds. *Children's Rights: Multidisciplinary Approaches to Protection and Participation*. Toronto: University of Toronto Press, 2008.
A collection of essays showing how states as well as families can benefit from the assistance of child rights workers under the auspices of the Convention on the Rights of the Child.

Pardeck, John. *Children's Rights: Policy and Practice*. Binghamtom, NY: Hathworth Press, 2006.
A book addressing social workers, child advocates, and juvenile justice practitioners.

Sloth-Nielson, Julia, *Children's Rights in Africa: A Legal Perspective*. Farnham, Surrey, UK: Ashgate Publishing, 1988.
A collection of essays looking forward to how international law can advance the cause of children in African culture, largely written by Africans from their individual perspectives.

Trindade, A. A. C. *International Law for Humankind: Towards a New Jus Gentium*. The Hague: Martinus Nijhoff, 2010.
A comprehensive book written by a visionary judge at the International Court of Justice for the general educated public.

UNICEF, *State of the World's Children*. New York: UNICEF, 1996-.
Every year since 1996 UNICEF has published a volume on the state of the world's children with a different special theme. UNICEF, known as the UN Children's Fund today, originally stood for United Nations International Children's Emergency Fund. As an emergency or relief

fund, it may be thought of as relating to the Convention on the Rights of the Child as humanitarian law is related to more general human rights law, although it is also committed to noncrisis participation rights. The series has included *Children in War* (1996), *Child Labor* (1997), *Nutrition* (1998), *Education* (1999), *The State of the World's Children at the Turn of the Century* (2000), *Early Childhood* (2001), *Leadership* (2002), *Child Participation* (2003) *Girls—Education and Development* (2004), *Children under Threat* (2005), *The Excluded and Invisible* (2006), *Women and Children—The Double Dividend of Gender Equality* (2007), *Women and Children—Child Survival* (2008), *Maternal and Newborn Health* (2009), *Child's Rights* (2010), and *Adolescence—An Age of Opportunity* (2011).

CONTRIBUTORS

CLARK BUTLER is a Purdue University Professor of Philosophy on the Indiana University-Purdue University Fort Wayne Campus (IPFW). Apart from contributions to Hegel studies, he has formulated and defended a contemporary normative ethical theory in the place of natural law ethics, utilitarianism, and other classical theories in *Human Rights Ethics: A Rational Approach* (Purdue University Press, 2008). He has directed the IPFW Human Rights Institute since 2003, and now its successor, the Center for Applied Ethics.

JENNIFER CASELDINE-BRACHT is completing a doctorate in Philosophy at Michigan State University. She is a Research Associate in the IPFW Center for Applied Ethics and teaches in the IPFW Department of Philosophy as well as Michigan State. She has previously contributed to *Guantanamo Bay or the Judicial-Moral Treatment of the Other* (Purdue University Press, 2007).

CLAIRE CASSIDY is Lecturer in the Department of Educational and Professional Studies at the University of Strathclyde in Scotland. She is the Course Director for the Postgraduate Certificate in Philosophy with Children, as well as a founding member of the Philosophy with Children and Communities group in Scotland. Following upon her Masters in Philosophy at the University of Glasgow, she completed her Ph.D. at the University of Glasgow with a thesis on the concept of the child. Besides numerous published essays and book chapters, her book, *Thinking Children* (London: Continuum) appeared in 2007.

KATHERINE COVELL is Professor of Psychology and Executive Director of the Children's Rights Centre at Cape Breton University in Canada. She also serves on the Board of Directors of the Canadian Coalition for the Rights of Children and represents North America on the NGO Advisory Council on Violence against Children to the Secretary General of the United Nations. She has coauthored three books with R. Brian Howe on children's rights, especially in the Canadian context.

MARIE-FRANCE DANIEL is Professor in the Department of Kinesiology at the Université de Montréal. She is a Research Associate at the *Centre de recherche en éthique* at the same university (CREUM) and at the *Centre de recherche et d'interventions sur la réussite scolaire* (CRIRES). Her major research projects include primary prevention of violence, the role of dialogue in the philosophical and pedagogical training of physical education teachers, and the development of critical thinking in children. Besides coauthoring a number of books in these fields, she has authored *La Philosophie et les enfants: Les modèles de Lipman et de Dewey* (Louvain-la-Neuve, Belguim: De Boeck Université, 1996).

STEPHEN L. ESQUITH is Professor of Philosophy and Dean of the Residential College in the Arts and Humanities at the Michigan State University. He received his Ph.D. in Political Philosophy from Princeton University. In 2010 he published *The Political Responsibilities of Everyday Bystanders* with the Pennsylvania State University Press. He has concentrated particularly on issues surrounding development ethics.

MICHAEL P. FARRIS, who received his Doctorate of Jurisprudence with honors from Gonzaga University, has successfully pleaded on behalf of homeschooling before the Supreme Court of the United States. He was the founding president of Patrick Henry College, where he is now Chancellor. He is Chairman of the Home School Legal Defense Association (HSLDA). In recognition of his work in home education, *Education Week* has named him one of the "Top 100 Faces in Education of the 20th Century."

PERRY L. GLAZNER is Associate Professor of Education at Baylor University. He received his Ph.D. in Social Ethics from the University of Southern California. Additionally, he served as a visiting professor at the Russian-American Christian University in Moscow. His research interests include moral education, religion and education, human rights in democratic societies, and comparative educational trends in both North America and Europe. He is a member of the Home School Legal Defense Association.

R. BRIAN HOWE is Professor of Political Science at Cape Breton University. He holds his Ph.D. from the University of Toronto. Howe teaches and publishes on public policy and law (especially dealing with public policy on children's rights), on children's rights education, on human rights legislation in Canada, and on the role of human rights commissions. With Katherine Covell, he has published *The Challenge of Children's Rights* (Waterloo, ON: Wilfrid Laurier University Press, 2001), *Empowering Children* (Toronto: University of Toronto Press, 2005), and *Children, Families, and Violence* (London: Jessica Kingsley, 2009).

KRISJON OLSON received her Ph.D. in anthropology from the University of California at Berkeley. Her published work is based on her extensive field work among children in war-torn regions of the world. She has served as Assistant Professor of Anthropology at Colgate University.

INDEX

www.ingramcontent.com/pod-product-compliance
Lightning Source LLC
Chambersburg PA
CBHW071850270326
41929CB00013B/2170